the Comprehensive Guide to
SmartSuite 97

For Windows 95
& Windows NT

the
Comprehensive
Guide to
SmartSuite 97

For Windows 95
& Windows NT

James Meade

toExcel
San Jose New York Lincoln Shanghai

This edition published by toExcel Press,
an imprint of iUniverse.com, Inc.

For information address:
iUniverse.com, Inc.
620 North 48th Street
Suite 201
Lincoln, NE 68504-3467
www.iuniverse.com

ISBN: 1-58348-552-X

About the Author

Jim Meade is a certified Lotus expert. His 18 computer book titles include two books on Lotus Freelance Graphics, two on Lotus Ami Pro, one on Lotus Word Pro, and one on LotusScript.

When he's not writing about Lotus, he still often writes about office products. He has produced two titles on Microsoft Excel, one on WordPerfect, and one on PowerPoint. He has even written specialty books on tax software (TaxCut) and accounting software (Peachtree Accounting).

All together, Jim's books have sold more than 600,000 copies. His bestsellers include *Using PowerPoint* (Que) and *Ami Pro for Dummies* (IDG Books/Dummies Press).

Jim also has been a columnist for several computer trade publications and a contributor to many, including *PC Magazine*.

Based in Fairfield, IA, Jim has headed up his own writing services company—Meade Ink, Inc.—since 1984. Before setting up on his own, he was an in-house writer with DEC (where his specialties were office products and introductory programming languages).

Jim has a Ph.D. in English from Northwestern University, where he specialized in American Literature. He coaches basketball and baseball, which he learned growing up in Syracuse, New York (a known basketball mecca).

You can contact him on the Net at words@lisco.com.

Acknowledgments

Talk about team computing. I can't express enough gratitude to the fine team at Ventana. It's the nature of books that they have the name of an individual author on the cover, but—make no mistake—a large group of people worked together to produce this book. I want to thank all of them.

Of course, I'll single out a few I worked with directly. Thanks to Neweleen Trebnik for the chance to work on this book and for steady (truly unrelenting) guidance as I raced to the finish. (By the way, many thanks to Bob Mullen for the introduction to Neweleen. I'm still in your debt for that.)

Thanks to Judy Wilson, project editor, who is as great a master of multiprocessing as any supercomputer. Thanks to Lynn Jaluvka, who guided me until Judy took over.

Also, thanks to Michelle Corbin Nichols, as sure-handed and insightful an editor and reviewer as one could find.

Thanks to my technical reviewer, Russ Mullen, who patiently went over the technical content of this book and checked for errors. Thanks to my perfectionist copy editor, Ellen Strader. Thanks to the desktop publishing team and the production artists.

And thanks to Karen Bluestein, my first editor at another publisher years ago, and now my publisher. I love reunions, and this one is special.

People at Lotus were helpful, as always. Thanks to Ed Thomas, of Lois Paul Associates (the Lotus PR firm). And thanks to Alexandra Trevelyan. They, too, were part of the team.

Especially, as always, I thank my family—Nina, Molly, Ben, Josh, and the extended family, too. Things get crazy writing these books, with their impossible deadlines. Without the soothing influence of my family, I'm sure I'd get crazy as well. (Some say I do anyway, but if so, that's really no fault of my family.)

Dedication

To Mom and John:
I don't ride around on top of the laundry in the red wagon anymore,
Mom, but I was never safer or happier than when I did.

Contents

4   Combining in the Suite: Freelancing 1-2-3   89

Part Two: Plugging into the Internet

5   Using the SmartCenter Internet Drawer 133

Part Three: Mixing SmartSuite Applications

9 Combining 1-2-3 & Word Pro 239

10 Combining Word Pro With Other SmartSuite Programs 261

Introduction

Wow! Have things ever changed in office suites . . . even since the days of SmartSuite 96. Lotus SmartSuite 97, the subject of the book you're holding, offers tools for a business environment more global, more dynamic, and more demanding than anyone envisioned even a couple of years ago.

Earlier versions of office suites seemed to be providing quite a lot by giving one common interface to a collection of standard office software products—a word processor, a spreadsheet, a database program, a presentation graphics program, and maybe one or two other "throw-ins." The office suite was a way to sit at your desk and work in one or two programs while being able to feel comfortable in the others (on the rare occasions you might use them).

Now the importance of individual products pales beside the overall power of the suite. Yes, you still use individual products—a word processor, a spreadsheet, a database program, a graphics program, and maybe one or two other "throw-ins." Those products are as important as ever. But the true power comes from the synergy among the programs as you use them in the suite. It comes from using the collection of powerful, feature-rich products as if they were a single powerful, feature-rich program.

In Chapter 1, I briefly introduce each product and talk about what each does. Here are the products in the suite:

- Lotus 1-2-3
- Lotus Word Pro
- Lotus Approach
- Lotus Freelance Graphics
- Lotus Organizer
- Lotus ScreenCam
- Lotus SmartCenter

The period from 1996 to 1997 (and from SmartSuite 96 to SmartSuite 97) might seem quite short. Just a year. In the evolution of software products, though, a whole new age has come up.

What's So Important About Lotus SmartSuite?

What matters now is the value of the whole. It's hard to be productive and competitive anymore while working, say, just with a word processor, or just with a spreadsheet. SmartSuite provides the combination of all the office products that you need. You get the benefit of all of them living and working together in an environment that includes the Internet and, often, Lotus Notes.

If you're working in a spreadsheet and want to create, say, a set of mailing labels, you should effortlessly enjoy the full power of the best mailing label maker in the Suite—Approach. If you're creating a Freelance Graphics presentation and want to store it in Lotus Notes or save it to the Internet, you should be able to do so as easily as saving it to your own hard drive. If you want to send a 1-2-3 spreadsheet for review to colleagues—over the Internet, perhaps, or using Lotus Notes—you should be able to do that readily, and pull reviewed copies back together without getting confused.

Lotus SmartSuite takes its proud collection of office products and blends them into a whole where you can perform the tasks I've just mentioned as easily as you can create and edit a spreadsheet or type a letter in your word processor.

Here are the capabilities of the SmartSuite 97 components, the things that make this newest office suite so revolutionary:

- **Internet Tools.** Just a buzz word a couple years ago, the Internet in business is becoming as well-known as the phone lines. It's a global way to share information instantaneously. SmartSuite keeps pace with the Internet revolution by putting at your fingertips the latest tools for building Web pages, saving to or searching the Net, sending mail over the Net, and retrieving information from the Net.

- **Intranet Tools.** For a certain segment of SmartSuite users, Lotus Notes is the central clearinghouse for all kinds of business activities. SmartSuite makes Notes just as accessible as the Internet.

- **Team Computing.** Another fledgling concept that has come of age, Team Computing is at the heart of SmartSuite 97. Whether you want to want to distribute documents using TeamReview, bring them together with TeamConsolidate, mail them using TeamMail, or simply keep track of multiple versions with Versioning, you can do so effortlessly in the newest SmartSuite. And you can use these powerful tools in whichever member of the SmartSuite family you're using.

- **Standard Tools.** SmartSuite has come of age, too, as a collection of products that truly is becoming a single product. SmartIcons, those great time savers, are uniform across all the products. You just point and click whether you're in Word Pro, 1-2-3, or wherever. SmartMasters make you an instant expert in any of the programs, even if you don't really know the tricks and techniques that went into making the SmartMaster. LotusScript is now a standard scripting language in all the products and across all the products (though the earlier macro languages in some of the products are still there for those who are used to them).

SmartSuite is still a collection of products. Those products are a new generation of office software tools, more powerful than ever. Above all, though, SmartSuite is a single entity with those individual products contained within it. The collection of parts has become a single whole, much more powerful as a totality than its components.

Who Needs This Book?

For the most part, SmartSuite isn't hard to use. Unless you get into advanced scripting with LotusScript or advanced spreadsheet design, you can do almost everything in SmartSuite with a few clicks and keystrokes. A late '90s office product has to be easy to use, and this product lives up to that obligation.

How do you know what to do, though? How do you know where to start? How do you know the shortcuts? How do you get the benefit of SmartSuite as an everyday way of life?

You need a guidebook for that. At least, a guidebook helps—saving you time, and pointing you in the direction of the powerful features of the program.

Sure, for instance, you can use Organizer on your own. But will you use it as just a wall calendar on your computer? To use its alarms and play tricks with it and have a ball with it, you can benefit from this book.

Sure, you can use 1-2-3 and Freelance. But do you know the best ways to use them together? Do you know when 1-2-3 is best, when Freelance is best? Do you know the quickest ways to get the two programs working together? You get the lowdown on doing that in this book.

A book justifies its existence by helping you do things faster and better than you ever would have on your own. This book points you toward what is most powerful and useful in SmartSuite and steps you through it.

The reader we envision is probably a beginning to intermediate SmartSuite user. If you're a SmartSuite trainer already, you might find a few tips and tricks in here that you've missed. This book might be helpful, but maybe not essential. If you're a rocket designer looking for the newest structured programming techniques to refine your desktop system, well, you won't find this book to be the best source of that material.

If you want to see how to be comfortable and productive with SmartSuite quickly, though, then this is the book for you—straightforward, clear, friendly, and to-the-point.

What's Inside This Book

This book is divided into five parts. You don't necessarily need all of them, though you'll probably find something you didn't know before in each. You don't necessarily need them in order, though we've tried to move from introductory to advanced material as we go. You can use the book as a reference; or you can read consecutively to find out about capabilities and techniques. Here is what's in each part:

Part One, "Getting a Feel for the Suite," helps you take the angle you should use if you want to get the most out of SmartSuite. It gets you up to speed with the main control center of SmartSuite—SmartCenter—and even gets you started at the all-important activity of using SmartSuite programs together.

Part Two, "Plugging into the Internet," plunges you into the powerful, richly rewarding world of the Internet. You find out about SmartSuite's convenient, well-designed tools for searching, sharing, linking, and publishing to the Internet.

Part Three, "Mixing SmartSuite Applications," leads you into what almost anyone sees as the heart of SmartSuite. Modern office computing isn't about using products. It's about using products together. In this section and the next, Part Four, "More Mixing SmartSuite Applications," you see every combination for using these sister products together.

Part Five, "Advanced Features," takes a direct look at capabilities you have no doubt begun to understand by the time you reach this part of the book. But these features are worth knowing thoroughly. You find out about Team tools, standard tools like the InfoBox, Lotus Notes, and—for the hardier among us—LotusScript.

You'll also notice that this book doesn't cover each individual application on its own. That's because in the world of modern office suites, you find solutions by integrating the best from multiple applications, not by force-fitting a solution from within a single application.

System Requirements

Basically, you need these things:

- A personal computer—at least a PC 80486/50.
- A monitor—VGA or higher resolution (with adapter).

- A mouse (or other pointing device, not counting your finger).
- A CD-ROM drive.
- MS Windows 95 or Windows NT 4.0.
- At least 8MB of memory, with 12MB recommended. For Windows NT 4.0, 16MB is the recommended minimum.
- 82MB of disk space for minimum installation. (If you want to run it from the CD-ROM, you need 22MB on the hard drive.)
- Access to the Internet (not required, but certainly helpful and fun).
- Lotus Notes (optional).

What's Around the Corner

Now that we've had this chance to get acquainted in this Introduction, I'd like to mention what's coming next as you continue with the book. In Chapter 1, I talk about what you gain by living in a suite like SmartSuite instead of just using individual products. (You gain a lot.) And in Chapter 2, I help you get to know the nerve center of the whole SmartSuite—SmartCenter.

I've known Lotus and its products for more than a decade. I enjoy the chance to share ideas and conclusions with the friends I meet through my books, too, so feel free to e-mail me at words@lisco.com.

Enjoy.

PART ONE

Getting a Feel for the Suite

The Advantages of Living in a Suite

Suites are for living in. It's useful for you to know that at the outset. To get the most out of SmartSuite, you should "live in it." Do everything in it. That doesn't mean you should use only Lotus programs. It does mean that you start in SmartCenter and get into the habit of working from there.

A suite in a hotel is not like, say, a single room—where you sleep but then go out when you want to eat or work or go to a meeting. In a suite you can cook, hold meetings, hold parties, do everything.

Whatever you want to do during your work day, you do it from within SmartSuite—and that includes even doing research at faraway places (over the Internet) and working with members of your team (who may also be in faraway places).

Because everything you need for working in business is in SmartSuite, you have no reason to go anywhere else. If something you need isn't in there, you can put it in.

Besides, because SmartSuite is a "first-class hotel," you can do anything better inside the suite than you can working by hand or using individual software tools outside the suite. Here is a summary of the advantages of working in the suite.

Advantage 1: Being Comfortable With Everything

When you're at home, you're comfortable. And you have the keys to everything. Because you live in SmartSuite, the Lotus office suite aims for the same comfort level.

Even the highest-level work (such as analyzing stocks and preparing a report) ought to be easy on every level . . . except perhaps for the intensive thinking that you do. You just crunch away, and the tools cooperate.

Lotus SmartSuite has at least three key ways of helping you feel comfortable as you engage in the business challenges (not the computer challenges) of your day:

- SmartCenter means you can get to your work readily and organize it easily.

- Lotus Organizer means that you do even petty day-to-day tasks in SmartSuite (like writing down an appointment), so that using SmartSuite becomes truly second nature.

- The Lotus Common Interface means that the stronger you become in using any one product (such as 1-2-3), the stronger you become using all the others as well.

Here's a little closer look at these SmartSuite capabilities that just tend to make you feel comfortably proficient.

Taking the Controls: SmartCenter

When you're at home in your suite, you have to be *in* something specific —a control center that eventually becomes as much an extension of you as your eyes, fingers, toes, and the mouse you hold in your hand.

That *something* you're in is SmartCenter. On the surface, it's simple enough. Figure 1-1 shows SmartSuite with one drawer open. (A "drawer," in SmartCenter, is a container for folders.)

Like the Windows 95 Taskbar, SmartCenter is what you turn to first when you want to do something. Essentially, it is a collection of file drawers that you can move around at will, rename at your whim, and in which you can place programs and documents.

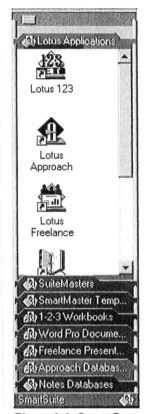

Figure 1-1: SmartCenter looks like a simple collection of drawers.

Chapter 2 covers SmartCenter, though devoting a whole chapter to the topic is deceptive in a way. It's not that SmartCenter is so hard that you need a lot of explanation. It's just that you ought to know its little ins and outs and make them second nature.

SmartCenter gives you that feeling of being in command.

Handling Even the Small Stuff—Organizer

I don't think there's anyone in business who doesn't, you know, call people up. There isn't anybody who doesn't have to keep track of appointments . . . even if some executive assistant does most of the writing.

Nobody is stopping anyone from writing phone numbers on the backs of envelopes or committing appointments to memory or just calling out to an associate in an emergency, "Hey, can you give me Jill's number?"

Organizer (which also has its own chapter in this book, Chapter 3), helps you organize and use all that "personal information." It handles the small stuff that maybe, before the era of suites, you didn't really handle on your computer at all. You may have done it by hand.

Getting into the habit of handling appointments and time management in SmartSuite, though, makes you all the more at home in SmartSuite, and all the more proficient.

In accumulating names, addresses, phone numbers, and e-mail addresses, you build up information that you can use in lots of other ways, too. Want to do a mailing to your marketing partners? If you have their addresses in Organizer, you can use the addresses from there and not have to re-key them.

Also, in applying the power of the suite to humdrum activities (such as by writing an ordinary letter but using a stunning Word Pro template), you elevate the level of the everyday "unimportant" work you do, too.

And, as with SmartCenter, the more you use Organizer for all those little things, the more settled in and proficient you become with the suite.

Not Having to Keep Learning—Lotus Common Interface

SmartSuite keeps empowering you as you work with its Lotus Common Interface. What used to be big, powerful, and distinct programs (1-2-3, Freelance, Word Pro), are now big, powerful common programs. They all work the same way.

When you're doing your work in the one that is most important to you, you become proficient at the one that you might not really have the time to master. For instance, an accountant uses 1-2-3 all day and can't take time to master Freelance. That person, though, already knows the basics of Freelance after using 1-2-3. To prepare an emergency presentation, he or she can turn to the less-used program and be productive quickly.

Extremely powerful features like SmartMasters and SmartIcons are the same in all the programs, so that once you know how to use one of them, you know how to use all of them. Once you know how to do advanced things in one of them (like create a table with a SmartIcon, or perform some drawing), you usually know how to do the same things in all of them.

Here's a quick look at some of the key tools in the interface.

SmartIcons

Hardly something new to experienced Windows users, SmartIcons like
the ones in Figure 1-2 are nevertheless an easy way to save yourself a lot
of time and trouble.

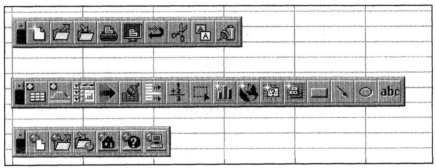

Figure 1-2: SmartIcons are the ultimate in "pushbutton living."

If there's a command to do something, there's a SmartIcon for it, too.
You can group the icons you use together into custom palettes. You can
create your own SmartIcons and attach your own scripts to them.

They're the ultimate in "pushbutton" computing, and they're in every
member of the suite. Chapter 15 talks about them in detail and explains
how getting to know them in any one SmartSuite program helps you in
all the others.

Whether they're any more powerful than the toolbars in Microsoft
Office is no doubt a matter of debate. But nobody does SmartIcons better
than Lotus.

SmartMasters

Calling these SmartMasters "templates" really doesn't do them justice.
SmartMasters don't just mean, anymore, that somebody who knows
something about fonts and page design has put together a form for you
to work on.

These SmartMasters, besides being artistic gems, have advanced
knowledge of the product and of whatever field the product aims at
(like preparing a budget or planning business strategy). There's even a
SmartMaster (in Word Pro) for creating a home page for the Web.

As examples of SmartMasters that are practically in-house consultants,
these are a few of the 1-2-3 SmartMasters:

- Amortize a loan, shown in Figure 1-3
- Calculate Loan Payments
- Create a Territory Sales Plan
- Create an Expense Report

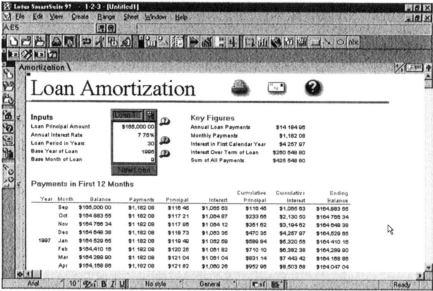

Figure 1-3: A SmartMaster like this is a lot more than just a "template."

Well, you get the idea. These templates don't just look nice. They help you do real work.

In Freelance, you select both a content topic *and* a look. Here are some sample Freelance SmartMasters:

- Business Plan
- Market Research
- Marketing Mix

And, for each of these content topics, you can select a look like these:

- Buttons
- Frame
- Gradate 1 (where the background shows gradated colors)

Figure 1-4 shows the Business Plan SmartMaster using the Buttons look.

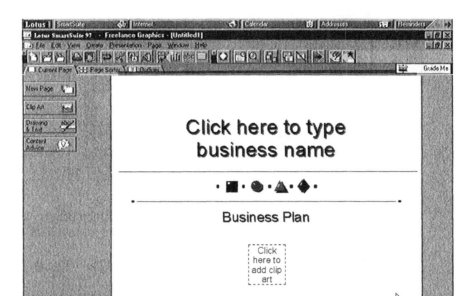

Figure 1-4: In Freelance, SmartMasters help with content and appearance.

Once you get accustomed to using these templates in one program, you'll turn to them readily in a less familiar program. In fact, you'll attempt work in those programs that you just might not attempt without these "advisors in a box" to help you.

Lotus InfoBox

If putting all the tools at your fingertips is the objective in Windows programs, the Lotus InfoBox may be the ultimate tool.

You can get to it by right clicking on an object you want to work with (like a Word Pro frame for inserting text, or just a document), then clicking the top choice from the pop-up menu. (The name of the choice varies depending on the program and the object selected, but the InfoBox works the same way everywhere. For instance, in Word Pro the choice is "Text Properties," where in 1-2-3 it is "Range Properties.") All the tools for your present task are before you in a tabbed dialog box. Figure 1-5 shows the InfoBox in Freelance.

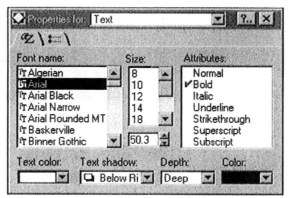

Figure 1-5: In the InfoBox, all the tools you need for a task are there before you.

When you make a change, such as selecting a different font, you see the change in the document. You don't have to do a document preview or anything else.

If you're making many changes, you can just leave the InfoBox open on the screen as you work.

Just as SmartMasters are not ordinary templates, the InfoBox is anything but your run-of-the-mill dialog box.

Advantage 2: Freedom in Using Products Together

The time is coming, at an incredible rate, when you will not use separate applications at all. You won't use a word processor for writing letters and a worksheet for doing calculations. You'll just work in a single, seamless application.

In SmartSuite, that time of working within a single application is practically here. Want to copy a range of data from 1-2-3 into a Word Pro document? You can just drag the range and drop it onto the Word Pro button in the Windows Taskbar.

Want to send out a mass mailing using Word Pro? You can merge in addresses from Approach.

Want to create a drawing and put it into Word Pro? Word Pro does have its own drawing tools. You used to have to use those. Now, though, you can use the more powerful tools, in Freelance, and then just paste your drawing from Freelance into Word Pro. In Chapter 10 I show how to copy a graphic from Freelance into Word Pro.

There are many other examples, and you'll be seeing them throughout this book.

The point is that in the suite you have the freedom to use everything together. You can use the most powerful tool for whatever you want to do—such as using 1-2-3 to apply a function to data in a table—while working along in other tools (such as Word Pro). When you're in a suite, everything is not just there. Everything works together.

Here is a summary of the products in Lotus SmartSuite 97, which, of course, you'll be free to mix together:

- **Lotus SmartCenter.** The "brains of the outfit," SmartCenter is the command center you use to work with all the other programs in SmartSuite. Created on the metaphor of a filing cabinet, it is the "collection of drawers" you see across the top of the screen as you work. I talk about it in detail in Chapter 2. You use it to organize programs, start programs, connect with the Internet, organize your time, give yourself reminders, and get help.

- **Lotus 1-2-3.** The great granddaddy of all Lotus programs, Lotus 1-2-3 is the 32-bit spreadsheet program you use to work with rows and columns of data. You can apply formulas and functions, create databases, create charts, and create maps. And 1-2-3 has the latest in Lotus Internet, Team Computing, and scripting tools.

- **Lotus Word Pro.** Word Pro is Lotus' powerful document processing software. OK. It's a word processor. But it's so powerful that it is more than just a way to get your words on paper. It's WYSIWYG from beginning to end. It has faster, easier spell checking than it ever had before. Its frames and tables make it an industry leader as a word processor useful for desktop publishing. And, like 1-2-3, it has those Lotus Internet, Team Computing, and Internet tools.

- **Lotus Approach.** If you don't want to do your database activity in 1-2-3 (which is a bit limited for that task), you can use Approach— the full-featured relational database. I like to think of it as Lotus' answer to Microsoft Access. You can use it for reporting and analysis, and it works nicely with SQL, DB2, and other existing database files. It provides LotusScript for creating custom applications.

- **Lotus Freelance Graphics.** If you want to present your findings and create a great impression with an audience, Freelance Graphics is your tool. You can use it for creating slides, diagrams, drawings, and screen shows. It allows you to use LotusScript. Because it is so visual and looks so neat, it's probably the most fun to use of any product in the suite.

- **Lotus Organizer.** Want an assist in managing your time? With Lotus Organizer, you can manage all your personal information—appointments, addresses, phone calls, anniversaries, to do items. It's about as easy to use as a pocket calendar. You can even scribble down notes and keep track of them.

- **Lotus ScreenCam.** Want to show someone how to use a program? ScreenCam is like a "VCR" for what you do onscreen. Use it to record keystrokes, then send them to someone else to play them back.

Advantage 3: Ease in Working With People

Lotus, the company that created Lotus Notes, clearly realized some time back that it has to develop a unique strength of its own to compete against a strong market presence like Microsoft. Lotus has developed Team Computing as one such specialty.

You'll meet the team computing tools in Chapter 14. The point here is that something important that has not generally been automated at all is automated in great detail in SmartSuite.

With TeamReview, covered in Chapter 15, you can send copies of, for example, a Word Pro document to several people, over e-mail if you like. They can mark their revisions with cool tools like a highlighter that puts yellow markings into the text. Colors can be different for each reviewer. You can go back over the document and choose the suggestions you want to include.

Then, with TeamConsolidate (Chapter 14), you can pull several documents together into the one final document. There are other cool team tools, too—especially ScreenCam, that lets you create "movies" of the sequence of screens you use to perform a task on your computer.

In SmartSuite, working with a team is not something you do outside your program. It's an integral part of what you are doing.

Advantage 4: Enjoying Easy Internet Access

Just because you are inside a suite, you are not isolated from the rest of the world. Quite aware of the Internet revolution, SmartSuite puts Internet tools at your disposal in SmartCenter and in individual programs.

After some configuration, you can check the weather, the news, or stock quotes from a SmartCenter drawer. Figure 1-6, for instance, shows stock quotes in SmartCenter.

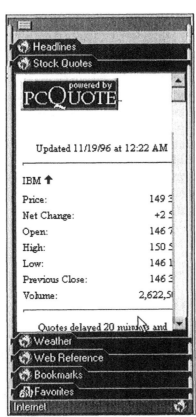

Figure 1-6: In SmartCenter, you have the Internet in a drawer.

You can connect with bookmarked pages in Netscape Navigator or Microsoft Internet Explorer. You can do Internet searches using specially tailored Internet SmartIcons.

And you can save a Web page, a presentation, or a 1-2-3 spreadsheet to the Web. In Word Pro, for instance, you open the File menu, click Internet, click Publish as Web Page(s), then follow the instructions to save your document in HTML format on a Web server.

Advantage 5: Using the Ultimate Intranet

You can readily save and retrieve documents from a company intranet. In many cases, for SmartSuite users, that intranet will be Lotus Notes. For instance, if you are running Notes on a network, as most companies do, you can combine 1-2-3 and Notes. Using TeamConsolidate in 1-2-3, you can use a Notes database to distribute 1-2-3 data to team members over the company network. Then, you can collect people's changes to the data and integrate everything into one spreadsheet again. Chapter 16 talks about Notes and the company intranet.

With the File-Open and File-Save dialog boxes in your SmartSuite applications, you can automatically open and save documents to a Notes database. Once they're in Notes, in the Lotus Notes format, you have complete Notes capability in working with them.

You can also exchange data between Lotus Notes and SmartSuite programs (Word Pro, 1-2-3, Freelance, and Approach). You can pass values from the SmartSuite program to Notes, or from Notes to the SmartSuite program. Though Notes is not a part of SmartSuite, you can set up links and readily use it to manage SmartSuite data.

Moving On

SmartSuite, then, isn't just a collection of handy tools anymore. You don't just "use" it. It's a complete style of working. And you live in it.

Every specialized tool helps you become more adept at working with the other specialized tools. The more you live in the suite, the more it becomes just an extension of you, the business professional.

It's most important, at the outset, to be adept at the central organizing principle of all the rest of the suite—SmartCenter, talked about in the next chapter.

2

Shopping in the SmartCenter

SmartCenter— the "filing cabinet" you use to start SmartSuite programs—has to be easy. There is no acceptable alternative. SmartCenter, shown in Figure 2-1, is the picture of a set of file drawers across the top of your screen. In the figure, I've opened one of the drawers. Inside the drawers are folders, just as in your metal filing cabinets in your office. In Figure 2-1, "Lotus Applications" is one folder, and "SuiteMasters" is another. You keep things inside the folders to help keep yourself organized. For instance, you keep your most-used applications in the "Lotus Applications" folder (and there doesn't really have to be just Lotus applications in there). You keep your Word Pro documents in, logically enough, the Word Pro Documents folder.

In SmartCenter, then, you do the same routine office activities you used to do by hand, like opening a file cabinet or opening a dictionary, but SmartCenter is an electronic version of those same things. It may be faster than the manual version. It may have extra capabilities such as, most obviously, the ability to search instantly for, say, a word in the dictionary.

But it has to be almost brainlessly easy, or nobody is going to do it. With time as scarce as it is in business, nobody has time to go out and relearn how to open a file drawer. Basically, to do anything, you should just point and click. For the most part, in SmartCenter, you do.

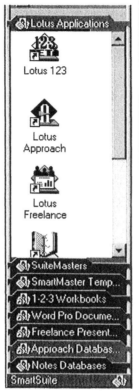

Figure 2-1: SmartCenter is a collection of "file drawers."

If all you do is point and click, you almost don't need a chapter on SmartCenter. Still, it is helpful to know where to point and click, and to know about easy-to-remember shortcuts (after you learn them the first time). Reminders are easy to create, for instance, but you may not know that you can drag them to the Desktop (or that you can't drag them to another folder). It's easy to open and read the Calendar, but you may not know how to move the Calendar forward or back a single day (by clicking in the corner of the icon of the current day). There are a lot of neat little things that make what's already easy still easier, and you pick those up by reading a chapter like this.

You can shape SmartCenter into whatever best suits your purposes, just as you do with your own filing cabinets and folders. In this chapter, though, you get a guided tour to the default drawers of SmartCenter (the ones you see when you first install it) and an introduction to the basics of using those drawers.

Starting SmartCenter

When you install SmartSuite, Lotus' install program places SmartSuite at the top of your screen, making it look just as permanent and unavoidable as Microsoft's Win 95 Taskbar at the bottom of the screen. (Lotus and Microsoft believe in friendly competition for your attention.)

It can happen, though, that SmartCenter may not be running for one reason or another. Maybe you close it for a time to create room on your screen. Or maybe—though of course this wouldn't happen—it "bombs" and you have to start it over again.

Here's how to start SmartCenter:

1. Click on the Win 95 or Win NT4 Start button.

2. Slide the mouse pointer to Programs, then to Lotus SmartSuite, as shown in Figure 2-2.

3. Slide the pointer to Lotus SmartCenter 97, and click to start the program.

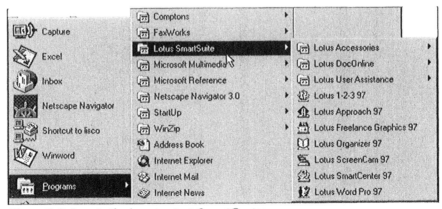

Figure 2-2: Locate the icon to start SmartCenter.

Starting Applications: "Hey, Open That SmartCenter Drawer"

The filing cabinets you have sitting in your office are pretty stationary. (If they've been there very long, the stuff in them is mostly pretty old, too. They are more like paperweights than useful furniture, for the most part, but that's a secondary point.)

Your SmartCenter filing cabinets, though, are quite movable. And, if you are in the habit of using them on a daily basis, they ought to be fairly up-to-date, too. You put things in and out of them by clicking on them.

Opening & Closing Drawers

You use the "Drawers" in SmartCenter to hold your work. They're not *really* file cabinet drawers, of course. They're the Lotus equivalent of the My Computer file in Windows 95 or Win NT4—a way to organize your work in categories that make sense to you.

To open a drawer, click on the colored area at the front of the drawer. Figure 2-3 shows an opened SmartSuite drawer.

Figure 2-3: Click a "drawer" to open it.

To close the drawer, click on the colored area again (which, in an opened drawer, will be at the bottom of the drawer).

Tip

SmartCenter is also a fancy scroll bar, like the ones you usually see along the right side or bottom in Windows programs. You probably can't see all the drawers at once. To move drawers into view, click on the scroll arrows on the right side of SmartCenter.

Starting an Application

You open drawers in SmartCenter, often, to start up the applications that are in them. For instance, to open Lotus Freelance from the Lotus Applications drawer, follow these steps:

1. Click on the colored area at the front of the drawer to open it.

2. Double-click the Lotus Freelance icon.

Using SuiteStart

Opposite the Start button on your taskbar is an icon palette of the six members of the SmartSuite. To start one of the programs, just click on the icon.

Tip

If you point to one of the icons in SuiteStart, a bubble appears over the icon and gives you the name of the program (very helpful, because the icons can be pretty small).

Adding & Removing Programs

You can add icons to SuiteStart, even icons for non-Lotus programs.
Here's how to add an icon:

1. Right-click any SuiteStart icon.

2. In the pop-up menu, click Add File.

3. In the Add File dialog box, shown in Figure 2-4, put in the application icon you want to add.

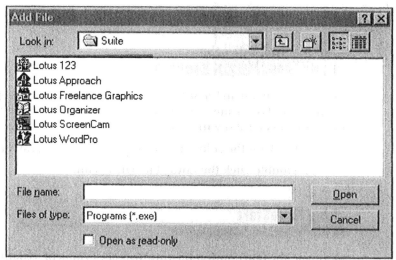

Figure 2-4: Locate the icon you want here.

You navigate in the Add File dialog box just as you would in any Win 95 dialog box. For example, click on the icon of a folder with an up arrow at the top of the box to move up one level. Double-click a folder to open it, and so on.

4. Click Open.

Here's how to remove applications from SuiteStart:

1. In SuiteStart, right-click the icon that you want to remove, such as Lotus Approach.

2. In the menu, click Remove Lotus Approach Icon (or whatever icon you have chosen).

In removing the icon, you are just removing the icon from SuiteStart. You still have it in the SmartSuite folder and in other places, and the application is still there.

Removing SuiteStart

Not everybody wants to have extra little icons on the Taskbar for starting programs. Maybe you don't use them and just find them annoying. Or maybe you want to be rid of them temporarily.

To remove SuiteStart from the taskbar, follow these steps:

1. Right-click any icon in SuiteStart.
2. Click Exit.

The icons disappear from the Taskbar.

To bring the icons back again:

1. Click the Start Menu.
2. Click Programs.
3. Click Lotus SmartSuite.
4. Click Lotus Accessories.
5. Click SuiteStart 97.

Getting Rid of SuiteStart When You Boot

As mentioned, the Lotus install program sets up Win 95 so that SuiteStart comes up automatically when you boot.

Some people (me among them, to be honest) prefer to have as few programs as possible start automatically when they turn on the computer.

You can use Windows 95 commands to remove SmartCenter and SuiteStart from the StartUp menu:

1. Click on the Windows 95 Start menu.
2. Click in Settings, then Taskbar.
3. Click the Start Menu Programs tab.
4. Click Remove, then click the plus sign to the left of StartUp.

The programs in the StartUp folder come into view, as shown in Figure 2-5.

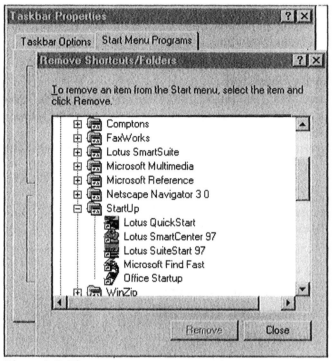

Figure 2-5: These programs start up with Win 95.

> 5. Click the programs you want to remove, and click the Remove button.
>
> 6. Choose Close, then OK.

To put them back into the StartUp menu, you would choose Add from the Start Menu Programs tab, click the Browse button and locate the command line for your program, and continue to use the wizard that guides you in the task. (That is, click the Next button in each dialog box and click the Finish button in the last box the Wizard gives you.)

Organizing Your "Filing Cabinet"

You have probably figured out the material so far in this chapter—how to open file cabinets, how to start applications. So now you have the basics.

Over time, though, you increase your effectiveness by finding ways to shape SmartCenter to fit the ways you work. This section looks at some of the ways you can do that.

Adding & Subtracting Drawers

If your metal file cabinets in the office have only three drawers, then you're pretty much limited to three drawers for eternity with that particular cabinet. In SmartCenter, though, you can add up to 50 drawers to the "cabinet" displayed on your screen.

Here's how to add a drawer:

1. Click the black Lotus button at the very left of SmartCenter, labeled "Lotus."

2. In the Lotus menu, shown in Figure 2-6, click New Drawer.

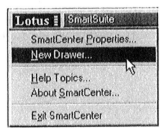

Figure 2-6: Use this menu to create a new drawer.

3. In the New Drawer dialog box (shown in Figure 2-7), click in the Drawer label box. Delete the existing label (usually "New Drawer"), and type in a label for your drawer.

4. Click OK.

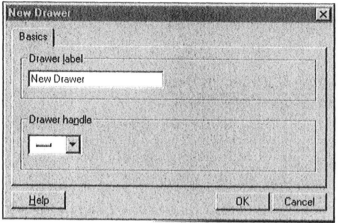

Figure 2-7: Name your new drawer here.

You don't have to use drawers just to hold, say, all your Reference programs. You can organize them around projects, for example. If you're preparing a presentation for the annual sales meaning, label the drawer "Sales Meeting," and put the documents and programs for that presentation into the drawer.

Dragging Drawers Around

In your metal filing cabinets, you could probably pull one drawer out and move it to the place of another one, though I've never heard of anyone wanting to do that.

In SmartCenter, though, you may decide to move drawers around to suit the way you work.

Here's how to move them:

1. With the mouse, point to the drawer you want to move. The drawer can be open or closed. It doesn't matter.

2. Drag the drawer to a new position.

Tip

If you want the drawer to be the first one on the left, drag it onto the SmartCenter menu on the left (the one labeled "Lotus").

Original File Drawers

Because it's so easy to change the folders around, you can quickly end up with a SmartCenter that has little correlation with your original set of drawers. You may even move drawers by accident.

There is nothing cast in stone about the original set, but if you want to restore it, here's the list of original file drawers:

- SmartSuite
- Internet
- Calendar
- Addresses
- Reminders
- Reference
- Suite Help

Changing the Size of Drawers

If you've used Windows before, then it will come as no surprise to you that you can drag the sides of these "drawers" to enlarge or shrink them. To change the width or length of a drawer:

1. Click the colored area to open the drawer.

2. In an open drawer, slide the pointer along the side or bottom of the drawer until the pointer becomes a double-headed arrow.

3. Drag the drawer to the shape you want.

Customizing Your Drawers

The handle that is on there probably suits you just fine. If you want to change the label or the handle for your drawer, though, it's easy enough to do:

1. Right-click the colored portion of the Drawer.

2. Click Drawer Properties.

3. In the Drawer Properties dialog box, shown in Figure 2-8, make your changes, and click OK. Basically, you can change the name of the drawer and the icon you use for the handle.

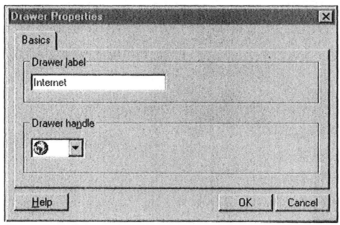

Figure 2-8: Change the drawer's name or handle here.

Getting Your Folders in Order

The SmartCenter drawers have folders in them. Each drawer has at least one folder to begin with. You can create additional ones—such as an imaginary one that says "Coffee Club Presentation." You can move the folders around within the drawer by dragging them. You can drag them to other drawers or to the desktop.

Most folders are file folders, for holding files and applications. (You can also keep Shortcuts in there, and Notes databases, and other folders.)

Folders can also be address folders (for keeping addresses, rather than files or folders), as explained later in this section.

Other types of folders, all explained in this section, are:

■ Internet folders

■ Dictionary and Thesaurus folders

■ Reminder folders

Creating Folders

What you can do with drawers, you can do with the contents of drawers—folders. You can add new ones, take undesirable ones away, drag
them around, and more.

Here's how to create a new folder:

1. Open the drawer where you want to add the folder.

2. Click the drawer menu button (an icon of a handle, at the top of
   the drawer).

3. From the menu, click New Folder.

   The New Folder assistant comes up (Figure 2-9) and, in its first
   step, asks you to choose the type of folder you want to create.

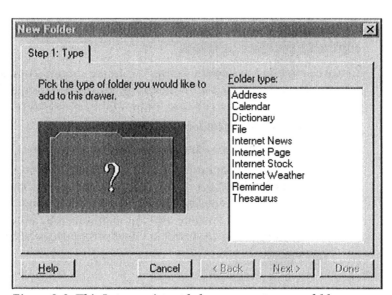

Figure 2-9: This Lotus assistant helps you create a new folder.

4. Choose a Type (usually a file folder), and click Next in the assistant.

5. In Step 2 of the assistant, click the Folder label box, and type in a
   meaningful label for the folder (such as "Coffee Club"). Click
   Next.

6. In Step 3 of the assistant, you can choose to display files in the folder as large or small icons and decide whether to arrange them by name or another criterion (such as date). Click Next to accept the defaults.

7. In Step 4, you can choose to create a new folder or use an existing one. For this example, click Done to accept the default.

The new folder appears in the Drawer you've chosen.

Moving Folders Around

The point with folders is to be able to move them freely. To move a folder in SmartCenter, just drag it to the new location.

You can drag a folder to a closed file drawer if you like.

Customizing Your Folders

Chances are you have better things to do than change the looks of your folders. You can change such things, though. As an example, here's how you change the 1-2-3 Workbooks folder in the SmartSuite drawer.

1. Right-click the folder.

2. In the menu that appears, click Folder Properties.

3. Change the properties you want to change—Folder label, the color of the folder, or the icon. You can also click the Display tab and choose to display files as large or small icons. And you can choose how to arrange files in the folder—by name, type, size, or date. Figure 2-10 shows the Folder Properties dialog box.

4. Click OK.

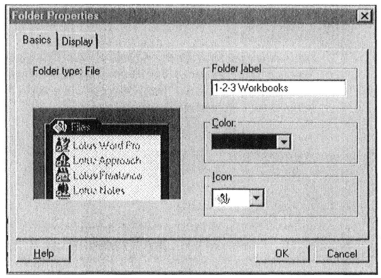

Figure 2-10: Change folder colors here.

Keeping Track of Time

For you to use an electronic calendar and address book instead of the dog-eared version you probably carry in a pocket or purse, the Lotus Calendar and Address book have to be incredibly accessible, as well as much more useful than the time-proven pocket version.

It's SmartCenter's mission to make the Calendar and Address book just *that* handily available, so you'll actually use them (a longstanding challenge, I must say, in the world of Personal Information Managers, "PIMs")

Setting Up Your Calendar

Before SmartCenter will let you use it, you have to set up your Calendar as either an Organizer file or a text file.

Tip

You can use the SmartCenter Address Book and Calendar as part of Lotus Organizer (the complete Lotus Personal Information manager, which I talk about in Chapter 3). Your SmartCenter calendar doesn't have to be the same as your Organizer calendar, though.

Default Installations & Organizer

When you install SmartCenter, the installation program looks to see if you're using Organizer already and if you have Organizer set up to open a .OR3 file automatically when you use Organizer. If you have that setup, the install program uses that same .OR3 file as your SmartCenter address file.

If you aren't already using Organizer, install sets up your address folder and your Calendar folder with its own .TXT file that is not part of Organizer.

Here's how to get set up:

1. With the drawer open, right click the area at the top of the Calendar drawer, next to the handle icon.

2. Click Folder.

3. Click Folder Properties.

4. In the Folder Properties dialog box, click Calendar.

5. In the Calendar dialog box , under File Type, choose text file if you don't want the file to be an organizer file.

   SmartSuite suggests a location for the text file, as shown in Figure 2-11.

6. Click OK.

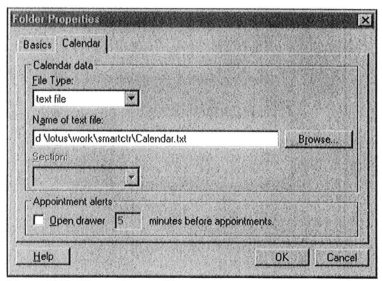

Figure 2-11: Choose the type file you want.

Adding an Appointment

Using the calendar is a matter of opening the drawer, clicking, and putting in appointments on the days that you want them.

Here's how to put in an appointment:

1. Click in the time slot where you want the appointment.

2. In the Create Appointment box that comes up, (shown in Figure 2-12), type in your appointment.

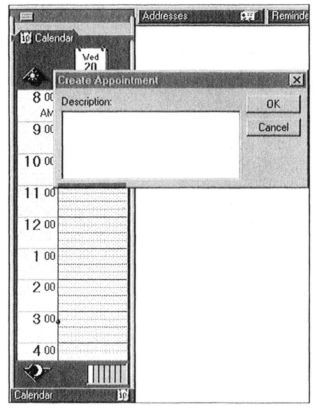

Figure 2-12: Type an appointment here.

Once you've put in the appointment, it appears as a white card covering a time period, as shown in Figure 2-13.

Here's a summary of what you can do with the calendar:

■ Click the scroll arrows (AM and PM buttons) to scroll through the appointments for the day.

■ Click the Date icon to display the whole month, then click on a day you want to work with.

■ Click the lower left of the Date icon to go to a previous day, the lower right to go to the next day.

■ Click on the "Days to display" icon (lower right) to select the number of days your calendar shows at a time.

■ Check the current time by seeing the position of the red dot.

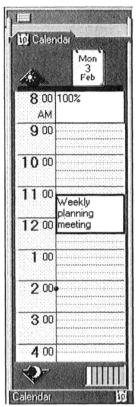

Figure 2-13: Appointments show up looking like this.

Keeping Track of People

Like the Calendar, the Address book is supposed to be as simple to use as the one you might carry in your briefcase. As with the Calendar, once you have the Addresses drawer set up, you click and type in addresses.

Setting Up Your Address Book

As with the Calendar, you can set up the Address book as a Lotus Organizer file or as an independent file. Refer to the Setting Up Your Calendar section above to see how to do that.

Adding Someone to Your Address Book

Here's how to put a name into your Address book:

1. Open the Address book, shown in Figure 2-14.

2. Click Add Name.

3. In the "address card" that comes up, put in the information for the person. Press Tab to move around the form, and press Shift Tab to move backwards.

4. Click OK.

Figure 2-14: Here's the open address book.

Tip

> *To add additional lines to Street Address, press Ctrl+Enter to start a new line. If you press Enter, Address Book closes the card as if you had completed it. To put in a tab, press Ctrl+Tab.*

Surfing the Net (From Inside a Drawer)

In C. S. Lewis' *The Lion, the Witch, and the Wardrobe*, a character walks to the back of a "wardrobe" (a "closet" to Americans) and keeps right on going into a fantasy world. When you are working in the SmartCenter Internet drawer, you almost literally walk into a fantasy world. At the time C.S. Lewis' book came out, the idea of just walking through the wall into a fantasy world was just imagination. It was for fun.

Now, it is pretty much literally true. I mean, you don't physically dive into your computer and walk around in Narnia. You go through a file drawer to get to computers and information all over the world, though.

You have to have an Internet browser in place already, usually Netscape or Microsoft Internet Explorer. And, of course, you have to have access to the Internet already through an Internet access provider of some sort.

If you have the Internet basics in place, though, you can click on the Internet drawer and then surf the Net to your heart's content.

Reviewing What's Available

Part 2 of this book, Chapters 5-8, looks at all the things you can do with the Internet from within SmartSuite. Connectivity with the wide world of the Web is a mainstream activity in business these days, and it's so important that it's worth covering the topic in those early chapters in this handbook.

Even in this introductory chapter on SmartCenter, you get a glimpse of what's in the Internet drawer in SmartCenter.

When you first click on the Internet drawer, you see a collection of folders, as shown in Figure 2-15. Each folder is actually a Web page. When you click on the folder, you open the Web browser and go to that page.

These are actual Web pages, not pages that Lotus has created just for SmartCenter.

Some of the folders require some initial setup, such as indicating the region where you want a weather report, or saying which stock quotes you want to see.

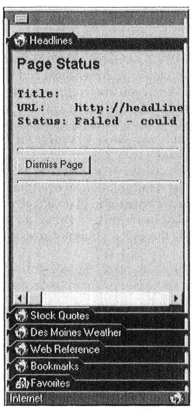

Figure 2-15: The Internet drawer is a collection of folders.

To set up an Internet folder:

1. Click the folder icon at the top of the folder.

2. Click Folder Properties.

3. Click a tab and provide information. For instance, you could click the Weather tab in the Weather folder, and select a region or city.

4. Click OK.

Once you have the Internet folders (Web pages), connected and set up, you just click the folder to see the contents.

The contents display using your default Web browser, and you can continue to use the browser in your usual way from within the drawer.

To use any of the folders, just click on the folder. Here are the initial folders you can use, with a sample view of each. You can add other Internet folders to display other Web pages.

Tip

When you first open a drawer, before connection to the Internet, you get a message like the one partially showing in Figure 2-15, that includes the words "Status: Failed."

To get to the Web page you want and eliminate the message, first be sure you are connected to the Internet. Then, if necessary, meet any special requirements for the drawer (such as providing the name of the stocks you want to check).

Then, click the folder icon for the Internet folder you're working with, and click Refresh. SmartCenter will display your Web page. Even after you disconnect from the Web, it will display the page until you exit from SmartCenter (or from Win 95).

Here are some sample Internet folders:

■ News

You can choose to show Top Stories, World News, Technology, Business, or Sports News. Figure 2-16 shows an example of Top Stories.

Figure 2-16: You can see the news "in a drawer."

■ Stock Quotes

You don't need the Wall Street Journal or even CNN Headline News. You can get the latest quotes straight from the Internet, shown in Figure 2-17.

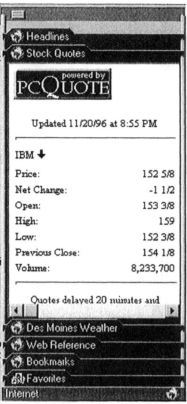

Figure 2-17: Just click to get the latest stock quotes (delayed 20 minutes, of course).

■ Weather

Choose your own region or city, or one you plan to travel to, and get up-to-date weather. Figure 2-18 shows an example.

Figure 2-18: Stuck inside? Look in a drawer to see what the weather's doing.

■ Web Reference (Search)

You can look up phone numbers, exchange rates, even clip art. Here's the Search page that appears when you start (Figure 2-19).

Figure 2-19: You can search Web reference materials.

■ Favorites

If you use Internet Explorer, SmartSuite displays a Favorites folder. If you use Netscape, it displays a Bookmarks folder. If you use both, it displays both. You can go to the Bookmarks just as you would when surfing the Net with another browser. Figure 2-20 shows an example.

Figure 2-20: You can go straight to Bookmarks (or Internet Explorer Favorites).

Tip

Besides the Web connections in the Internet drawer, you can click the Suite Help drawer, then Helpful Web sites to connect with Lotus Internet pages, shown in Figure 2-21.

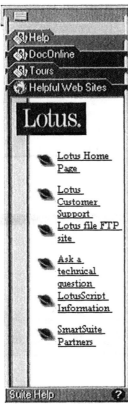

Figure 2-21: The Lotus Web pages are in the Suite Help drawer.

Adding Other Internet Page Folders

You can add folders for other Internet pages, so that you can go directly to those Web pages just by clicking the folders that contain them:

1. Right-click the Internet drawer.

2. Choose New Folder.

3. In the New Folder assistant, click Internet Page.

4. In the Assistant, shown in Figure 2-22, click Next to customize the folder. For Folder label, type in a meaningful name. The example uses *USA Today*.

5. Click Next again to type in the URL (the Internet address of the site). The example uses http://www.usatoday.com.

6. Click Done.

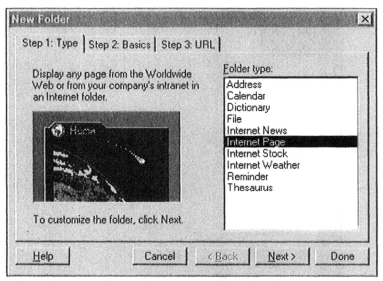

Figure 2-22: Use the Assistant to customize the folder.

SmartCenter creates the folder. If you click the Internet drawer, you see your new folder added to the Internet folders, as shown in Figure 2-23.

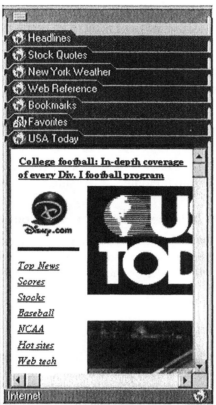

Figure 2-23: You can put a Web page in a folder.

Remind Me What I'm Supposed To Do

You already have a Calendar in SmartCenter. "What do I need reminders for?" you might wonder. Well, you don't, and it's up to you whether you put them anywhere. But what do you do with things like, "Write that letter to Janie" or "Set up a dentist appointment" or "Call a guy about the car"? These aren't things you have to do at any particular time, so you don't have to put them into a slot on the calendar. They may not even be particularly important, except in a nagging "got-to-remember-that" way. Or they may be critically important, such that you probably wouldn't forget them anyway.

The Reminders folder is a pretty cool way to handle such stuff that you really don't want to forget but may not want to be bothered with either.

Creating a Reminder

If you've created entries in the Calendar or Addresses, you know how to put entries into the Calendar. Just click and write. Here are the formal steps:

1. With the Reminders drawer open, click the folder you want to put the reminder into ("Home" or "Business" until you create other folders).

2. Click the blank box in the folder, and type in your reminder.

Figure 2-24 shows the box you type your reminder into.

Note that if you press Enter, SmartCenter marks the note as completed. If you want to put an Enter or Tab inside your reminder, press Ctrl+Tab or Ctrl+Enter.

Tip

You don't have to stick with just the folders in the Reminders drawer. You might want a folder for a project you're working on, such as "Lion's Club Paper Drive Folder" or whatever. Create a new folder in the same way explained earlier in this chapter. Click on the drawer handle at the top, then click New Folder, and go from there.

Figure 2-24: Type a reminder here.

Dragging Reminders Around

Reminders, by nature, have to be portable and pretty subservient. In ordinary life, people stick reminders on refrigerators, on front doors, on car seats, or in any unlikely place where the reminders are likely to catch their attention at the right time.

In SmartCenter you can drag your reminders around, but only to two places—from one Reminder folder to another, or to the desktop. Figure 2-25 shows a reminder being dragged from a folder to the desktop.

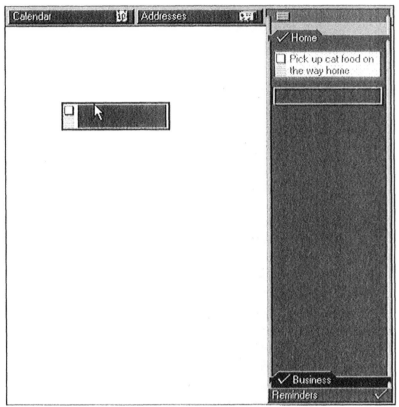

Figure 2-25: You can drag reminders around.

Warning

If you drag a reminder to another (non-Reminder) folder, it may appear to be in the folder. But it isn't. It's on the Desktop and will show up there when you close the folder. That is a useful feature in the reminder; it tends to get in the way and persistently nudge you to do something.

Dragging Text to Create a Reminder

Just as you can drag reminders around, you can drag other text into the reminders folder.

It's pretty automatic, but you do have to follow a couple of steps to be able to drag the text successfully:

1. Click the minimize button (the middle of the three buttons at the top right of the application window) so that your program is open but doesn't take up the full screen.

2. Open the Reminders drawer and the folder you want to drag to.

3. Drag the text into the folder. It appears as a reminder.

Changing Your Reminder

You're of course always free to change a reminder once you've created it. Here's what you do:

1. To edit a reminder, double-click it. A cursor appears inside the reminder box.

2. Delete any text with the Del key or other techniques you may like. Type in new text.

3. When you're done, press Enter, or click somewhere outside the Reminders drawer.

Trashing Your Reminder

Deleting a reminder is also probably automatic if you are used to Win 95:

1. Right-click the Reminder.

2. Click Delete Reminder.

3. Choose Yes.

Marking the Reminder Completed

Some people get a real sense of satisfaction from looking back over tasks they've completed. Others, with grander aspirations, want to be able to look back over the small things in their life so they can pull them together into an autobiography. (Most people want to delete reminders once they're done with them, of course.)

If you want to mark a Reminder as completed, click the check box to the left of the reminder.

Looking Up Words

You use the Reference drawer to look up, well, words.

The Internet may be the latest and greatest in research tools. You can look up anything about anything there. Want to find out about the mating habits of Yaks? Check it out. Want to find a husband or wife? Use an Internet dating service.

However, widespread as the search for yaks, husbands, or wives may be, the most common form of research is still using the dictionary to find out what some strange word means. Also important, though a distant second, is using a Thesaurus to find out another word to use for a word you know.

SmartCenter gives you a separate file drawer for your dictionary and thesaurus. These are not Internet folders. When you use the dictionary and thesaurus, you can have SmartCenter look up the words on the SmartSuite CD-ROM. Or, if you want to have the dictionary on your hard drive, run the Install program, select Customize features, and select Dictionary.

Here's how to use the Dictionary and Thesaurus:

1. Open the Reference drawer. The cursor is in a blank box, waiting for you to type in a word.

2. Click either the Dictionary folder (for a definition) or the Thesaurus folder (for a synonym).

3. Type in the word, and press Enter. A definition comes up. Figure 2-26 shows a sample Dictionary entry.

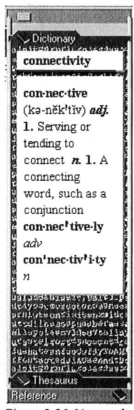

Figure 2-26: You can look up words in a flash.

Getting Suite-style Help

Win 95-style Help has become standardized over the years, and
SmartSuite Help is no exception.

To start Help, click on the SmartCenter drawer (the black one labeled
"Lotus"), then on Help Topics. Windows 95-style help comes up, shown
in Figure 2-27. Click on Contents, Index, or Find, and use the Help file
just as you use Win 95 Help.

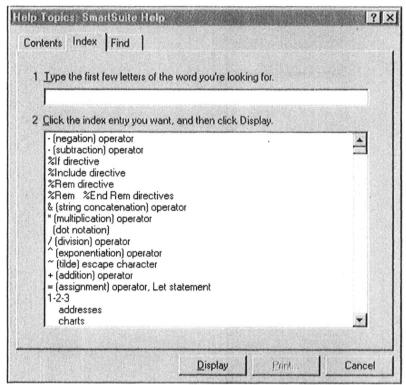

Figure 2-27: SmartCenter Help works the same as Win 95 Help.

There is also a separate drawer dedicated to Help, and it includes Tours and a few other Help items not in the SmartCenter Help file. Click on the Suite Help drawer to see the choices, shown in Figure 2-28.

Figure 2-28: The Help drawer offers cool options.

Managing the "Manager"

Your office furniture may be too bulky to move around very much. SmartCenter, though, is just some electronic shapes on your computer screen. You can bend it to your will. You can move the drawers around, change their positions, and change their handles and colors, as the following sections explain.

Dragging Your Set of File Cabinets Around

Once you decide where you want your SmartCenter "file cabinet," you'll probably want to leave it there most of the time. That way, you can click there unconsciously to accomplish what you want.

At first, though, you may want to try both of the available locations—top of the screen, or bottom.

To move SmartCenter to the top or bottom, double-click on the area between drawers or the blank area to the right. The other figures in this chapter show SmartCenter at the top of the screen. Figure 2-29 shows SmartCenter at the bottom of the screen.

Figure 2-29: You can have SmartCenter at the top or bottom of the screen.

Warning

You can also use the menus to move SmartCenter. Click the SmartCenter menu, then SmartCenter Properties, and, in SmartCenter position, click Top of screen or Bottom of Screen.

Customizing SmartCenter

Though the sound of the drawer opening sounds pretty cool at first, it may start to jar on you or someone else after a while. Or, if you find the sounds really fun, you may want to change them a lot just to keep yourself amused.

To change sounds and other properties:

1. Click the SmartCenter menu (labeled Lotus).

2. Click SmartCenter Properties.

3. Click the Effects tab.

4. Make your choices in the tab shown in Figure 2-30.

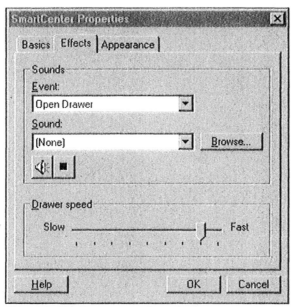

Figure 2-30: Change sounds and other properties here.

Moving On

SmartCenter, as I say, is pretty much of a no brainer. I'm sure that the primary, ongoing charge for SmartCenter programmers is, "Make things so ridiculously simple that absolutely anybody can do them without training."

Still, it's nice to glance through the drawers and see what's there. Reminders are great, for example, but you'll never use them if you don't know they're there. It's nice to be able to have all your most-used Internet stuff already before you, at a glance. But, again, you won't use it if you don't know about it.

So, in this chapter, you've had the chance to get to know that part of SmartSuite that's always around as you work—the nerve center of all the rest.

If you would like to get even more organized with your calendar, appointments, and reminders, there is a better way than SmartCenter. It's called Organizer, and I'll talk about it next.

3

Organizer: Finally Getting Organized

Organizer can't really solve things like problems in your love life or bad relations with a co-worker (though it might be able to help). It is a Personal Information Manager (PIM), but it's not *that* personal.

But Organizer does have an awful lot to do with making you efficient and with helping you get the most out of SmartSuite.

First of all, by using Organizer you automate and systematize things that you otherwise would probably not automate—addresses, phone numbers, appointments, and anniversaries. Then, you can use those collections of information in other places—such as doing a Word Pro mailing to clients you've listed in Organizer.

Second, using Organizer gets you truly "living in the suite," as explained in Chapter 1. The more you organize mundane activities in Organizer, the more you become an unconsciously proficient SmartSuite aficionado. You get into the habit of using SmartIcons, dialog boxes, menus, and all the electronic tools in the suite.

Tabs in Organizer seem to be in the order of importance (and, not incidentally, in the order of the likelihood of people using them). People are much more likely to put appointments into a calendar than to track their calls or, certainly, to write down anniversaries. The topics in this chapter, likewise, are in the order of decreasing importance—except for the customizing topics at the end, which can be fairly important to some people.

Doing Anything in Organizer: Basic Steps

If you learn a few simple steps, you can use them throughout Organizer. For whatever you want to do, the steps are basically the same:

1. First, open Organizer by clicking on its icon (an open address book) on the SuiteStart bar or in one of the other standard places for starting a program (such as the SmartCenter file drawer). Figure 3-1 shows Organizer when you first open it—an open appointment book with tabs on the sides.

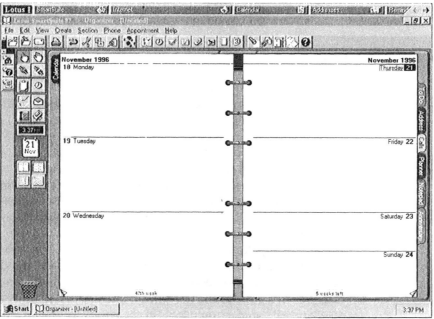

Figure 3-1: Organizer looks like a plain old appointment book.

2. Click on the tab for the activity you want, unless it's Calendar, which you're already in when you start. Figure 3-2, for instance, shows the To Do list.

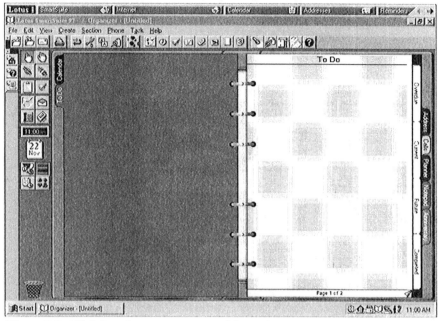

Figure 3-2: Click its tab to see any part of Organizer.

3. Double-click in the area where you want to make an entry. A dialog box comes up like the one in Figure 3-3, for creating a To Do list item.

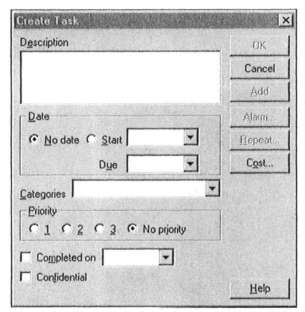

Figure 3-3: To put in information, complete the dialog box.

4. Type in the information you want, and click OK.

Things can get a lot more complicated than you see in just these four steps. There are at least two ways to open any section, for instance: clicking on the tab for it, or choosing from the menu. You have lots of choices in some dialog boxes. You can get involved with the Internet or mail. There are SmartIcons all over the page you can click (and I encourage you to do that).

But the basics remain pretty simple: click a tab, double-click, type in your information, choose OK.

Deleting is particularly important when organizing your time. You have to throw things away when you're done with them or when you change your mind. To delete anything, point to it until the mouse pointer takes that shape of a hand, then drag the item to the little wastebasket icon at the bottom left of Organizer. If you don't like drag and drop, you can just click an item to select it, then press the Del key.

Tip

If you delete something by accident, as often happens in the frenzied world of personal planning, click the Undo SmartIcon (two arrows) to undelete it. You can undo only the last action (not multiple actions as in some other programs, like Word Pro). So try to make up your mind right away if you want to undo something. Besides the SmartIcons available in any Lotus program, Organizer comes with a Toolbox of shortcuts to the things you do most commonly in Organizer.

Here's a table of the tools in the toolbox and what they do:

Tool	What It Does
Pointing Finger	Select or drag and drop an entry
Hand, no pointing finger	Move an entry
Picture of a chain link	Create a link
Picture of links with line through them	Break links
Picture of clipboard	Drag an entry to it to copy it, drag one from there to paste it
Clock in Calendar (icon changes in various Organizer programs)	Create a Calendar appointment
Picture of a notice	View meeting notices
Open envelope	Send or open mail
Phone dialer	Drag an entry there to dial
Printer	Print information
Clock	Show current time

Table 3-1: The Organizer tools and what they do.

Working With the Organizer File

When you work in a paper planner or address book, you probably just have one of them. Though Organizer may look like a single book, it can be as many books as you want. That is, you save your information in files, just as you save word processing documents in individual files. You could have one organizer file for personal things, one for business. You could have one for your daytime business, another for your moonlighting job. But you can have more than one.

In many respects it's practical to have just a small number of Organizer files, though. It's convenient to have all your entries in one place and not have to redo them in a separate file.

You save your Organizer file just as you save a word processing or 1-2-3 file, or a file from about any other program. Then, you can open the file later to work with it.

Here's how to save a file:

1. From the Organizer File menu, choose Save.

2. In the Save As dialog box, shown in Figure 3-4, type a name for the file, and click Save.

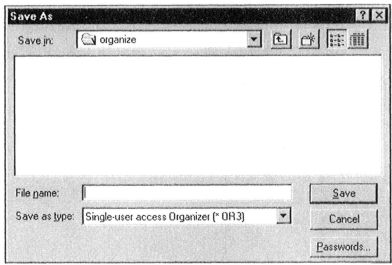

Figure 3-4: The first time you save a file, you see this Save As dialog box.

Organizer saves the file with the extension .OR3. If you plan to create many organizer files, you may want to make note of the name you used for your primary one.

"Hey, I Already Have a Calendar in SmartCenter."

If you wish, you can just use the basic calendar in SmartCenter, and leave your calendar activities at that. Also, you can use just the Address Book from SmartCenter, if you wish.

As explained in Chapter 2, you can set up the SmartSuite Address Book and Calendar as .TXT files and use them outside Organizer.

However, you increase your possibilities in working with them if you set up your SmartCenter Address Book and Calendar as Organizer files. Then you can open them in Organizer and use the additional capabilities available in the full-featured time management program, such as having entries "show through" into other parts of Organizer, or using Addresses in your database program. Also, items you add in SmartCenter show up in Organizer, and vice versa.

Setting Appointments: Calendar

Use the Calendar section to book appointments and set alarms. Here is a look at a few of the special things you can do with Calendar.

Creating Appointments

You use the standard steps to create an entry. Here they are for Calendar:

1. Click on the day where you want to schedule the appointment, such as November 14.

2. Click the Create an entry icon in the toolbox (a picture of a clock).

3. In the Create Appointment dialog box, shown in Figure 3-5, type a description for the appointment, such as "Restructuring committee."

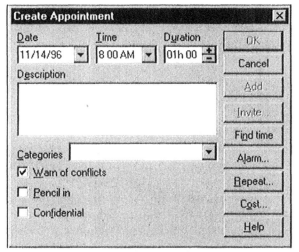

Figure 3-5: Set up appointments here.

4. If you want to choose a different day, click the Date drop-down box and select the date.

5. Use the list box for Time to select a time, and the box for Duration to choose duration.

6. Choose OK. The entry appears on the Calendar, as shown in Figure 3-6.

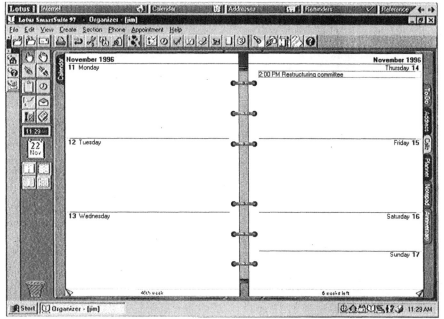

Figure 3-6: Your entry appears in the calendar.

Picking a View

Organizer has really cool views you can use when making your entries. They are similar to the Special Views on the View menu in Word Pro, though not as ambitious as those in the word processor.

Click on the view icons below the toolbox on the left to create the views. Here are the four views:

- Day per page
- Week per page
- Work Week
- Month

Figure 3-7 shows week per page.

Figure 3-7: Here is a view of a week per page.

To move backward or forward in the view that you're in (day, week, or month), click on the "curled corner" in the lower left or right of the calendar.

Tip

> *If you want to see the whole year, click on the Planner tab. I'll talk about the Planner later in this chapter.*

Creating Repeating Appointments

Do you, like people at many companies, have a Monday morning meeting where you plan the week's activities? You can set up your Calendar so that the repeating meeting shows up every week automatically:

1. Double-click on the time and date when you want to create the first of the repeating appointments—for the example, Monday, Dec. 2, 1996.

2. In the Create Appointment box, put in Date, Time, Duration, and Description as for a regular appointment. For time, use 8:00 AM. For duration, use 01 00. For description, type **"Weekly org meeting."**

3. Click the Repeat button.

4. In the Repeat dialog box, Figure 3-8, use the list boxes to choose how often it repeats, the Starting date, and the duration (such as a year). In the list boxes for Repeats, select Weekly from the first box, Every from the second, and Monday from the third. In the list boxes for Duration, click on the list box next to For, and choose Year. (The Until box then automatically puts in the data a year later.) Choose OK.

5. In the Create Appointment dialog box, choose OK.

The weekly appointment appears at the designated time each week for a year, which is really pretty useful for those nagging, recurring meetings.

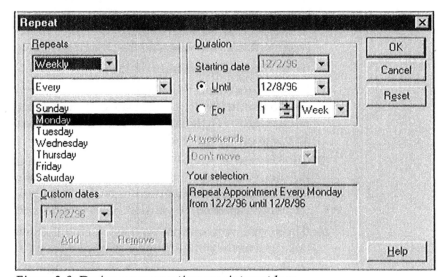

Figure 3-8: Design your repeating appointment here.

Rescheduling Appointments

It seems to be the nature of appointments to change. To move an appointment, follow these steps:

1. Right-click the appointment to display the menu.

2. Click Cut.

3. Click where you want to place the appointment—another date and time.

4. Right-click, and choose Paste.

Setting Alarms

When you create an appointment, you can also set up an alarm to go off to remind you of the appointment:

1. Double-click a date and time to create an entry, such as 11/22/96 at 2:00 P.M.

2. In the Description box, type a few words to describe the Appointment. (You can't create an alarm without typing in some description. If you want an alarm without a description, just type anything you want into the Description box.)

3. In the Create Appointment dialog box, click the Alarm button.

4. In the Alarm dialog box (Figure 3-9), if necessary, click the arrow next to the list box to change Date or Time. Click the plus or minus sign to the left of Before and After to have the snooze alarm go off before or after the designated time.

5. Click the arrow on the Tune list box to choose a tune, and click the tune you want. (Tunes are really fun. Choose one and click Play to hear what an alarm sounds like. Tunes play through the computer's speaker, so you don't need a sound card to hear them.)

6. If you wish, you can type yourself a reminder in the Message box, such as the phone number you want to call at that time.

7. In the Start box, you can type in an application that you want to start up when the alarm goes on, such as the 1-2-3 worksheet you want to discuss at that time. (Use the Browse button to navigate to the application, if you like.)

8. When you've set up the details, click OK.

9. Click OK in the Create Appointment box. The box closes, and the alarm will go off at the designated time.

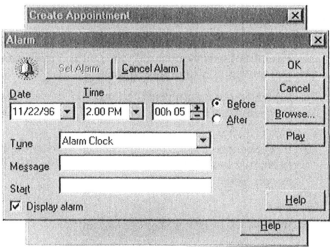

Figure 3-9: Set up alarms here.

Tip

You can also set alarms in the To Do, Calls, Planner, and Anniversary sections.

Finding an Available Time

If your calendar is really full, you may not be sure when you have time to meet with someone for, say, an hour.

In the Create Appointment box, you can specify a duration for the appointment, then click Find Time. Organizer searches through the coming days until it finds an opening of the right duration, and it displays the date and time settings in the dialog box for that time.

If you don't like the suggested time, just click Find Time again, and repeat as often as you have to.

Using Time Tracker

SmartSuite tries to automate as many things as possible, because typing can often be a waste of time. You don't even have to type in the starting and ending times for an appointment. You can use Time Tracker to change the times for an appointment.

Here's how:

1. First, double-click on a date to create an appointment, like the one shown earlier in this chapter.

2. In the Create Appointment dialog box (shown earlier in Figure 3-5), click the Time drop-down box. Tracker comes up, shown in Figure 3-10.

3. Drag the top clock to change the start time, the bottom clock to change the end time, or the center bar to move the whole appointment.

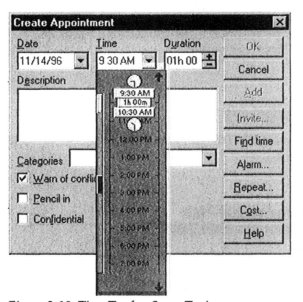

Figure 3-10: Time Tracker Saves Typing.

Printing a Calendar

Maybe you aren't going to be at your computer all day. You'll be in meet-ings, out to lunch, at a trade show, in the car.

You can print out your scheduled work for the day, and you can choose which Organizer tasks to print.

Here's how:

1. Click the Print information SmartIcon (picture of a printer).

2. Click the drop-down box for Section, and select what you want to print. Figure 3-11 shows the Section drop-down box.

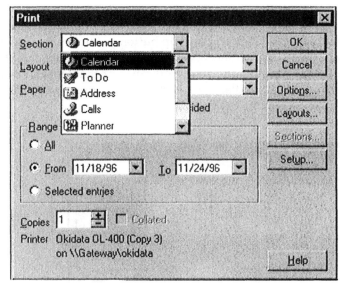

Figure 3-11: Pick a task to print.

3. Click the Layouts button, and use the drop-down list to choose a layout (such as Daily Calendar/To Do/Calls), and click OK.

4. Under Range in the Print dialog box, choose the current date (or whatever range of dates you want to print).

5. Click OK.

Organizer prints out your calendar, and you can put it in your pocket.

Much To Do About Nothing: To Do Lists

A calendar, of course, isn't the same as a simple "to do" list. Organizer recognizes that and offers a separate To Do tab. Sometimes you just want to list the things that you have to do, without setting them for a particular time and other such details.

Creating a To Do Item

To create an entry in your To Do list, click the To Do tab, then double-click. Figure 3-12 shows the Create Task dialog box that comes up. Type in the description for your task.

As in the Calendar, you have a number of optional choices when you create an item. Click on the Help button in the Create task box to read about them. For instance, you can assign a Start date or a Due date for the item. If you assign a date, you can click the Repeat button and have the item repeat, as discussed in the Calendar section in this chapter. Or, you can assign the To Do item a priority.

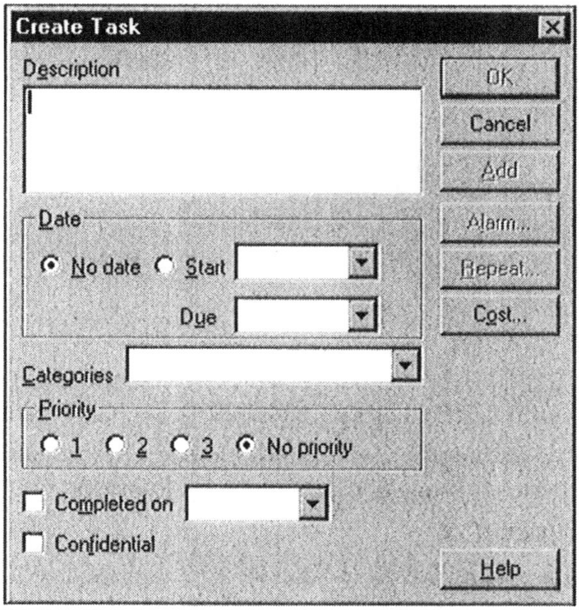

Figure 3-12: Create To Do items in this box.

Once you have an item in your To Do list, you have several choices for dealing with it.

If you maintain a fairly short list of To Do items, you may just want to click in the box next to completed tasks to mark them as done, and leave it at that.

It's fun, and sometimes helpful, to mark down when you completed a task.

Here's how:

1. Double-click your completed To Do task.

2. In the Edit Task box that comes up, click the Completed on drop-down box.

3. Click on the date you want.

4. Click OK.

Picking a View

If you work with many To Do items, you can even sort them by priority, status, start date, or category.

To sort your To Do tasks, from within the To Do section, choose View.

From the View menu (Figure 3-13), click how you want to display the items on the list. Figure 3-13, for instance, shows To Do items by status. Notice that the tabs on the right are for Overdue, Current, Future, and Completed. (The tabs change if you choose a different View, such as By Priority.)

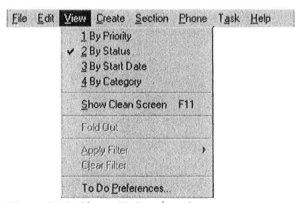

Figure 3-13: Choose To Do views here.

Addressing the Address Book Question

For someone who uses the entire SmartSuite, the address section may be the most important one in Organizer, because you can use the addresses over and over again with other SmartSuite programs. Use them with Word Pro to send out a mail merge. (Chapter 12 talks about doing a mail merge using a Word Pro form letter and an Approach database of addresses.) Import the addresses into the main database program (Approach) and have full relational database power over them. Use them with 1-2-3 to copy addresses into the spreadsheet program.

Creating an Address Entry

You put entries into the Address Book the same as into any other section: click on the tab for Address book, double-click, then fill in the form (shown in Figure 3-14).

Tip

Notice that there are tabs for Business and Home. You may complete both, if you have the information. The Business and Home information (i.e., personal information) show up as separate entries in almost all views in the address book. Don't be confused if you're in the Home tab and you don't see information you put into the Business tab.

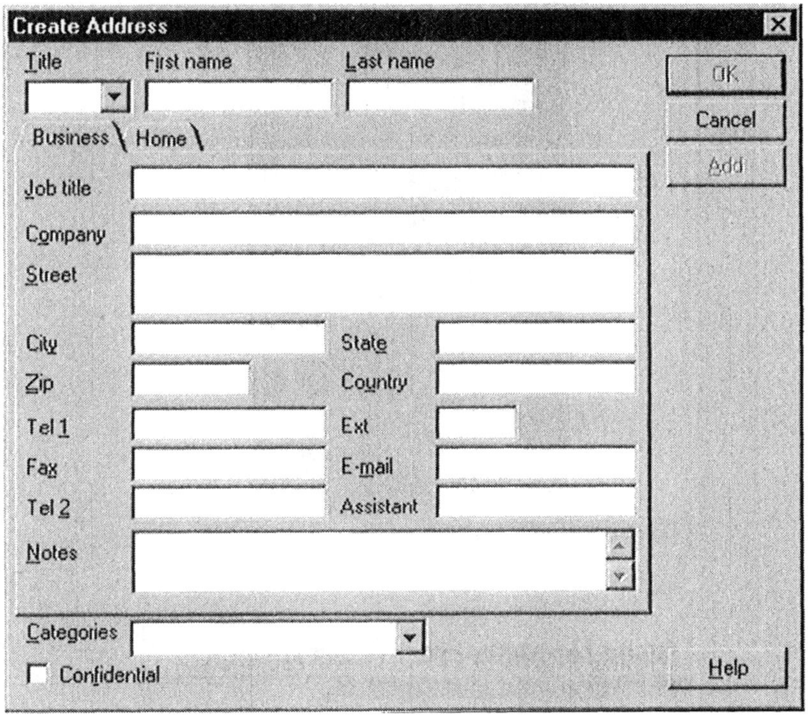

Figure 3-14: Fill in this form to add an address.

Picking a View

Another primary way to use addresses is to sort them in some meaningful way. You can do more elaborate sorts in Approach and 1-2-3 than in Organizer, but the Organizer sorts may well be all you need on many occasions.

You may want to sort by last name, just to put addresses in order. You may want to sort by company so that you can plan a systematic sales approach by company, for instance.

Here's how to sort addresses:

1. From the main menu at the top, choose View.

2. From the View menu (Figure 3-15), choose a style of sort, such as By Company.

Organizer sorts the records according to your criteria.

Figure 3-15: Choose Sorts here.

Dialing Numbers From Address Book

The most common reason to look up anyone's address in the address book, I would venture to guess, is to call that person.

If you have a modem installed and set up properly, you can call automatically from Address Book (and also from To Do, Calls, or any other section):

1. Select the entry that has the phone number.

2. From the Phone menu, choose Quick Dial.

3. In the Dial dialog box, shown in Figure 3-16, click Dial.

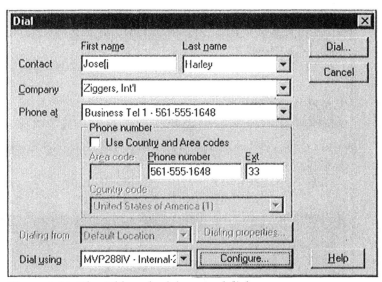

Figure 3-16: The Address book is a speed dialer.

4. When the Call Status dialog box comes up and says "Lift the receiver and talk," do as directed. It's a SmartSuite form of speed dialing.

Tip

If you find yourself using Quick Dial often, add a SmartIcon for the capability to your primary SmartIcon bar.

Or, if you like Drag and Drop (as I do), you can drag an address to the Toolbox icon of a phone (on the left of the screen), with the label Drag an entry here to dial. The Dial dialog box comes up, and you follow step 4 just listed.

Keeping Track of Calls

If you have to just call someone, then the Address book is all you need. Look up the number and Quick Dial it.

Sometimes, though, you have to call someone repeatedly—to check the progress of a proposal, for instance, or to make initial and follow-up calls for an interview.

Use the Calls section to track both your incoming and outgoing calls.

Creating a Call

You create a call as in any of the other sections: click the Calls tab, then double-click on the page.

Figure 3-17 shows the form for creating a call.

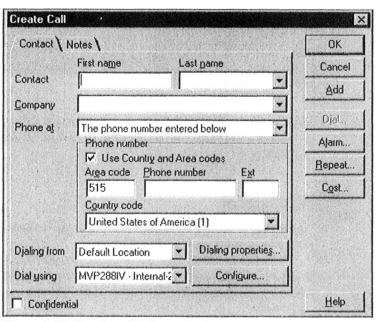

Figure 3-17: Type in call information here.

To put in information about the call, click the Notes tab, and type the information under Notes.

Type your Notes into the Create Follow up Call box.

As with addresses, you can click the View menu to choose how to view your Calls: by person, company, date, or category.

Creating a Follow-up Call

You can track follow-up calls to a person:

1. Click Call on the Menu Bar at the top.

2. Click Follow Up.

3. In the Create Follow up Call box, Figure 3-18, type in notes about the call, and use any other options in the dialog box that you want.

4. Click OK.

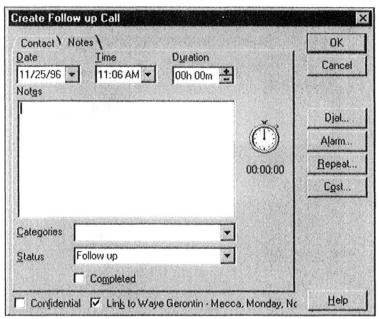

Figure 3-18: Use this for follow-up calls.

Putting In Some Planning: Planner

You may not turn to the planner every day, or even every week. The planner shows long-term commitments of various sorts—vacations, that annual trip to a trade show, company meetings. Planner shows events that take all day or more than one day, not just an hour or 15 minutes.

Creating an Entry

You make entries into the Planner the same as in every other section. Figure 3-19 shows a Create Event dialog box for the planner.

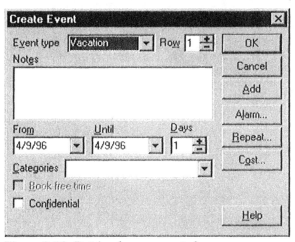

Figure 3-19: Put in planner events here.

You can type in entries, but much of the fun in planner comes from dragging and dropping instead of typing in entries. Click on a colored category at the bottom, and drag over a time frame to "block out" that time period.

Picking a View

You can view the Planner by year or by quarter. Click on the icons on the left, just below the date, to change the view.

Scribbling, Scribbling: Notepad

Most of us, when working by hand, scribble down notes on envelopes, Post-it notes, napkins, or whatever we can find in the heat of the moment. Then, later, we sort through them in various ways (if they have survived the latest visit of the cleaning person and other risks of being on a busy desktop).

Organizer Notepad offers a better way to note down those random (but important) thoughts and find them later. When you put them in Notepad, you give them a title, and you can readily view them later in a number of ways—by Page Number, by Title, by Date, or by Category.

Nobody says the napkin will ever go out of style for taking down those random jottings, but Notepad offers certain efficiencies.

Creating an Entry

You can use the Notepad in a free-form way. Just click the tab, double-click, name your project in the Create Page dialog box, and type in information.

Figure 3-20 shows a new notepad page with a brief entry.

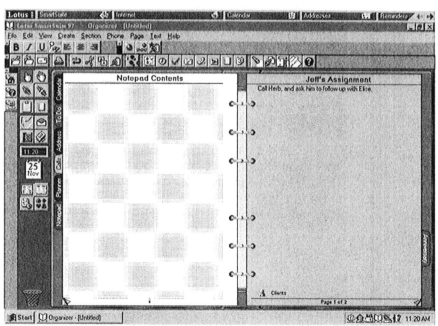

Figure 3-20: You can create a page, and just type.

Once you've created your pages, you can find them again on the Contents page. Just click the Notepad tab to see the Contents page, shown in Figure 3-21.

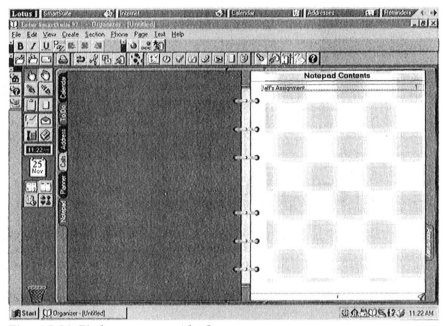

Figure 3-21: Find your notes on the Contents page.

Picking a View

Once you have a number of entries in the Notepad, you can choose to view them a number of different ways—by Page Number, by Title, by Date, or by Category.

Use the View menu to choose a view (Figure 3-22), or click on the icons below the calendar icon on the left.

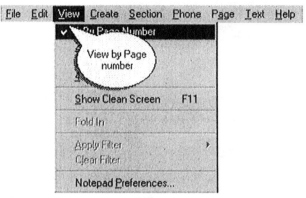

Figure 3-22: You can view the Notepad various ways.

Other Neat Notepad Options

You may want to set up a link to a World Wide Web browser, so that the browser is visible right in your Notepad. (Of course, thanks to the Internet drawer in SmartCenter, you may not need to set up the link this way.) Chapter 7 talks about using Notepad with the Internet.

Remembering Birthdays & Such: Anniversary

Not everybody seems to remember birthdays and anniversaries. Organizer isn't likely to change that widespread failing in human nature, but it may make forgetting birthdays a little less common. If you remember a birthday once, and put it into Organizer, all you have to do in the future is remember to look in Anniversary to see the data. In fact, you don't have to remember to look in Anniversary, because you can have information from Anniversary show through automatically into Calendar or Planner.

Double click in Anniversary to enter an anniversary, and fill in the Create Anniversary box, shown in Figure 3-23.

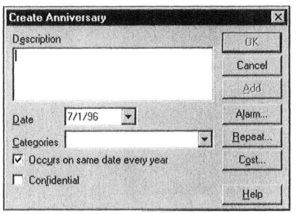

Figure 3-23: Put in Anniversaries here.

Here are a few cool things you can do with Anniversary:

■ Have the date carry through from year to year.

■ View by Month, Year, Zodiac sign, or Category (using either the menus or the icons just below the calendar).

■ Set alarms to remind you of dates.

■ Have anniversaries show through into the calendar (which you probably check more regularly than anniversary).

Customizing Organizer

You can make all kinds of fine distinctions in how your Organizer displays. Most people, at first, probably don't care about the tiny details and just want to put in their appointments or their To Do items.

As you begin to realize how you work, though, you may see that you can set up Organizer so that it displays the way you most often use it. You can set up preferences for each tab in Organizer—Calendar, To Do, Address, Calls, Planner, Notepad, and Anniversary.

The menu choice is the same in each case. Click View in the menu at the top, then click the last item—Calendar Preferences (or preferences for whichever part of Organizer you're using).

For example, to change your Calendar Preferences, follow these steps:

1. Click the Calendar tab to open the Calendar.

2. Click View.

3. Click Calendar Preferences.

4. Make your choices in the Calendar Preferences dialog box, shown in Figure 3-24.

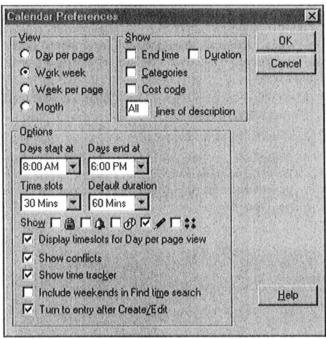

Figure 3-24: You can control all kinds of preferences here.

Advanced Topics

Once you get used to a few things about your paper steno pad or address book, you probably stop your learning process right there. What's left to master, in the case of those simple objects?

With your electronic information manager, though, you can get the best of both worlds. You can get started using it pretty quickly, by creating entries and viewing them different ways.

Once you own the basics, though, you can continue to find new capabilities and new ways to let Organizer make you more efficient. Here, in the following sections, are a few of my favorites.

Starting Other Applications Automatically

You can have Organizer automatically reach out to start other applications—just the type of activity that SmartSuite is all about.

Here's how:

1. Create or edit an entry in the Calendar, To Do, Calls, Planner, or Anniversary section.

2. Click the Alarm button.

3. In the Start text box, put in the path and filename for the application you want to start. (Use the Browse button to be sure you get the path and name right.) Figure 3-25 shows the Alarm dialog box.

4. Click OK.

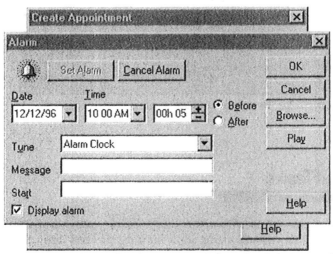

Figure 3-25: An application can start when the alarm goes off.

Being in One Task, Working in Another

Let's say you are in the Calendar section, and you remember a task you must complete before you go to the appointment you've just scheduled:

1. From the menu, Choose Create | Entry In. Figure 3-26 shows the menu.

2. Click on the task you want, such as To Do.

Even though you are still in the Calendar section, the Create Task dialog box appears where you can enter your task information without leaving the section you're in.

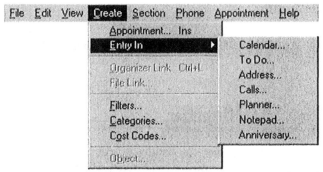

Figure 3-26: Use this menu to make an entry in a task you're not in at the moment.

Displaying Information From Other Sections

When you're in one task in Organizer, you can sometimes get useful information from other sections. In Calendar, you can get information from the To Do, Calls, Planner, and Anniversary sections.

Suppose you want to be able to see your To Do items in the calendar:

1. From the date in the Calendar you want, click the Section menu, then Show Through.

The Show Through dialog box comes up, shown in Figure 3-27.

2. Click the item or items you want to have show through— To Do for this example.

3. Click OK.

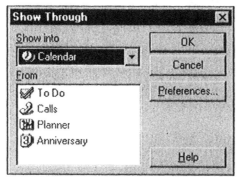

Figure 3-27: Choose what you want to have show through.

Linking Parts of Organizer

SmartSuite is all about using different programs together as if they were one, and the principle applies even when within Organizer. You can link different parts of Organizer together.

For instance, you can link an appointment scheduled in calendar to an address record of someone you're going to meet with.

Here's how to create a link:

1. Click on the entry that you want to Link to another.

2. Click on the Create Links tool.

3. Click on the entry that you want to link to, either in the same section of Organizer or a different section. A picture of a chain link appears next to any linked information.

Taking Organizer on the Road

Calendars are all about portability. You carry them around. Often, you need them most when you are scurrying around airports or sitting in a strange office across the country from your home office.

You don't have to abandon Organizer when you're traveling, though. You can use Organizer on your laptop and keep yourself up to date. Of course, you have to have Organizer installed on the laptop.

Here's what to do:

1. Copy the most recent version of the Organizer file to your laptop before you go.

2. Make entries into the file on the laptop for To Do tasks, calls, Addresses, Notepad, or whatever as you travel.

3. When you get back into the office, open the original Organizer file on your main computer or network.

4. Choose File, then Merge.

5. In the Merge dialog box, choose the name of the file on the portable that you want to merge and the one on the main computer that you want to merge into, and press Merge.

Tip

You can use the Browse button to find the file on your portable that you're going to merge. Most likely it will be on the A: drive and have the same name as the one you're merging it into.

Moving On

Once you get into the swing of it, doing anything in Organizer is pretty much of a cinch. Organizer may seem more ambitious at first than the Addresses and Calendar in SmartCenter. But really, it isn't. Organizer lets you do more than SmartCenter alone, but just by making simple choices from dialog boxes you can link Organizer files, have parts of Organizer show through into other parts, start up other applications, and do some other advanced-sounding activities.

Using tools together as if they were a single tool is really the main idea of SmartSuite as a whole. Having had a taste of using programs together within Organizer, you get down to that in earnest in the next chapter, where you use Freelance and 1-2-3 together.

4

Combining in the Suite: Freelancing 1-2-3

Probably the most important benefit of working with a suite of products instead of individual products is the ability to use applications together.

Even as the members of SmartSuite continue to become more and more similar in their interface, they continue to have "specialties." Say what you will, for instance, but 1-2-3 is still better than any other member of the suite at putting numbers into a table and applying formulas and functions to them. For its part, Freelance—though it has pretty nifty tables for a graphics program—really can't compare with 1-2-3 as a number cruncher.

Freelance, meanwhile, is the cat's meow at presenting information so that people can grasp its meaning right away. It creates great bullet charts, title pages, and all the rest that has to do with great graphics. 1-2-3, though it creates nice graphics, really can't compare.

SmartSuite gives you the best of both worlds. Want to crunch some numbers, then present them? Use 1-2-3 first, then present them in Freelance.

Using 1-2-3 and Freelance as an example, this chapter gets you started thinking of the multiple programs in SmartSuite as almost a single program.

Using 1-2-3 Data in Freelance

1-2-3 is the place to work with data. Freelance, though, is the right place to present that data effectively to others. Using 1-2-3 and Freelance together in SmartSuite, you get maximum power in both working with data and presenting it.

Copying 1-2-3 Data to a Freelance Table

The easiest way to display your 1-2-3 data in Freelance is simply to cut and paste it. Thanks to the Windows Clipboard, you can cut and paste between programs just as if you are working with one program.

Here's how to display 1-2-3 data in Freelance.

Starting 1-2-3

For many of the examples throughout this book, you start programs and work with a program that is running. Though starting programs may soon become automatic for you, here is a step-by-step guide to starting 1-2-3 and, in this case, opening the first workbook:

1. In SmartCenter (the "file drawers," usually across the top of the screen), click the SmartSuite drawer to open it.

2. Find the icon for 1-2-3, the one labeled Lotus 1-2-3, and double-click it. The Welcome to 1-2-3 screen comes up.

3. Click the tab for Create a New Workbook Using a SmartMaster.

Your screen should now be similar to the one shown in Figure 4-1. Click the Create a Blank Workbook button at the bottom. A blank 1-2-3 workbook comes up, where you can create the table you'll later present using Freelance.

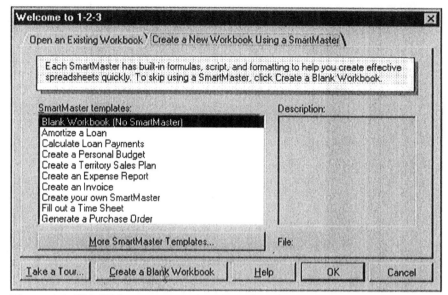

Figure 4-1: This Welcome screen comes up when you start.

Creating a Sample Worksheet

As I explain in the Introduction to this book, this book covers SmartSuite and doesn't give detailed information about all of the programs in it. There's just too much to cover. 1-2-3 alone could be the subject for a book at least as long as the one you're reading.

Figure 4-2 shows a basic sales worksheet, of the kind many companies keep.

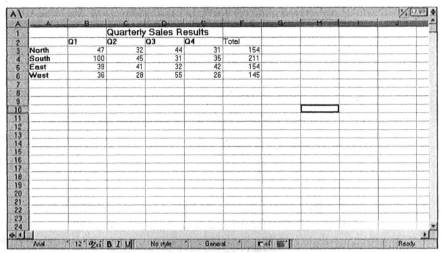

Figure 4-2: Sales worksheets like this are common.

To create the sheet yourself, follow these general steps:

1. Click in a cell where you want to enter data, and type the data.

2. Press Enter when you've finished the data for each cell.

3. At the top of the sixth column of data (in cell A:F2 in the example), type the word Total. With this neat new feature in 1-2-3, totals for each of the rows appear automatically in column F.

4. Save the worksheet with the name sales_results.

5. To save the workbook, click the SmartIcon for Save the Current File (an arrow pointing into a file folder). In the Save As dialog box, choose a location for the file, if you wish. Type in the name next to File name. If you like, type in a description next to Description and click Save.

To make the worksheet attractive and easy to read, I have put the row and column heads in bold type and have used a large font for the title. You probably know how to use such formatting. You don't have to use it, though, for the example to work.

Starting Freelance

To copy between two programs, you have to have both of them running. Since I just showed you how to start a program using SmartCenter, I'll show you a different method for Freelance. You can start it using SuiteStart. Here's how:

1. If you have SuiteStart running (the small Lotus icons—originally on the right side of the Windows 95 Taskbar, next to the time, though you may have moved them), click on the Lotus Freelance Graphics icon (a picture of three people behind a bar chart).
   As with 1-2-3, a Welcome screen comes up.

2. Click on the tab labeled Create a New Presentation Using a SmartMaster.

3. For Select a content topic, leave the choice as is.

4. For Select a Look, have some fun and choose a look. Each time you click on a look, you see an example of it in the Sample box in the lower right of the dialog box. The example uses the "shadowbx" look.

Figure 4-3 shows the Welcome screen with the look selected:

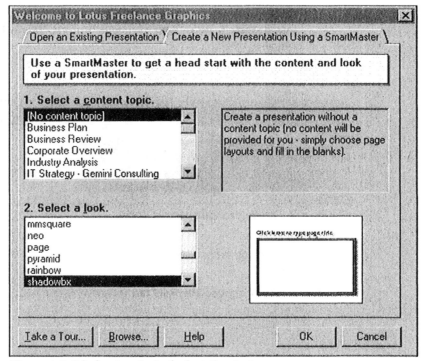

Figure 4-3: It's fun to select a look at the start.

5. Click OK in the Welcome screen to start the program.

6. When Freelance starts, a New Page screen comes up. For now, just click the OK button to accept the selected page type—Title.

7. If you like, save the presentation. The example saves the presentation with the name sales_table.

Once you have both programs running, you're ready to get to the fun part—copying from 1-2-3 to Freelance.

Selecting a 1-2-3 Range to Copy

When you're working on your own, don't be surprised if you end up experimenting a little when choosing what to copy. For instance, you may or may not want to copy the title from 1-2-3 into Freelance, or you may or may not choose to include the Total.

Here's how to copy sample material for this example:

1. Click on the 1-2-3 button on the Windows 95 Taskbar to return to 1-2-3.

2. Click and drag across the cells you want to copy. The example selects cells A:A2 to A:E6 (not selecting the title or the Total column).

Figure 4-4 shows the selected cells.

A	A	B	C	D	E	F	G
1			Quarterly Sales Results				
2		Q1	Q2	Q3	Q4	Total	
3	North	47	32	44	31	154	
4	South	100	45	31	35	211	
5	East	39	41	32	42	154	
6	West	36	28	55	26	145	
7							

Figure 4-4: Drag across cells to select them.

3. Right-click the selected cells, and click Copy on the shortcut menu.

You have now copied the selected material to the handy clipboard.

Tip

Remember that the clipboard holds only one item at a time, so your selected material stays there only until you copy something else to the clipboard.

With the selected cells nicely copied to the clipboard, you're ready to paste them into a Freelance table.

Pasting 1-2-3 Data Into a Freelance Table

There are a few preparations for pasting, such as creating the right Freelance page to paste into. Here's what to do:

1. Click on the Freelance Graphics button in the Windows 95 Taskbar to return to Freelance.

2. In Freelance, click on the New Page button (top left) in the presentation where you want to create the table.

3. In the New Page dialog box, click Table as your page layout (Figure 4-5), and click OK.

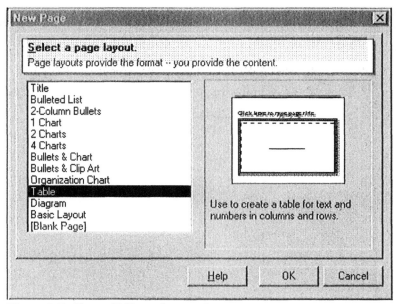

Figure 4-5: Choose Table as the page layout.

4. On the Table page, click where it says, "Click Here to Create a Table."

5. In the Table Gallery box (Figure 4-6), click on a table style—the first one, for the example, with lines around all cells.

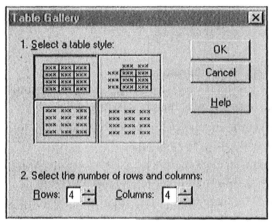

Figure 4-6: Choose a table style.

6. Click the up and down arrows to put in the number of rows and columns—five of each for the example (the number of rows and columns copied from 1-2-3 to the clipboard).

7. Click OK. The empty table appears on the page.

8. Click in the top left cell of the blank table to place the cursor there.

9. Right-click, and choose Paste. The 1-2-3 cells become a Freelance table, where you can apply Freelance's graphics power to them (Figure 4-7).

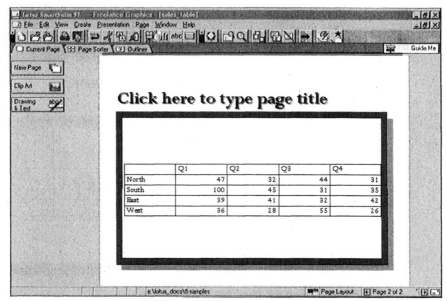

Figure 4-7: The 1-2-3 cells become a Freelance table.

Enhancing the Table in Freelance

The main reason to put 1-2-3 cells into Freelance is to be able to apply the power of the graphics program to them. For instance, you could put a frame around the table as follows:

1. Click in the top left cell to put a frame around the table.

2. In the example, you didn't copy the title from 1-2-3. Instead, you can use the "Click here to type page title" block in Freelance to put in a nicely preformatted title.

3. Click on the 1-2-3 button in the taskbar. Then, select the title (Quarterly Sales Results), right-click, and click Copy.

4. Click on the Freelance button in the taskbar. Then, click where it says Click Here to type a page title.

5. Right-click in the click here block in Freelance, and click Paste.

6. The title appears in Freelance. Click outside the click here block to see what the table looks like with these simple enhancements, as shown in Figure 4-8.

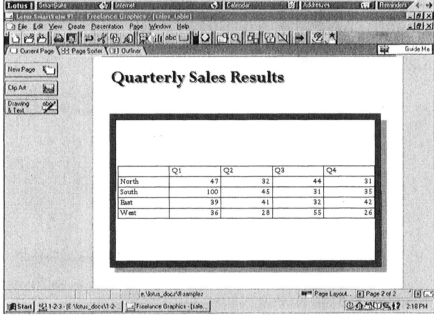

Figure 4-8: Use Freelance to enhance the 1-2-3 data.

Applying More of the Power of Freelance

You can improve colors and lines in the table, use drawing tools to call attention to parts of the table, and in general enhance the table better than you could in 1-2-3 alone (which does share some of the same graphics tools).

Suppose, for instance, you wanted to add a colorful border to the table:

1. Click the table to select it.

2. Right-click, and choose Table Properties to bring up the Lotus InfoBox.

3. Click on the fourth tab from the left, for Color, Pattern, and Line Style.

Figure 4-9 shows the InfoBox with the tab displayed for color, pattern, and line style.

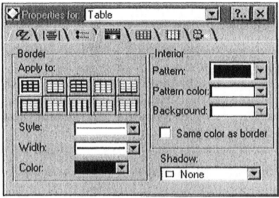

Figure 4-9: Use the InfoBox to change pattern and colors.

4. In the Interior box, click on the list box next to Pattern Color, and choose Teal (or another color that appeals to you). This is just for fun. Even for serious presentations, color is mostly for fun.

5. Under Border, click on Color, and choose orange.

6. Click the X in the top right of the InfoBox to close it. Or, if you like, you can leave the InfoBox open. You can click on the Title bar at the top and drag the box to different parts of the page to keep it from blocking your view of the page.

Tip

As you make changes in the InfoBox, they show up in the table itself, and not just in a sample box within the dialog box as they do when you choose a SmartMaster. You can use this feature of Lotus products to experiment with changes before making final selections.

You could continue to experiment in the InfoBox with various looks and effects for the table. And you could use other Freelance capabilities, such as adding clip art to the page. The specific changes are not the point here, though. The idea is that once you have copied the 1-2-3 data to Freelance, you have all the power of Freelance at your disposal for making the data look good.

Dragging & Dropping Data From 1-2-3 to Freelance

You don't even have to use the Copy and Paste commands to copy data from 1-2-3 to Freelance. You can use drag and drop.

For the example, I again used the sales_results worksheet in 1-2-3 and the sales_table presentation in Freelance. Refer to the sections "Starting 1-2-3," "Creating a Sample Worksheet," and "Starting Freelance" if you want to see how I created the sample files.

First, in Freelance create a fresh page to which you'll drag the 1-2-3 data:

1. In Freelance, click the New Page button to create a fresh page.

2. In the New Page dialog box, click Table, and choose OK.

3. Before doing this step, you might want to close any other open programs, besides Freelance and 1-2-3, so your screen will be easy to read. Right-click the Windows 95 Taskbar, and click Tile Horizontally. The two applications appear so that you can see both, as shown in Figure 4-10.

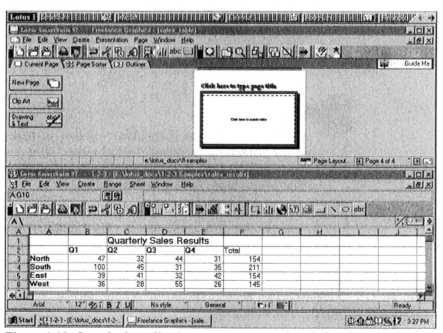

Figure 4-10: Open both applications so you can see them before dragging and dropping.

4. Click and drag across the 1-2-3 cells you want to copy.

5. Position the pointer on the border of the selected cells. Be sure that the pointer changes to a hand.

6. Hold down the left mouse button, and drag the selection to the Freelance page.

7. Release the mouse button. The cells appear in the Freelance table, as shown in Figure 4-11.

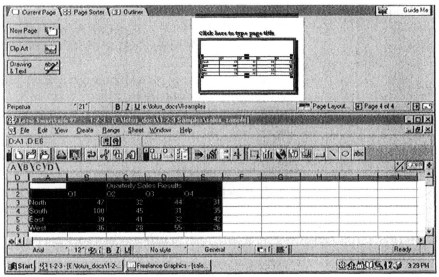

Figure 4-11: The dragged cells appear in Freelance.

When you finish, you may want to save the changed Freelance Graphics file. Click the Save SmartIcon (an arrow pointing into a file folder). If you've saved the file previously, then Freelance saves the file and you don't have to supply filename, location, or description again.

Linking 1-2-3 Data to a Freelance Table

In the previous example in this chapter, when you paste the 1-2-3 data into Freelance, the data becomes Freelance data. If you change the data in 1-2-3, you don't change the data in Freelance at the same time.

However, you can link the Freelance data to 1-2-3 data, so that if you change the 1-2-3 data, the Freelance data reflects the change. Linked data can be useful, for instance, for a weekly report where you want to have Freelance reflect the latest data recorded in 1-2-3.

Here's how to link a Freelance table to 1-2-3:

1. If you don't have Freelance running already, start it in one of the usual ways—such as by clicking the Lotus Freelance Graphics icon in SuiteStart.

2. In the Welcome screen, open a presentation or create a new one. The example uses the existing presentation used already in the chapter sales_table.

3. Click on the New Page button.

4. In the New Page dialog box, choose [Blank Page] for the page layout, and click OK.

You're ready to set up the link. The steps are similar to those for copying data, but you will use Paste Special instead of just Paste. Here are the steps to establish the link:

1. Be sure that the 1-2-3 file has been saved (that is, that it has a name and is not an untitled file). Be sure to keep the 1-2-3 file open as you set up the link. For the example, use the sales_results workbook from earlier in the chapter. If you have it running already, click on the 1-2-3 button in the taskbar to switch to 1-2-3.

2. Drag across the data you want to copy, as shown earlier in the chapter in Figure 4-4.

3. Right-click, and click Copy in the shortcut menu. You have placed the data in the Win95 clipboard.

4. Click on the Freelance Graphics button in the taskbar to switch back to that application.

5. From the Edit menu, choose Paste Special.

6. In the Paste Special dialog box (Figure 4-12), click the Paste Link to Source radio button.

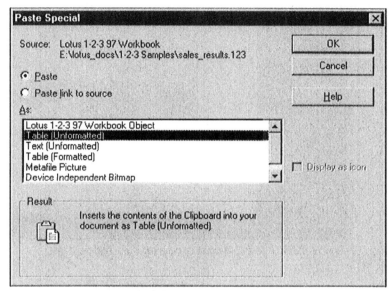

Figure 4-12: Set up the link here.

7. Be sure that the item you want is highlighted: Linked Lotus 97 1-2-3 Workbook Object. Click OK. The linked object now appears on the page in Freelance, as shown in Figure 4-13.

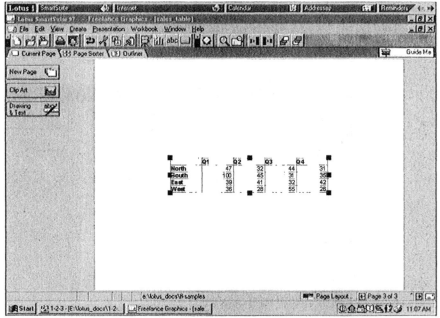

Figure 4-13: The 1-2-3 data is now on the Freelance page.

The linked data is an OLE (Object Linking and Embedding) object. You can drag the handles to resize it, and you can drag the complete object to reposition it. Changes in 1-2-3 show up in the Freelance table. When you click in the Freelance table to work with the data, you return to 1-2-3.

Linking 1-2-3 Data to a Freelance Chart

1-2-3 specializes in handling data, and Freelance is best at presenting the data. Therefore, you often may choose to work with data in Freelance and present it directly as a Freelance chart. This section shows you how to do this. You may have created a chart in 1-2-3 already; if so, you can still use the chart in Freelance.

More powerful than copying the data once from 1-2-3 to Freelance is linking the 1-2-3 data to a Freelance chart. You may have a table of data that you maintain all the time, changing the table as the data changes. A linked Freelance chart would then reflect these changes. Here is how to work with charts (as opposed to tables) in 1-2-3 and Freelance.

To link 1-2-3 data to a Freelance chart, you don't have to have both applications open. From within Freelance itself you get a view of the 1-2-3 worksheet and you can select the cells you want to link. You will see in Freelance an Edit Data dialog box that gives you a view of the 1-2-3 data, as you see in the steps that follow.

Creating a New Page in Freelance & Setting Up the Links

To link a chart to 1-2-3 data, you create a page, then set up the link. Here I again used the Freelance presentation sales_table. You can refer to the section "Starting Freelance" earlier in the chapter to see how to set it up.

1. If you haven't done so already, start Freelance and choose a presentation to work with. The example continues to work with the "sales_table" presentation in Freelance.

2. In your Freelance presentation, click New Page, select 1 Chart as the page layout, and click OK. Figure 4-14 shows the blank chart page.

Figure 4-14: Create a chart on this page.

3. Click the block that says "Click here to create a chart."

4. In the Create Chart box (Figure 4-15), choose a chart type and style if you like. The example uses the default—a bar chart using basic style. Click OK.

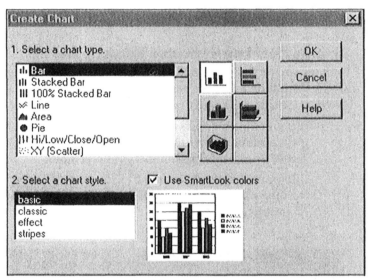

Figure 4-15: Choose a chart type here.

5. In the Edit Data box, Figure 4-16, click Import Data.

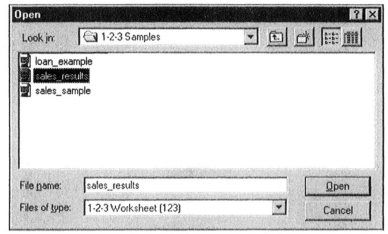

Figure 4-17: Find the file to which you want to link.

7. Click Open to open the file. The Edit Link dialog box comes up.

Editing the Links

You may want to experiment a bit when doing a chart yourself, to get the look you want. You can set up links not only to the 1-2-3 data, but also to the title, the legend, and the X-axis labels.

In the Edit Links dialog box (Figure 4-18), select the range or ranges you want to link. Here's how the example sets up the links:

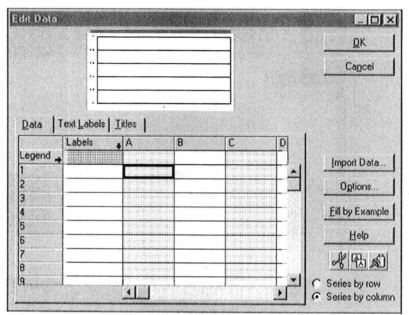

Figure 4-16: Use this box to choose the data to import.

6. In the Open dialog box, find the 1-2-3 file you want to link, and click Open. The example uses the sales_results worksheet from earlier in the chapter, as shown in Figure 4-17. (As I mentioned, the 1-2-3 file doesn't have to be open for you to use it. That's kind of cool.)

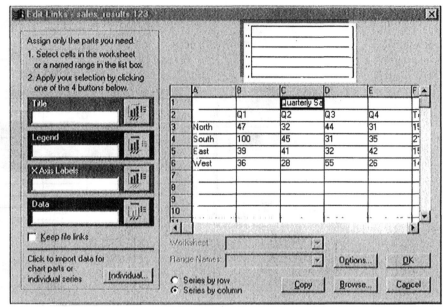

Figure 4-18: Select ranges to link.

1. For the example, click on the title ("Quarterly Sales"), and click the button next to Title on the left of the dialog box. The cell address appears in the title.

2. Drag across the four column labels (Q1 to Q4), and click the button for Legend.

3. Drag across the four sales districts (North, South, East, and West), and click the button next to X-axis labels.

4. Drag across the data in the four columns (don't drag across the title, the labels, or the data in the Total column), and click the button for data.

Figure 4-19 shows the Edit Links dialog box so far.

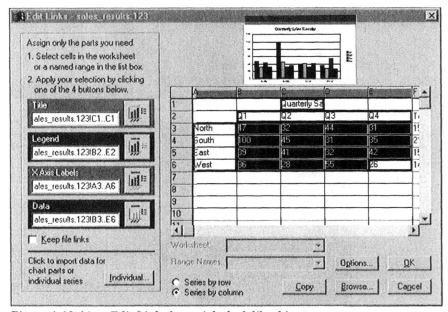

Figure 4-19: Your Edit Links box might look like this one.

5. Click to select "Keep file links."

6. Click on either Series by row or Series by column, using the preview at the top of the box to be sure you're getting what you want. For the example, click Series by column.

7. Click OK. You return to the Edit Data dialog box.

8. Click OK. The chart is now a Freelance chart, as shown in Figure 4-20. The data is linked. If you change data in the worksheet, the changes show up in the chart right away (if the chart is open), or the next time you open the Freelance Presentation containing the chart.

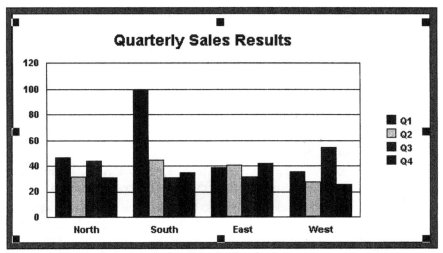

Figure 4-20: The linked data shows up in the chart.

Though you can preview the chart in the Edit Links and in the Edit Data dialog box, you often discover things you'd like to change once you've created the actual chart. If you want to make changes, do this:

1. Click to select the chart.
2. From the Chart menu at the top, click on Edit data.
3. You return to the Edit Data dialog box, where you can make your changes.

Copying a 1-2-3 Chart to a Freelance Presentation

You may be in the habit of creating your charts in 1-2-3, not Freelance. Previously, people might have opted to do everything in 1-2-3, even though Freelance has more powerful charting. You may have a large collection of 1-2-3 charts that you may, on occasion, now want to use in Freelance.

You may decide after the fact to use the more powerful charting in Freelance. You can copy a 1-2-3 chart into Freelance.

Getting Ready in Freelance

You need to display the page you want to use in Freelance when you copy the chart. Here's how to get set up:

1. With both 1-2-3 and Freelance running, open the Freelance presentation where you want to display the 1-2-3 chart.

2. Click New Page, select 1 Chart as the page layout, and click OK.

Creating the 1-2-3 Chart

For this example, you can create a chart in 1-2-3 using the sample "sales_results" from the chapter. To create the chart:

1. Click on the 1-2-3 button in the taskbar (or start 1-2-3, if you haven't done so already, and display the sales-results sample data as explained at the start of the chapter).

2. Click the Create a chart SmartIcon (a picture of a bar chart).

3. The Chart Assistant comes up, shown in Figure 4-21.

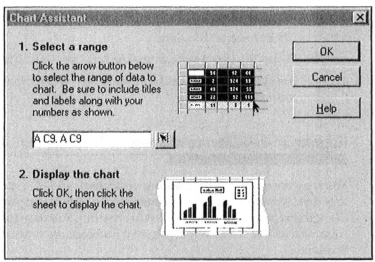

Figure 4-21: Create 1-2-3 charts with the Chart Assistant.

4. Drag over the cells you want to chart—in the example, all cells but the Total column.

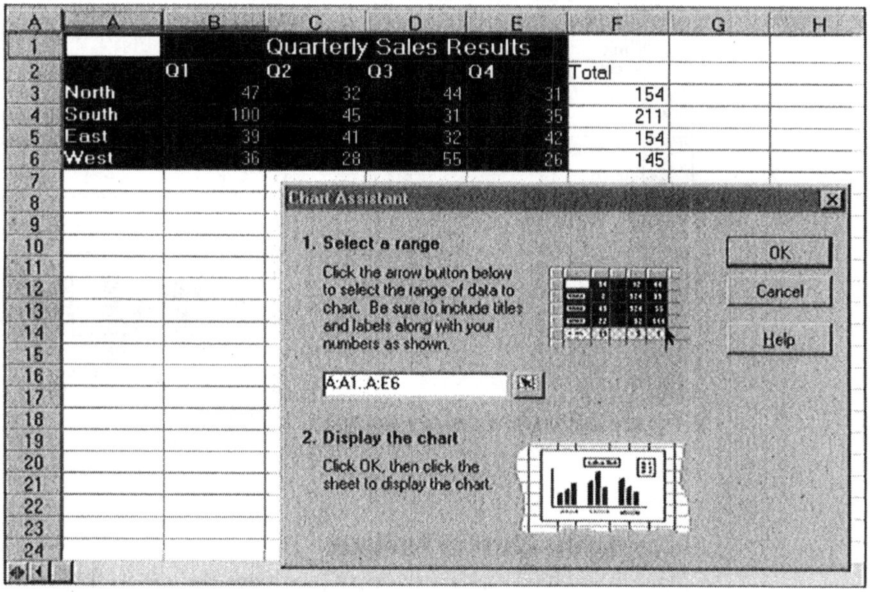

	A	B	C	D	E	F	G	H
1			Quarterly Sales Results					
2		Q1	Q2	Q3	Q4	Total		
3	North	47	32	44	31	154		
4	South	100	45	31	35	211		
5	East	39	41	32	42	154		
6	West	36	28	55	26	145		

Chart Assistant

1. Select a range

Click the arrow button below to select the range of data to chart. Be sure to include titles and labels along with your numbers as shown.

A:A1..A:E6

2. Display the chart

Click OK, then click the sheet to display the chart.

OK

Cancel

Help

Figure 4-22: Select the cells you want to chart.

5. Click OK.

6. Click and drag in the worksheet to create the chart.

Figure 4-23 shows the completed 1-2-3 chart.

7. You don't have to save the worksheet for the example to work, but you may want to click the Save SmartIcon to avoid any risk of losing your work.

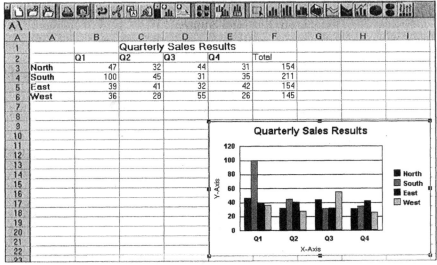

Figure 4-23: Here's a nice sample 1-2-3 chart.

Copying the Chart to Freelance

Once you have a chart to copy (such as the one in this example), you can readily copy it to Freelance. Here's how:

1. Click on the chart in 1-2-3 to select it. (If you have just created it in the previous example, the chart is already selected. A selected chart has selection handles on the sides.)

2. Click on the Freelance Graphics button in the Windows 95 Taskbar.

3. With Freelance running, click on New Page to create a new page.

4. In the New Page dialog box, click 1 Chart, and click OK.

With the new page in place, you are ready to copy:

1. Right-click the page anywhere outside the Click here block, and click Paste. The 1-2-3 chart appears in Freelance.

2. To position the chart on the page, click Edit, then Select, then All.

3. Drag the chart to the desired position on the page.

Figure 4-24 shows the copied chart in Freelance.

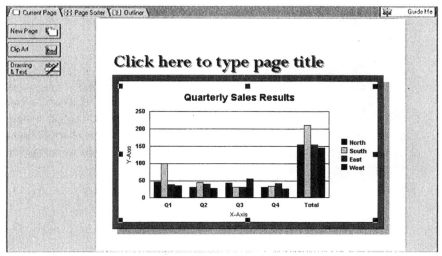

Figure 4-24: You can copy a 1-2-3 chart to Freelance.

You can drag a 1-2-3 chart to Freelance. It's really fun to do that, too. The chart is just a copy, though, not a link. Changes you make in 1-2-3 won't show up in Freelance. Here's how:

1. In Freelance, click on the New Page button, choose 1 Chart as the page layout, and click OK.

2. Click on the 1-2-3 button in the Windows 95 Taskbar to move to 1-2-3. Create the chart in 1-2-3, as described in this section.

3. In 1-2-3, click on a blank area of the chart so that the mouse pointer takes the shape of a hand.

4. Drag the chart to the Freelance Graphics button on the Windows 95 Taskbar. Continue to hold down the mouse button. Freelance becomes the active program. Drag the 1-2-3 chart to the Freelance box that says "Click here to create chart." When you release the mouse button, the 1-2-3 chart appears in Freelance.

5. Dragging and dropping the chart actually works a bit better than using menu commands to copy and paste. You don't have to select and position the chart in Freelance. It goes nicely into place in the Click Here block.

Linking Charts

You can link a Freelance chart to a 1-2-3 chart. In most cases, though, you might as well link to 1-2-3 data instead of linking to a 1-2-3 chart. The fact is that when you link a Freelance chart to a 1-2-3 chart, you are actually linking to the 1-2-3 data anyway. For instance, you could link a 1-2-3 bar chart to Freelance, and then change the 1-2-3 bar chart to a pie chart. The Freelance chart would continue to be a bar chart.

Using Freelance Material in 1-2-3

Truthfully, there would seem to be many more occasions when you might use 1-2-3 materials in Freelance than the other way around. The most common pattern is to accumulate data and perform analysis in 1-2-3, often working in the spreadsheet on a daily basis. Then, on occasion, you might want to use the data in a Freelance presentation.

Nevertheless, you might want to work the other way. Another member of your team, for instance, might specialize in Freelance and compile a valuable table there. Or, a colleague in another department might put together a presentation with a chart that is a big hit with your boss. The boss might want you to maintain the data in 1-2-3 on a regular basis. If you want to use the table in 1-2-3, you can do so.

Or, you might just want to use one of the advanced graphics in Freelance—a nice piece of clip art, for instance—in a 1-2-3 worksheet. If the occasion calls for it, you can move Freelance materials into 1-2-3.

Copying Data From a Freelance Table into 1-2-3

To copy data from a Freelance Table into 1-2-3, you follow basically the same procedures you're probably familiar with in copying from 1-2-3 to Freelance or in exchanging data between other SmartSuite programs. You can drag and drop the table, or you can use the menus to copy and paste it. You can copy all of a table or part of it.

The most fun part of copying—as in copying from 1-2-3—is dragging selected data to the 1-2-3 icon in the Windows 95 Taskbar, then pasting it automatically into 1-2-3. (Not everybody finds that fun, I guess, but I do.)

Tip

Caution: Remember that copying data is not the same as linking data. Copied data doesn't change if you change the source data; linked data does. Although you can link 1-2-3 charts and data with Freelance, you can't link Freelance charts and data with 1-2-3, at least not in the present version of SmartSuite. Once you have pasted a Freelance table into 1-2-3, the 1-2-3 table won't reflect changes you make to the Freelance data.

Starting Freelance & Creating a Sample Table

Freelance tables don't allow you to use functions. In this case, you're not being unfair to Freelance if you say, "Its tables are just for show." In fact, Freelance is proud of that. However, suppose you had a table in Freelance that you wanted to enhance in 1-2-3 by adding numbers and "crunching" them. You could copy a Freelance table to 1-2-3. Here's how to create the sample table:

1. Click its icon in SuiteStart to start Freelance.

2. In the Welcome to Lotus Freelance Graphics screen, click the tab labeled Create a New Presentation Using a SmartMaster. In the Select a Content Topic box, click Industry Analysis. Just for fun, click a look in the Select a Look box—click 3line. Click OK.

Figure 4-25 shows the completed dialog box.

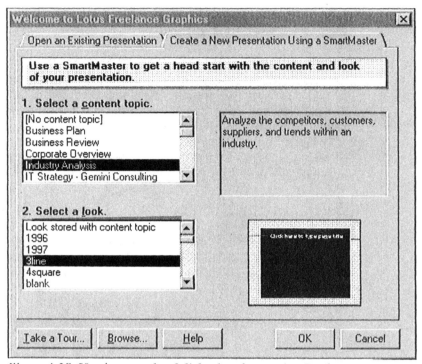

Figure 4-25: Here's a completed dialog box for starting Freelance.

3. In the New Page box, in the Content Pages tab, click Competitor
    Strategies as the content page. See Figure 4-26.

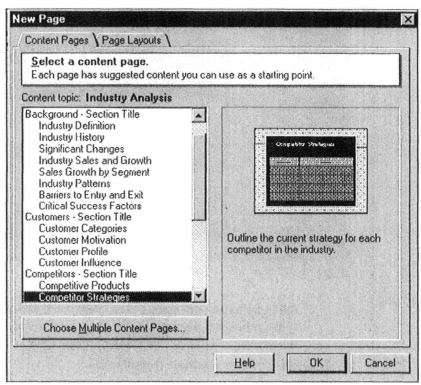

Figure 4-26: Select "Competitor Strategies" as the content page.

4. Click OK. A blank table comes up, shown in Figure 4-27.

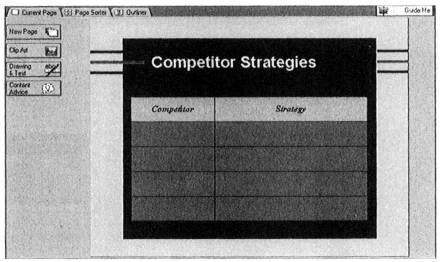

Figure 4-27: Start with a blank table like this.

5. Fill in the table with sample data. Double-click to place the cursor in the initial cell, and type in the contents. Use the arrow keys to move from cell to cell. I saved the presentation as "competitors."

Figure 4-28 shows a sample completed table.

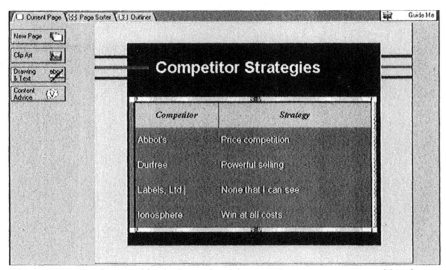

Figure 4-28: Freelance tables look so nice, it's tempting to create your tables there.

Dragging & Dropping the Table Into 1-2-3

You can drag and drop material from Freelance to 1-2-3, just as you can drag it from 1-2-3 to Freelance. Suppose you wanted to copy the sample list of Competitor Strategies into 1-2-3, where you might perform additional analysis on the list. (And, of course, the list might be much longer than the four entries in the example. Copying would save typing time and prevent errors.)

To drag and drop the table into 1-2-3:

1. Start 1-2-3 by clicking on its icon in SuiteStart.

2. In the Welcome to 1-2-3 box, click Create a Blank Workbook. 1-2-3 starts up and displays a blank page 3. With both Freelance and 1-2-3 open to the pages you want to work with, select the table you want to copy. (Be sure there are selection handles on all four sides of the table. If you have been typing in the table, first click outside it, then click in it once to select it.) Figure 4-29 shows a selected table.

Tip

If you want, you can drag and drop just a portion of the table. Simply drag across the cells to select them, then follow the same steps as for dragging and dropping the entire table.

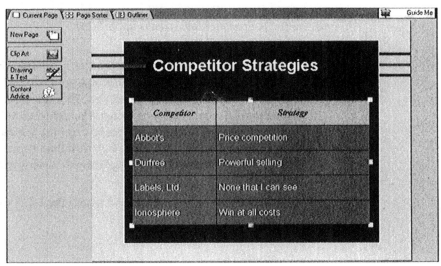

Figure 4-29: Select the table to copy.

3. Drag the table to the 1-2-3 button in the Windows 95 Taskbar, and continue to hold down the button. When 1-2-3 becomes active, position the pointer where you want the table to appear in 1-2-3, and release the pointer. The table appears in 1-2-3, as shown in Figure 4-30.

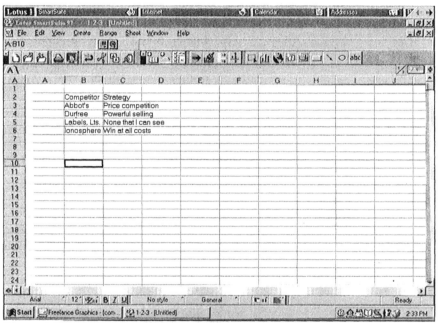

Figure 4-30: The Freelance table shows up in 1-2-3.

The Freelance table becomes actual 1-2-3 data that you can work on in 1-2-3, not just an OLE object on top of 1-2-3, unlike Freelance tables copied to Word Pro. Though there are advantages to OLE, such as the fact that it is linked directly to the source, there are also advantages to copying the data into 1-2-3. You're free to work with it just as if you had typed it into 1-2-3 in the first place, instead of having to work with it in the source application.

4. I clicked the Save SmartIcon and saved the 1-2-3 workbook as "competitors."

After you have the table in place, you may want to enhance it. I placed the column heads in bold type and resize the columns so that all the text shows.

Using the Menus to Copy & Paste

Some people don't like drag and drop. They prefer to use the menus or keyboard commands to copy and paste. Here's how to use the menus to copy and paste:

1. In Freelance, select the table you want to copy.

2. From the Edit menu, click Copy.

3. Click the 1-2-3 button on the taskbar to switch to 1-2-3.

4. Position the cursor where you want the table to appear in 1-2-3. From the 1-2-3 Edit menu, choose Paste.

Copying a Graphic From Freelance Into 1-2-3

Freelance, the drawing specialist, has more powerful drawing and graphics than 1-2-3, of course. If you want to create a good drawing, you'll find it easier and more satisfying to work in Freelance than in 1-2-3. Once the drawing is done, you can readily copy it into 1-2-3.

For instance, if you're graphically inclined, you might want to create your own drawing of a topic you're discussing in 1-2-3—such as a large dollar sign when you're talking about "price competition." If you like diagrams, you may want to use Freelance's impressive collection of diagrams—branch diagrams, flow charts, pyramids, and a number of others. You can work with them readily in Freelance. To create them, you would click Create, then Drawing/Diagram, then use a ready-made diagram. Click OK. In the dialog box labeled "Add Clip Art or Diagram to the Page," you would select the diagram you want, and click OK. The diagram would appear on the page, and you could use Freelance drawing tools to modify it, if you wished.

Also, 1-2-3 doesn't have clip art of its own, but there could be many occasions when you might want to enhance a chart or worksheet with clip art. Cartoons are great. Arrows make a neat addition to a somewhat drab chart. Although you can insert pictures directly into 1-2-3, one of the easiest ways to import high quality pictures is to drag them from Freelance.

Creating a Sample Graphic in Freelance

Often, there is an existing graphic you'll want to copy. For this example, though, I created a graphic. Here's how:

1. If you don't have it running already, start Freelance. A good way to start it is to click its icon in SuiteStart. For the example, I had Freelance running already and used the Presentation titled "competitors" created earlier in this chapter.

2. To create a sample graphic, click the New Page button at the top left. In the New Page dialog box, click the Page Layouts tab, (see Figure 4-31), and click "Bullets & Clip Art." Click OK.

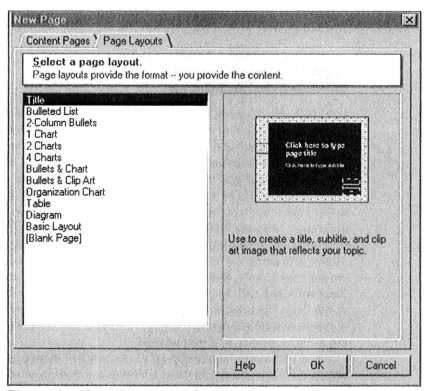

Figure 4-31: Choose Page Layouts here.

3. For the example, I typed in sample text. Click where it says Click Here to Type Page Title and type a title. I typed "Our Best Strategy."

4. Click where it says Click Here to Type Bulleted Text and type text to go with the bullets. I typed "Catch the wave" for the first bullet and "Go with the flow" for the second.

5. Add a graphic to the sample. Click where it says Click Here to Add Clip Art. In the Add Clip Art or Diagram to the Page dialog box, click cartoons in the Category box. Use the scroll arrows to move through the possible selections. Click Surfer Pete (8 of 46.) Figure 4-32 shows the selected cartoon.

6. Click OK to place the cartoon on the Presentation page. Then click outside the cartoon to deselect it.

Now you have a sample graphic to use in the example, shown in Figure 4-33.

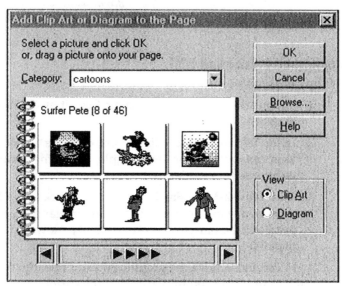

Figure 4-32: Pick clip art that you like.

Figure 4-33: With a graphic this nice, you might want to copy it to 1-2-3.

Copying the Graphic Into 1-2-3

To copy the graphic into 1-2-3:

1. You must first have 1-2-3 running. Start it by clicking its icon in SuiteStart.

2. In the Welcome to 1-2-3 dialog box, click the Create a Blank Workbook button. For the example, I used the "competitors" worksheet from earlier in the chapter.

3. With both 1-2-3 and Freelance running, click the cell in 1-2-3 where you want the upper left of the Freelance graphic to appear. For the example, I clicked cell E8 (below and to the right of the table).

4. In Freelance, click the graphic you want to copy to select it. For the example, I used the cartoon of the surfer.

Figure 4-34 shows the selected graphic.

Figure 4-34: Select the graphic you want to copy.

5. Drag the graphic to the 1-2-3 button in the Windows taskbar.
    Continue holding down the mouse button until 1-2-3 becomes
    active, then drag the pointer to the active cell and release it. The
    cool Freelance graphic appears in 1-2-3, as shown in Figure 4-35.

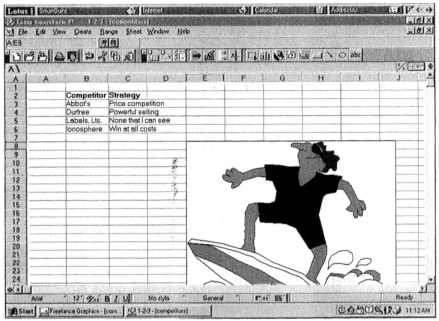

Figure 4-35: The graphic appears in 1-2-3.

Editing the Graphic in 1-2-3

Once the graphic is in 1-2-3, you can edit it back in Freelance. (For the example, first close Freelance by right-clicking its button in the taskbar and clicking Close.)

To edit the graphic in 1-2-3:

1. Double-click the 1-2-3 picture. Freelance starts and displays the image.

2. In Freelance, double-click the image to edit it. In the Lotus InfoBox that comes up, shown in Figure 4-36, make whatever changes you want in the Freelance Object. For the example, I clicked the arrow next to the Pattern color box, and clicked a blue color. The surfer became a solid blue color.

3. Click the 1-2-3 button in the taskbar. The 1-2-3 spreadsheet reflects the change. See Figure 4-37.

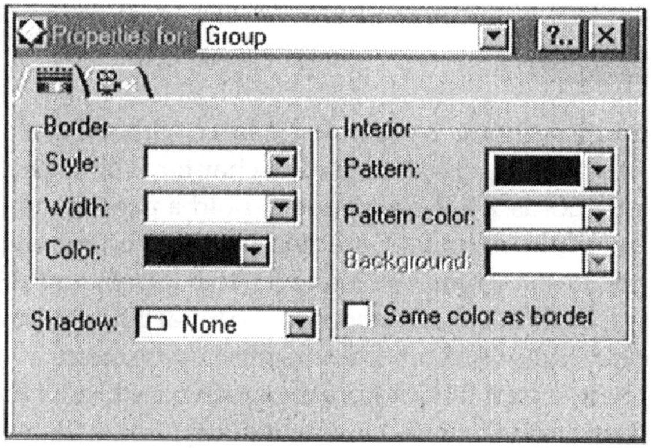

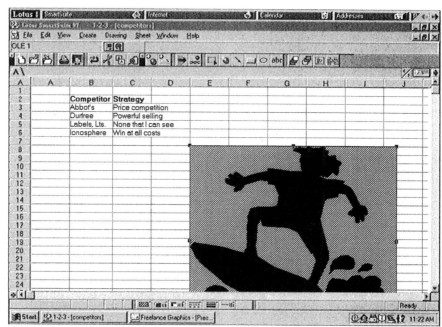

Figure 4-36: Use the InfoBox to make changes to the graphic.

Figure 4-37: Changes made in Freelance show up in 1-2-3.

Moving On

Using programs together is truly at the heart of SmartSuite, and you have had a taste of doing just that in this chapter. The grandfather of all Lotus programs, Lotus 1-2-3 continues to hold a prominent place in the SmartSuite family of products. Here you have seen how you might use another SmartSuite program—Freelance—to support and enrich 1-2-3.

By adding capabilities to one another, the SmartSuite programs become more than simply the sum total of the separate programs.

The chapters in Part 3 talk more about using programs together. But first, the next section talks about a new activity that is also quite close to the heart of the new SmartSuite—the Internet.

In the next series of chapters, you see how to have the World Wide Web be an integral part of your desktop as you work within SmartSuite.

Plugging into the Internet

5

Using the SmartCenter Internet Drawer

In Chapter 2, when talking about SmartCenter, I introduced the subject of the SmartCenter Internet drawers. You may have found out enough in that chapter to be having quite a lot of fun with the Internet. (Oops. Did I say "fun?" I mean "to be getting a lot of productive work done with the Internet.")

Before going into subjects such as publishing for the Internet (Chapter 8), I take time in this chapter to look a little more closely at those Internet drawers than in Chapter 2. Here you'll see, for instance, how to set up the type of news displayed in the News drawer and how to put in the stocks displayed into the Stock Quotes drawer.

You can set up SmartCenter so that you can check the weather at a click of the mouse. Unless you're a pilot or a weatherman, you probably don't have to spend too much time with the weather page, though. But you have the option.

There's so much more than the weather you can find yourself engrossed in. You can check the news headlines. Sports. Stock quotes. Travel. You name it.

The matter of temptations aside, though, the fact is that access to the Internet is indispensable these days. Good business has everything to do with getting information, and the Internet is nothing if not information.

In Chapter 2, we looked at surfing the Net from within SmartCenter drawers. In this chapter I talk about customizing the Internet drawers and creating Internet folders of your own.

Overview: The Initial Internet Drawers

"I already have a browser," you might think. "Why would I need SmartCenter drawers?" "Quick access" is the answer.

In your browser, you have to enter an address for a Web page and wait for the Web page to load. In SmartCenter, you can load multiple pages when you start your session, and then you can readily move from one page to another by clicking on the SmartCenter folder for that page.

The Web sites installed with SmartCenter offer a second advantage, too—ready access to useful sites you might not have known about otherwise. Lotus has researched the question and put useful sites at your disposal.

Tip

To use the Internet from SmartCenter, you have to have a connection to an Internet provider, whether a dial-up connection over a modem or a direct connection. And you have to have a Web browser (with, of course, Netscape Navigator and Microsoft Internet Explorer being the best-known).

Starting the Session & Loading Multiple Pages

When you use the SmartCenter Internet folders, you work with your regular Internet browser. To start an Internet session, if your browser is not already running and connected to the Internet, start it in the usual way—for instance, double-click the icon for Netscape Navigator or Microsoft Internet Explorer on the Win 95 Desktop. Put in your user name and password, the phone number if necessary, and click the Connect button. Your browser and your Internet connection will then be in place.

With the browser and connection in place, you click on the Internet drawer to open it, then click on the tab for the folder you want to use, such as "News—Top Stories." If the folder doesn't have current information, you click the Folder icon, then click Refresh, as I show in the section "Refreshing the Information in a Drawer" in this chapter.

Repeat the process for each Internet folder you want to work with. Most browsers actually store versions of the Web page on your hard drive, to help save in downloading time for working with the page. If you download it once, you don't have to download it again to work with it. Once you have opened multiple Web pages and placed them in folders in your Internet drawer, you can quickly move from one to another without having to wait for the pages to download each time.

You can make Internet drawers of your own. To create new folders, click on the icon for the drawer, then click on the type of folder you want to create. I talk about creating new folders in Chapter 2 and give an example later in this chapter, too.

Before you add additional folders of your own, you have these Internet folders in your SmartCenter drawers:

- In the Suite Help drawer in SmartCenter, there is a folder labeled Helpful Web Sites.

- In the Internet drawer, you'll find these folders:

  - News

  - Stock Quotes

  - Weather

  - Web Reference

  - Bookmarks (if Netscape is your main Web browser) or Favorites (if Internet Explorer is your main Web browser). If you have both browsers, you'll have both folders—Bookmarks and Favorites.

You'll probably find them all by looking through the drawers on your own. It's sometimes helpful to have a list, though.

Refreshing the Information in a Drawer

When you connect to a Web page in a folder, you have to refresh the connection so that you display current information from the Internet. As explained in the section "Starting the Session & Loading Multiple Pages" above, you have to give SmartCenter the opportunity to download a Web page to your hard drive the first time. Once it has done so, it keeps the page on your hard disk and you can continue to work with it, though you'll want to refresh it from time to time to get the latest information. If you click a link inside the drawer (text underlined in blue), the page refreshes automatically.

To use any drawer, follow these steps:

1. Click on the drawer to open it—the SmartCenter Internet drawer for this example.

2. Click on the folder you want, which is News—Top Stories for this example.

3. If you want the most current information, click on the icon on the folder tab (a globe, unless you change it, as I explain in the section "Changing the Icon for a Folder" later in this chapter).

Tip

If you like to right click as a shortcut, you can use that technique to refresh the drawer. Right click anywhere on a tab, then click Refresh.

4. In the pop-up menu, shown in Figure 5-1, click Refresh.

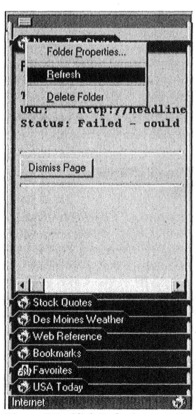

Figure 5-1: Click Refresh to get the latest info.

Getting to the Lotus Home Page

In another drawer, the Suite Help drawer in SmartCenter, you can quickly get to the Lotus home page.

Getting in touch with Lotus may not be the biggest thing on your mind most of the time. If you need tech support or a quick piece of information, though, you may want to have Lotus at your fingertips.

Here's how to get to the Lotus Web sites right away:

1. Click on the Suite Help drawer in SmartCenter.

2. Click on Helpful Web Sites.

3. If necessary, click on the folder icon and click Refresh.

Figure 5-2 shows the list of links that become available.

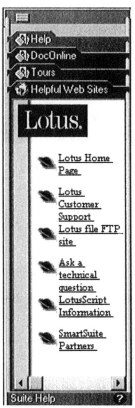

Figure 5-2: Use these links to Lotus sites.

To get technical support, for instance, you can click on Ask a Technical Question to bring up the screen shown in Figure 5-3, where you can then continue to pursue an answer.

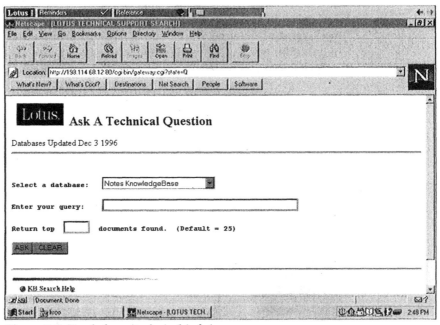

Figure 5-3: Track down technical info here.

A few other things you can do at the Lotus site are:

- Get Customer Support.
- Download updates to Lotus products.
- Browse through frequently asked questions.
- Read press releases.
- Get phone numbers if you prefer to get in touch the old-fashioned way.

Tip

When you click on a topic in one of the Internet folders, your browser opens if it is not already running, and the browser takes up the full screen. To be able to work with the drawer again while keeping the browser open, click the minimize button (a dash) on the top right of the browser.

Choosing Your News: Top, Tech, or Sports

Lotus does you the service of providing a ready connection to one of the many news sources available on the Internet—top headlines from Yahoo, a customized database of Internet information based on the computers at Netscape Communications in Mountain View, California.

You don't have to use just the initial news source, though. You can select one of several offered in the drawer. Here's how:

1. In SmartCenter, click on the Internet drawer.

2. Click on the icon (a globe) on the tab for the News folder.

3. From the menu, click on Folder Properties.

4. In the Folder Properties dialog box, click on the News tab.

5. On the News tab, shown in Figure 5-4, click the button for the type of news you'd like to display when you open the News drawer, and choose OK.

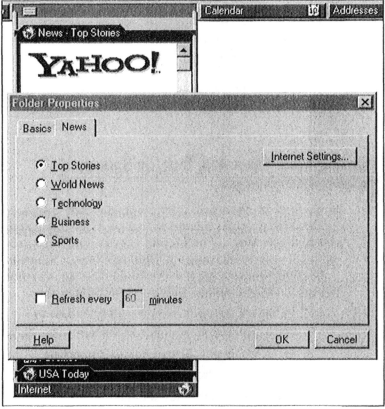

Figure 5-4: Choose your type of news here.

Tip

Notice in the Folder Properties box, shown in Figure 5-4, that you can choose how often to have the News folder automatically refresh. Just click the Refresh every box, and type in a number of minutes.

Taking Stock of the Stocks

If you're in the habit of checking stocks on the Internet using your browser, you probably have to click several times to find the information you need. With SmartCenter, though, you can display your stocks quite readily, and display the very stocks you're interested in.

Adding Stocks to Stock Folders

Nobody else knows which stocks you own (or wish you did). Here's how to add your own stocks to the Stock Quotes drawer:

1. Click the Internet drawer.
2. Click the Stock Quotes folder.
3. Click the icon for the folder.
4. Click Folder Properties.
5. In the Folder Properties dialog box, click Stocks.
6. In the Stocks tab, as shown in Figure 5-5, click Add.

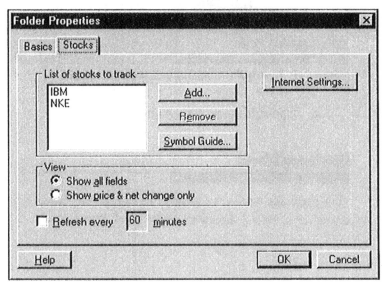

Figure 5-5: Use the Stocks tab to add stocks.

7. In the Add Stock Symbol dialog box, type the symbol for the stock you want to add, and click OK.

If you don't know the symbol for your stock, click the Symbol Guide button in the Stocks tab. You can then use a search engine to find your stock. Figure 5-6 shows the stock symbol search page.

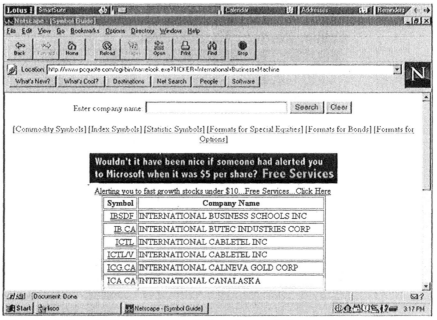

Figure 5-6: Type in the company to look up its symbol.

8. Click OK to close the dialog box.

Displaying Stocks

To display stocks you've already added to the drawer, just click on the drawer. Figure 5-7 shows a sample stock quote.

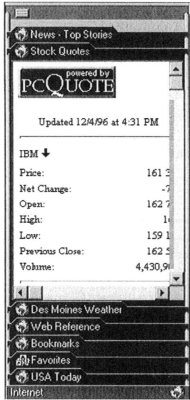

Figure 5-7: Quotes are just a click away.

Getting Rid of Stocks in Your Stock Folders

Removing stocks from your folder is similar to adding them.

After all, maybe you've just lost your shirt on a stock, have sold it, and don't want to be reminded of it each time you see the stock drawer. Or, on a happier note, maybe you've made a bundle with it and, pleased with that, sold it off.

Here's how to get a stock out of your stock folder:

1. In the Stock quotes folder, click the folder icon at the top.

2. Choose Folder Properties.

3. Click the Stocks tab.

4. In the Stocks tab, shown previously in Figure 5-5, click the stock you want to remove.

5. Click Remove.

6. Click OK to return to the drawer.

Changing the Weather

You use the Folder Properties dialog box to choose the site for your weather report.

The weather report doesn't do you much good unless it's from your own area. If you're going to a ski area, you may want to check for fresh powder there. If you have relatives living in Florida, you may want to see how they're doing. Or, if you live in Florida, you may want to gleefully see about the blizzard that's hitting your friends in the North. Of course, if you're going away on a business trip, you'll want to check conditions where you'll be traveling.

Here's how to set the Internet Weather drawer:

1. In the Weather drawer, click the folder icon, and click Folder Properties.

2. In the Folder Properties dialog box, click Weather.

3. In the Weather tab, shown in Figure 5-8, click the arrow next to each list box (for region and for city) and click the location you want.

4. Click OK.

The settings appear in the weather folder.

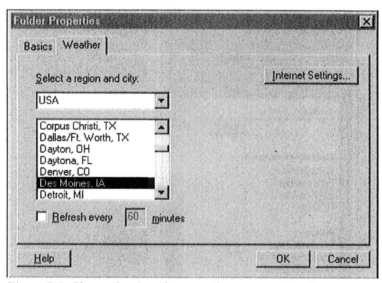

Figure 5-8: Choose the city whose weather you want to view.

Searching the Web From SmartCenter

You can search the World Wide Web from SmartCenter using the Web Reference folder:

1. Click the Internet drawer to open it.

2. Click the Web Reference folder.

3. Do one of the following:

    • In the white "Search the Web" box, type a topic that interests you, and click Search Web. Web Reference produces a list of matches.

    • Click one of the blue, underlined links to a Web page that interests you, such as "Encyclopedia" or "Currency converter." Figure 5-9 shows the Web Reference folder.

4. Click the drawer to close it.

Figure 5-9: Use the Web reference folder to do research.

Tip

Web Reference is not available in all countries.

Putting In Your Own Web Sites

You can add Internet folders to SmartCenter that link to your favorite Web sites.

As with the rest of SmartCenter and all of SmartSuite, you are quite likely to set up your Internet connections so that they have very little resemblance to the initial, installed settings. Maybe you live in San Diego, where it's always nice, and could not care less about the weather report. You'd just as soon remove the Weather drawer altogether. Maybe, for your Web Reference, you don't use Yahoo but some other source.

Maybe (if you're lucky) you're a sports writer and spend all day reading sports. Or you're a fashion expert and need instant links to fashion sources. Whatever your preferences, you can set up SmartCenter so that what you want is a click away.

Adding an Internet Folder

To add an Internet folder, you add the folder to a drawer, then assign an Internet address to it. Here's how:

1. Click the drawer where you want to put in a new folder, such as the Internet drawer (or any other drawer).

2. Click the icon for the drawer (not for a folder.) The menu for the drawer comes up, shown in Figure 5-10.

3. Click New Folder.

4. In the New Folder assistant, select Internet Page as the type of folder, as shown in Figure 5-11, and click Next.

5. If you wish, select a label, color, and icon, or just click Next to accept the defaults. For the example, type the folder label Boston Sports.

Tip

It's a good idea to type in a new, meaningful label so you'll remember what's in the folder.

6. In the Internet Location box, type in the URL path (Uniform Resource Locator, that is, the Internet address) of the Web site you are adding. The example uses http:// www.bostom(boston)com.

7. Type in the URL for the Web site.

8. Click Done.

   The new folder appears in the drawer.

Figure 5-10: Create a new folder here.

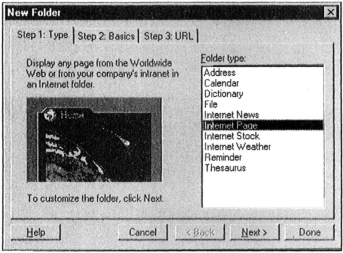

Figure 5-11: Select the folder type.

Dragging Your URL Links to SmartCenter

Instead of creating a new folder for an Internet page, you can just drag a URL link to a folder.

The URL for the Lotus home page is http://www.lotus.com. To go to the location, you type the address into the Location box in your Web browser (if you're using Netscape Navigator) or click File, then Open Location, and type the URL into the Open Location dialog box.

When you type in the URL and press Enter or click OK, the Web browser locates the Web page you've specified and displays it.

When you're working on a Web page, you see numerous highlighted or underlined terms you can click on to move to other Web pages. These terms are links (also sometimes referred to as "hypertext"). When you drag a link in SmartCenter, you are dragging the reference to a particular Web page. You can then click on the link in SmartCenter to open the Web page. And links are friendlier to work with than URL addresses, because they are in English (as in "Lotus Home Page") instead of technospeak as they are in URLs (as in http://www.lotus.com).

Now, dragging links in SmartCenter is easy and quite cool—a neat way to keep track of some of the zillions of good Web pages you discover in your Web travels:

1. Click the drawer and file folder where you want to place the URL. The example uses a folder labeled CNN News in the SmartSuite drawer.

2. Using your Web browser, find the URL link you want to include as a shortcut. (A URL link appears as highlighted text in your browser.)

3. Drag the link to the file folder you have open.

The URL link displays as a shortcut in the folder, as shown in Figure 5-12.

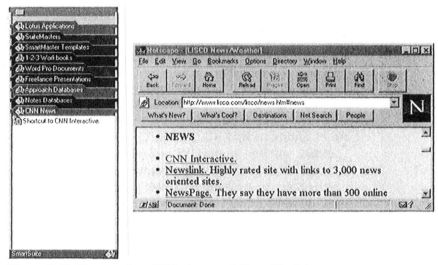

Figure 5-12: You can drag URLs to your folders, like this.

Customizing Folders

You can use the Folder Properties dialog box to change the color of a folder and to change the icon. Color coding has become a time-honored way to differentiate file folders from one another, and you can continue to use the approach in SmartSuite. With paper folders, too, people attach various clever stickers to the tabs. Customizing the icon on a folder comes from honest precedents.

Changing the Color of a Folder

Color has two values to the SmartCenter user. First of all, color is pretty. You can use various colors for your folders just to have them look nice. Second, though, color is useful for coding. You might assign a unique color to a folder just to make it stand out, or you might assign the same color to all folders of a certain type (such as all Internet News folders). The example uses the Boston Sports folder I created in the Internet drawer in this chapter. Here's how to change the color of a folder:

1. Click the drawer containing the folder to open the drawer.
2. Click the folder to open it.
3. Right-click the folder label to bring up the menu.
4. Click Folder Properties.
5. In the Folder Properties dialog box, click the arrow for the Color list box. A palette of colors comes up. Figure 5-13 shows the palette.

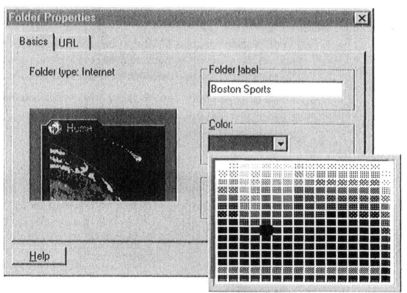

Figure 5-13: Choose colors from this palette.

6. Click the color you want.
7. Click OK to close the Folder Properties dialog box. Your folder now has the new color.

Changing the Icon for a Folder

You can choose an icon that gives you clues to the contents of the folder. SmartCenter offers several icons to choose from— a check mark, a calendar, a book, a silhouette of three heads, and others.

The steps for changing folder icons are similar to those for changing folder color:

1. Click the drawer containing the folder to open the drawer.

2. Click the folder to open it. The example again uses the Boston Sports folder.

3. Right-click the folder label to bring up the menu.

4. Click Folder Properties.

5. In the Folder Properties dialog box, click the arrow for the Icon list box. A list of icons appears. Figure 5-14 shows some of the icons. (You can click the up and down scroll arrows to see more icons.)

6. Click the icon you want—a check mark for the example.

7. Click OK to close the Folder Properties dialog box. Your folder now sports the new icon.

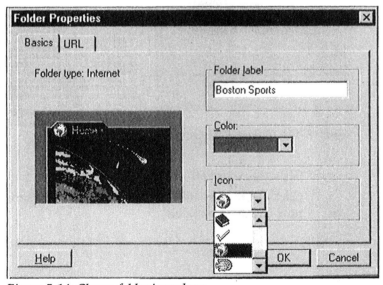

Figure 5-14: Choose folder icons here.

Moving On

In SmartCenter alone, then, you can enjoy all the tools of your familiar Web browser and a whole lot more. You can place news, stock quotes, weather, and anything else you want so that it is a single click away. You don't have to navigate with your browser to get to it each time. The advantage is speed and convenience.

As powerful as SmartCenter alone is, though, it's just a beginning in using SmartSuite with the Internet. You can also use individual SmartSuite applications (like Lotus 1-2-3 and Word Pro) with the Internet.

The next chapter talks about searching and linking to the Internet in programs like 1-2-3 and Word Pro.

6

Searching the Net From Within SmartSuite Programs

Getting news from the Internet or doing research there can certainly be useful. (Also, as I mentioned, it can be distracting and burn some valuable time.) Much of the time while using SmartSuite, though, you focus within a single program. That is, you might be working on a detailed forecast in 1-2-3, or you might be preparing a research paper in Word Pro.

You still might want to have the advantages of the Internet as you work, but you don't really want to go "out" to SmartCenter or take time to fire up your Web browser. SmartSuite now puts important Internet capabilities a simple click away as you work in your SmartSuite program. One useful capability is just the ability to search for information.

In the age of paper (before the Internet), searching for information was time consuming. It was often a job to pass off to a research assistant, because it took so long. And, look, I hate to be hard about it, but a lot of useful research just never got done, because nobody had the time to do it.

Thanks to the Internet and electronic searching, though, there can be a lot less "fudging" and other evasive tactics in business. People can go out on the Net and find information quickly just by highlighting text in a document, then clicking an Internet SmartIcon.

Tip

Remember, you have to be connected to the Internet to be able to do the things in this chapter. You have to have a working modem. You have to have Netscape Navigator, Internet Explorer, or another browser. And you have to have an account on the Internet.

Looking Over Internet Capabilities

In SmartSuite products, you can publish materials to the Internet without leaving the individual product. You can open files from the Internet (commonly referred to as "downloading"). You can go directly to the Lotus home page, customer support page, and FTP site. You can search the Net, and more.

As is usually the case with SmartIcons, Lotus has one available for every command you might use. The next section summarizes the SmartIcons on the Lotus Internet Tools bar.

Displaying the Internet SmartIcons

All your SmartSuite applications have a palette of icons just for working with the Internet. Here's how to turn on the SmartIcon palette, using 1-2-3 as an example:

1. Start 1-2-3. Click the SmartSuite drawer in SmartCenter and double click the Lotus 1-2-3 icon. In the Welcome to 1-2-3 screen, click Create a Blank Workbook.

2. Click the arrow at the left of the main SmartIcons palette to show the list of SmartIcon palettes, as shown in Figure 6-1.

3. Click Internet Tools.

The Internet tools appear on the left, as shown in Figure 6-2.

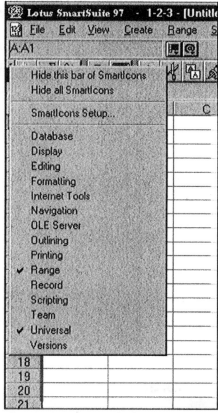

Figure 6-1: You can find the Internet SmartIcons listed here.

Figure 6-2: Internet SmartIcons (on the left) give one-click Internet Access.

Reviewing the Internet SmartIcons

You can see what each tool does by putting the pointer over the tool and reading the Bubble help. Table 6-1 lists the Internet SmartIcons and tells what each does.

Icon	What It does
	Publishes a range to the Internet, as discussed in Chapter 8. Name changes in various programs. In Word Pro, name is "Publish as Web Page(s)."
	Opens a file from the Internet. Means opening from an FTP server, as discussed in Chapter 7.
	Saves a file to the Internet. Means saving to an FTP server, as discussed in Chapter 7.
	Goes to the Lotus home page, as discussed in this chapter.
	Goes to Lotus Customer Support page, as discussed in this chapter.
	Goes to the Lotus Customer Support FTP site, as discussed in this chapter.
	Goes to the SmartSuite Reference Library page, as discussed in this chapter.
	Searches the Internet for selected text, as discussed in Chapter 7.
	Creates a button with a link to a URL. Specific to Lotus 1-2-3. See Chapter 7.

Table 6-1: The Internet SmartIcons and what they do.

Tip

You may want to drag the SmartIcon for showing and hiding the SmartIcon toolbar to your main SmartIcon palette. You would then click it to show or hide the Internet SmartIcons. Chapter 15 talks about how to set up and modify SmartIcon palettes.

Basically, here's how to add a SmartIcon to a bar:

1. Click on File, then on User Setup, then on SmartIcons Setup.

2. In the SmartIcons Setup dialog box, scroll in the Available Icons box to display the icon you want. Figure 6-3 shows the SmartIcons Setup box with the Show or hide Internet SmartIcons icon showing.

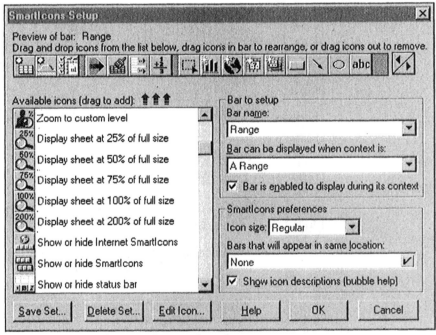

Figure 6-3: Drag the SmartIcon to the palette you use most.

3. Drag the icon for Show or Hide Internet Icons to the palette you use most often.

4. Click OK to close the dialog box.

In many cases, the Internet SmartIcons give you a one-click way to work with the Internet from within your application.

Tip

Many of the Internet options are available from the menus as well. Figure 6-4 shows the File/Internet menu in 1-2-3.

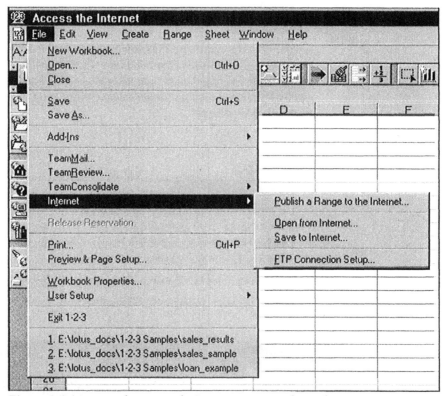

Figure 6-4: You can also get to the Internet commands on the menus.

Searching the Internet

Before the Internet came along, you could do such things within a single application as search for words and phrases in your application, check the spelling of a term, or locate synonyms. Now, though, you can call upon the resources of the World Wide Web as you're working.

If you are connected to the Internet and have a Web browser, then searching the Internet from within a SmartSuite program isn't much different from searching in your browser. In SmartSuite programs, you click on a SmartIcon and perform a search. The advantage is that you never have to leave your SmartSuite program to perform that search.

Warning

The command for searching the Internet is not on the File/Internet menu in any of the SmartSuite programs that offer the capability for Internet Search. To perform the search, you have to use the SmartIcon on the palette of Internet tools. Its Bubble help in Word Pro is "Perform Internet search on selected text."

Searching in 1-2-3

Suppose, for instance, you wanted to research the Taguchi Loss Function (well known to marketing researchers) while working within 1-2-3.

What goes on behind the scenes is pretty ambitious, but the steps themselves are quite simple. Here's how to perform the search in 1-2-3:

1. Highlight the term you want to search, as shown in Figure 6-5.

2. Click the Search Internet for Selected Text SmartIcon.

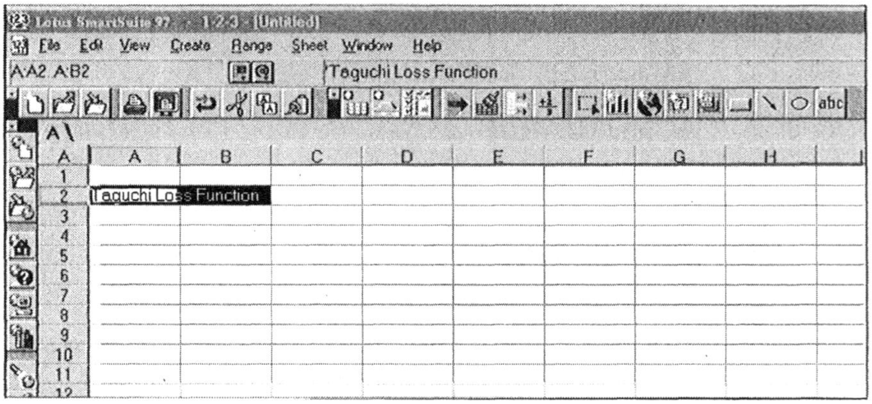

Figure 6-5: Highlight the term you want to search.

SmartSuite does the rest. It starts up your Browser, if it's not already running. It connects you to your Internet server, if necessary.

Then, as shown in Figure 6-6, it displays an Internet search engine with search results on the item. 1-2-3 uses the Yahoo search engine for its search.

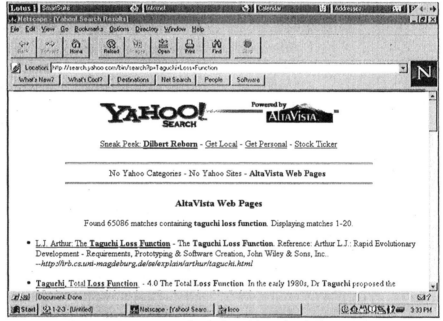

Figure 6-6: You get Internet search results without leaving your program.

You can read documents and continue to navigate the Web. If you want to copy and paste something into your 1-2-3 worksheet, here's how:

1. Select the material you want to copy.

2. Press Ctrl+C (the keyboard shortcut for copying). The material goes to the Win 95 Clipboard.

3. Click the 1-2-3 button in the Win 95 Taskbar.

4. Click where you want to place the material.

5. Press Ctrl V (the keyboard shortcut for pasting.) The material appears in the worksheet.

6. If you like, save the worksheet. I saved the example as Taguchi.

Searching in Word Pro

Searching in any of the SmartSuite programs that offers the capability follows the same steps as just shown for 1-2-3. Be sure you have your Internet SmartIcons showing. (The section "Displaying the Internet SmartIcons" earlier in this chapter tells you how.) Highlight the search text and click the appropriate SmartIcon. Here's an example from Word Pro:

1. Start Word Pro in one of the usual ways, such as by clicking the Word Pro icon in SuiteStart.

2. Type in some text. The example uses these words, in a fictitious literary essay, "People might think a lot more highly of Herman Melville if they didn't have to read Moby Dick in high school."

3. If you like, save the document by clicking the Save SmartIcon (an arrow pointing into a folder), and typing a name for the document in the Save As dialog box. I named my sample document "Moby Dick."

    Now you're ready for the actual search.

4. Click and drag across the term you want to search, to highlight it. For the example, I highlighted Moby Dick. See Figure 6-7.

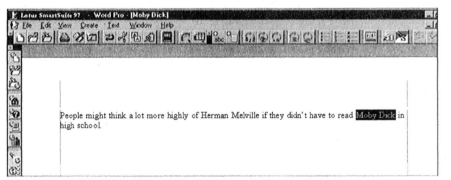

Figure 6-7: Highlight the text you want to search.

5. Click the Internet Search SmartIcon on the Internet SmartIcons palette (a flashlight shining onto a globe).

Your Internet browser comes up (I use Netscape Navigator) and performs a search using the Yahoo search engine. Figure 6-8 shows the search page. Once the page comes up, you're on your own on the

Internet. Click any URL (underlined text) to go to a different site. If you want to copy text into your Word Pro document, follow the same steps just explained for 1-2-3.

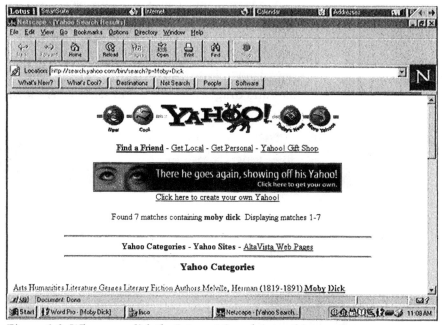

Figure 6-8: When you click the Internet Search icon, this page comes up.

Highlight the text. Press Ctrl+C to copy it. Place the cursor where you want it in Word Pro, and press Ctrl+V to paste the text into Word Pro. When you're done with the browser, you can click the dash in the top right to minimize it or the X in the top right to close it.

Searching in Freelance

To search the Internet from Freelance, you again click the SmartIcon and use the Yahoo search engine that comes up. When you're working with a graphics program, your search needs will probably be different from when working with Word Pro or 1-2-3. Perhaps you'll search for pictures to paste into the presentation. Nevertheless, the search capability will be no less useful.

Here's how to search the Internet from Freelance:

1. Start Freelance using any of the usual methods. For instance, click the SmartSuite drawer in SmartCenter, then double-click the Lotus Freelance icon. Click Create a New Presentation Using a SmartMaster, then click OK. In the New Page dialog box, choose any page layout. I clicked [Blank Page]. Click OK.

2. To type in the text you want to search, click the Drawing & Text button, then click the button labeled ABC, and then click in the current page. Type the search text. I typed "clip art."

3. Click and drag across the text to select it, as shown in Figure 6-9.

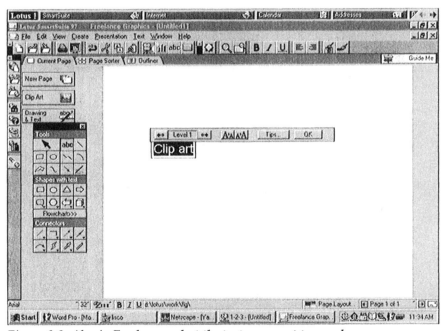

Figure 6-9: Also in Freelance, select the text you want to search.

4. Click the search Internet SmartIcon (identical to the one in Word Pro or 1-2-3—a flashlight shining on a globe).

Your Internet Browser comes up and performs a search using the Yahoo Internet search engine. Figure 6-10 shows the result.

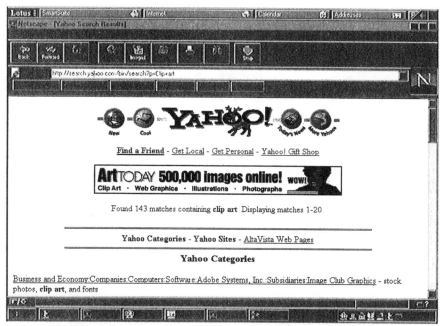

Figure 6-10: You see the results on the Internet of your search from within Freelance.

Tip

When you're done with the search, click the dash or the X in the top right of the browser to minimize or close it. Click the X in the top right of the Freelance title bar to close Freelance as well.

Surfing the Net With the Approach Database of Web Sites

Approach doesn't offer the SmartIcon for searching the Internet that appears in 1-2-3, Word Pro, and Freelance. But Approach is no slouch when it comes to searching the Internet. In fact, if you want to surf the

Net in SmartSuite, the best tool of all may be the Approach database of Web sites, available by using an Approach SmartMaster.

To be able to use the database, you first have to create an Approach database based on the Internet WWW Sites SmartMaster. Then you can start that Approach application and use it to find and go to Web sites.

Creating the Approach Database

Before you can use the database of Web sites, you create it using a SmartMaster. Here's how:

1. Start Approach using your favorite method, such as clicking its icon in SuiteStart.

2. In the Welcome to Lotus Approach dialog box, click the Create a New File Using a SmartMaster tab, as shown in Figure 6-11.

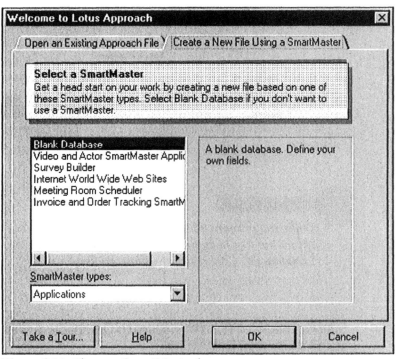

Figure 6-11: Choose a SmartMaster here.

3. In the Select a SmartMaster list box, click Internet World Wide Web Sites. Click OK. The Approach database comes up using the SmartMaster. Figure 6-12 shows the Main Menu for the Approach database based on the SmartMaster.

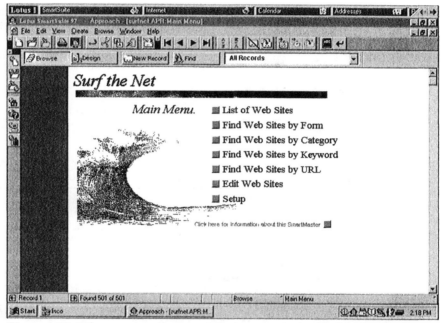

Figure 6-12: When you use the SmartMaster, you start with this Approach database.

4. If you like, click File, then Save As, and type a name for the database. I used the name "surfnet." Approach adds the extension .APR. Click Save.

Thanks to Lotus SmartMasters, you now have a neatly developed database application of Internet locations. You use the application to find Web sites by category, keyword, and location. Once you locate a site you want, you can connect to it using a browser.

Accessing Web Sites From the Approach Database

Once you've created the database of Web sites using the SmartMaster, you get the fun of looking up Web sites and connecting to them.

Try out the application a bit, if you like:

1. On the Surf the Net main menu, click the box next to List of Web Sites. A page comes up showing List of Web Sites by Title, as shown in Figure 6-13.

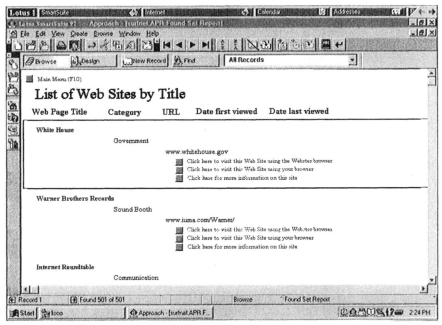

Figure 6-13: You can pick from a list of Web Sites by title.

2. For one of the sites, such as White House, click the appropriate button. I clicked the one that says "Click here to visit this Web Site using your browser." The nifty Approach application fires up your browser (if it isn't already running), and takes you to the chosen Web site, shown here in Figure 6-14.

3. Click the dash or the X at the top right of the browser to minimize or close it. You return to the Approach page labeled List of Web Sites by Title.

Figure 6-14: You go straight to the chosen Web site, like this one.

Thanks to the SmartMaster, you have a completely developed list of Web sites at your disposal. You can play with the possibilities to your heart's content, by clicking on the Main Menu button and making selections, as in the example.

4. Click File, then Exit Approach to close Approach and the application.

Approach, then, may not offer the ability to search for phrases the way its companion programs 1-2-3, Word Pro, and Freelance do. It does offer something the others don't, though, when it comes to surfing the Net—it gives you a database of useful sites and an easy way to connect with them.

Getting Lotus Support on the Internet

One form of Internet search, of course, is the search for useful information from Lotus. In SmartCenter or any of the SmartSuite applications, a connection to Lotus Customer Support is just a menu choice away. You don't have to leave the application to get to the Lotus site.

Getting Lotus Support From Within a SmartSuite Program

Getting Internet support from a SmartSuite program is a matter of clicking the right SmartIcon, then surfing around the Lotus sites if you like. You can also get to Lotus support using menu choices.

Here's how to connect to Lotus support using the 1-2-3 menus:

1. Start 1-2-3.

2. Click the Help menu.

3. Click Lotus Internet Support.

A submenu comes up (see Figure 6-15) showing all your choices for Lotus Internet Support, the Lotus Home Page, Lotus Customer Support, and the Lotus FTP site.

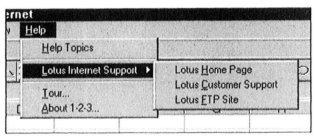

Figure 6-15: Choose Internet sites from this menu.

4. Click the type of support you want. For instance, click Lotus Home Page.

Your browser kicks in, if it isn't active already, and it goes to the URL with the address www.lotus.com, as shown in Figure 6-16.

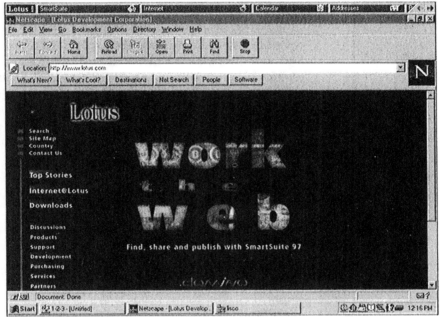

Figure 6-16: You can start at the Lotus Home Page.

You can use similar menu choices from Freelance, Word Pro, Approach, and Organizer.

Tip

You can always use SmartIcons to get to Lotus sites on the Web. Each of the SmartSuite programs has icons for the Lotus Home page, Lotus Customer Support, and the Lotus Customer Support FTP server. See Displaying the Internet SmartIcons at the start of this chapter for help with displaying the Internet SmartIcon bar.

Getting Lotus Support From SmartCenter

You don't even have to open one of the SmartSuite programs to get to Lotus support. You can get there directly from SmartCenter. Here's how:

1. In SmartCenter, click the SuiteHelp drawer.

2. Click Helpful Web Sites.

3. Click the folder icon, and click Refresh to get the up to date version. A list of Lotus Internet support sites comes up, including those from the 1-2-3 menu: Lotus Home Page, Lotus Customer Support, and the Lotus file FTP site. See Figure 6-17.

Figure 6-17: You can go from SmartCenter or any of the SmartSuite programs directly to SmartSuite Support.

4. To go to one of the sites, click its link. For instance, you could click Lotus Customer Support. Figure 6-18 shows the result.

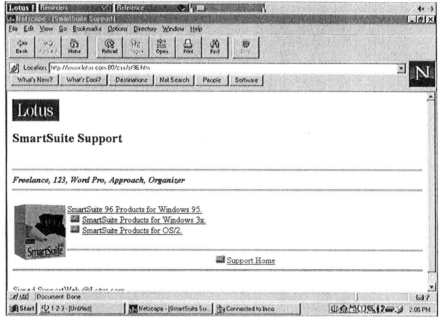

Figure 6-18: You can go to SmartSuite Support.

Going to the Lotus FTP Site

An *FTP site* is a remote computer site using a particular, widely-used protocol (File Transfer Protocol). You can connect to an FTP site if your computer meets these quite common criteria:

- Your own computer and the FTP site must both be on the Internet.

- Your computer has to have a WinSock-compatible TCP/IP stack. (Most do.)

- The server has to support anonymous FTP (which means that you don't have to log in and give a password), or else you have to have a login name, a password, and an account you're authorized to use.

To connect to the Lotus FTP site from one of the SmartSuite programs, such as 1-2-3, click on the SmartIcon that says Go to Lotus Customer Support FTP site on the Internet SmartIcon bar.

Figure 6-19 shows the site you go to.

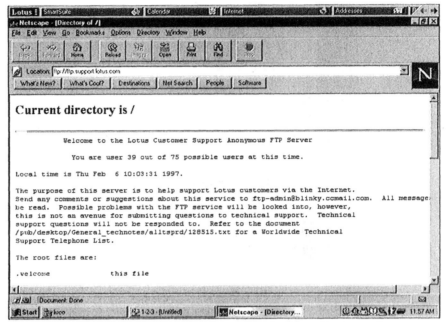

Figure 6-19: You begin at this page when using the Lotus Customer Support FTP Server.

To stop using the site, just click the dash or the X in the top right of your browser to minimize or close it.

You can enjoy all the resources of the computer maintained by the company that has the site, such as Lotus in this example. That is, you can enjoy all the resources the company lets you use. You can browse around looking for files, and you can download the ones that you want.

Moving On

You don't even have to leave your SmartSuite program, then, to enjoy the resources of the Internet. Using the Internet SmartIcons, you can search the vast Internet resources for information on a subject you select inside 1-2-3, Word Pro, or Freelance.

If you really want to go in depth into Web sites, you can use a SmartMaster in Approach to create an application that lists them. Then you can use the application to take control of Web sites.

If you want to get Lotus Internet support, you can click SmartIcons without your program to have it happen. And you can go directly to the Lotus FTP site to enjoy its resources.

Searching the Net, fun and useful as it is, is just the beginning of what you can do on the Internet in SmartSuite. You can also set up live links to the Net and share documents from several of the SmartSuite Programs, as I talk about in the next chapter.

7

Sharing & Linking on the Internet

"S haring" documents on the Internet means putting your documents on an Internet computer so that others can copy them to their own computers and use them. Team tools in SmartSuite (which I talk about in Chapter 13) turn such sharing into quite an art, because you can do some nice things with distributing and revising documents. This chapter shows how to make a document accessible to others in the first place by copying files to and from an FTP site.

Putting a document on the Internet for others to read isn't the same as putting a Web Page out there, which I talk about in Chapter 8. When you put a document on the Net, others download it to their computers and read it. When you create a Web page, you place your document at an address on the Internet for people to read right there (no downloading necessary). Your Web page itself resides at a URL (Uniform Resource Locator—an address of the form "http://www.address.com"). Also, your Web page may contain links to other URLs.

People "surfing the Net" can read your Web page and click links in the document to go to other Web pages. *Linking* means putting "live links" (URL addresses) into your documents so that users can go to Internet sites at a click of the mouse.

The computer you connect with is usually an *FTP site*, though it may occasionally be a World Wide Web site. The name "FTP site" sounds rather technical, as if it's something only somebody else would use.

Actually, though, an FTP site is just a computer somewhere using a commonly used protocol (File Transfer Protocol).

As I mentioned in Chapter 6, you have to meet these basic (and widespread) criteria to exchange files with an FTP site:

■ Your own computer and the FTP site both have to be on the Internet.

■ Your computer has to have a WinSock-compatible TCP/IP stack. (If you use Netscape Navigator, Internet Explorer, or another major browser, you have it, because those browsers also require it.)

■ The server either has to support anonymous FTP (which means that you don't have to log in and give a password), or else you have to have a login name, a password, and an account you're authorized to use. You can't control what the server allows; the system administrator for the Internet computer handles that. The best way I know to find out if the Internet computer will let you exchange files is to try it out.

Setting Up FTP Connections

Using any of the four main SmartSuite programs—Word Pro, 1-2-3, Approach, or Freelance—you can connect to an Internet computer and then either copy files from the Internet computer (*download* them) or save files to it (*upload* them). Once you get set up to connect to a remote computer in one of the programs (such as Word Pro), you are set up in the others as well.

You should be aware, though, that you need permission to upload files to most FTP sites—permission that such sites are stingy in granting. You can readily download files, but you may not be able to upload them.

Setting Up a Connection

You have to set up a connection to each remote computer you need to transfer files to.

In the example below, I'll explain how to set up an FTP connection using Word Pro. Once you've set up the connection in Word Pro, it's available in any of the other SmartSuite programs that allows FTP connections.

1. Start the program and, for the example, create a plain document.

2. Click File, then Internet.

3. From the submenu, shown in Figure 7-1, click FTP Connection Setup.

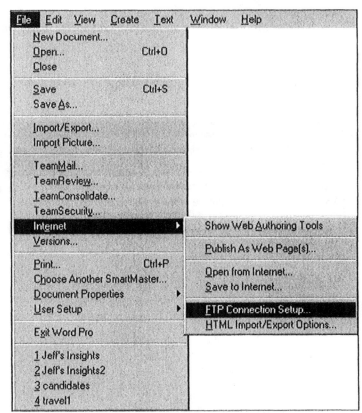

Figure 7-1: Choose Internet commands from this menu.

4. In the FTP Connection Setup dialog box, see Figure 7-2, click the Hosts button.

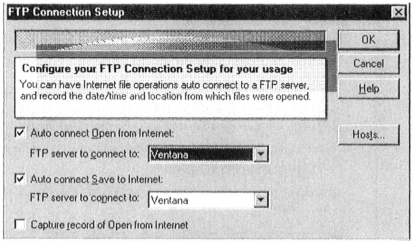

Figure 7-2: Use this dialog box to set up connections to a host computer on the Internet.

5. In the FTP Hosts dialog box (Figure 7-3), click the New button.

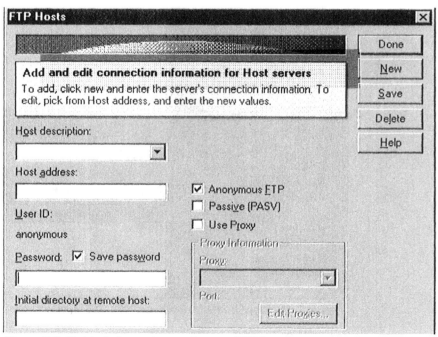

Figure 7-3: Put in information on the new FTP host here.

6. In the Host Description box, type a description for the computer. For the example, I used Ventana.

7. In the Host Address box, type in the computer's address. For the example, the address is ftp.vmedia.com.

8. Click Done.

9. In the FTP Connection Setup box, click OK.

Autoconnecting to Open Files From the Internet

There may be one Internet computer that you connect to all the time. You can set up your FTP connections so that you automatically connect to that computer when you open a file on the Internet:

1. Start Word Pro (or Freelance, 1-2-3, or Approach) and click File, then Internet, then FTP Connection Setup.

2. In the FTP Connection Setup box (Figure 7-2), click Auto connect. Open from Internet. Then, if you choose Open from Internet from the menu (or use the SmartIcon), you automatically log in to the server you've specified. Pretty cool, if you use the same remote computer a lot.

Looking Over Connection Options

There are a few options in the FTP Hosts dialog box (Figure 7-3). You may have to talk with the systems administrator for your host computer to see which ones apply to you. You have to get them set up properly to be able to use the host.

Here's a brief description of them:

■ **User ID.** The ID identifies you as a user on the FTP host you're connecting with. A system administrator for that computer assigns you the ID. You don't need one for anonymous FTP. That is, if you select the Anonymous FTP box, the word "anonymous" appears automatically. If you deselect the Anonymous FTP box, a text box appears under User ID for you to type in your ID.

Not all sites allow anonymous FTP. If they do, they generally allow it only for downloading files, not uploading them.

- **Password.** If you need a password, you have to get it from the FTP computer's administrator. Or, you can use your e-mail address.

- **Initial directory at remote host.** You can put in the address to a particular subdirectory you often use on the host.

- **Anonymous FTP.** Means that the remote FTP site allows anonymous FTP (doesn't require a user ID or password. It's a common practice to use your e-mail address as the password.)

- **Passive (PASV).** Means that your internal network is connected to the Internet using a firewall that supports passive transfers. If you want to use this option, check with your system administrator to see if it's available.

- **Use Proxy.** If you select this option, you're saying that your internal network is connected to the Internet using a firewall that is a proxy server. If you want to use this option, check with your systems administrator to be sure it applies.

Finding the Connection Log File

For each time you connect with the Internet, the program you're using (such as Word Pro) keeps a log of the messages you send to and from the Internet server. The name of the log file is LTSNET.LOG, and it appears in the Win 95 temporary directory (for instance, a directory named C:\WINDOWS\TEMP). There is a log of only the most recent session. If you log out and connect again, the SmartSuite program deletes the record of the previous session.

Changing Connection Information

If you decide to start using a password or want to make another change to a connection profile you've set up, you can edit connections information. Here's how:

1. From the File menu, click Internet.

2. Click FTP Connection Setup.

3. Click the Hosts button.

4. In the Host Description list box, click the Internet computer you want to modify.

5. Make your changes, such as typing in a new password.

6. Click Save.

7. Click Done.

8. Click OK.

Deleting an Internet Host From the List

You may begin to accumulate more FTP sites than you need or for some other reason may want to delete one. Here's how you do it:

1. From the File menu, click Internet.

2. Click FTP Connection Setup.

3. Click the Hosts button.

4. In the Host Description list box, click the Internet computer you want to delete.

5. Click Delete.

6. Click Done.

7. Click OK.

Copying an Internet Document (Downloading)

Internet computers set up as FTP sites usually have collections of files on them for users to download. They are "one-stop shopping centers." The Lotus site, for instance, offers user documentation for Lotus products and downloads of Lotus products, among other things.

Opening an Internet Document From an FTP Site

With the main SmartSuite Programs (all but SmartCenter and Organizer), you can open a document from the Internet. That is, you can open the file from the remote computer and save it to your own computer.

Once you're set up and have the privileges to use the Internet computer, opening and saving files from an FTP site is not that different from doing so on your own computer. Here's what you do:

1. First start the program you want to use—1-2-3 for this example. You can use any workbook but for the example, just create a blank workbook.

2. From the File menu, click Open.

3. In the Open dialog box, shown in Figure 7-4, click the Internet button.

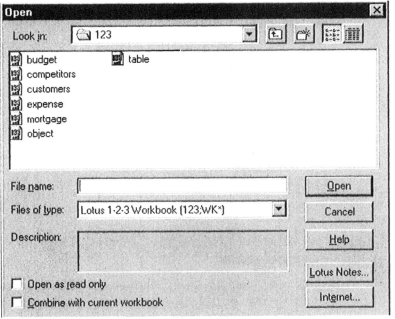

Figure 7-4: Click the Internet button in this dialog box.

4. In the Open from Internet dialog box (Figure 7-5), make sure the FTP button is selected.

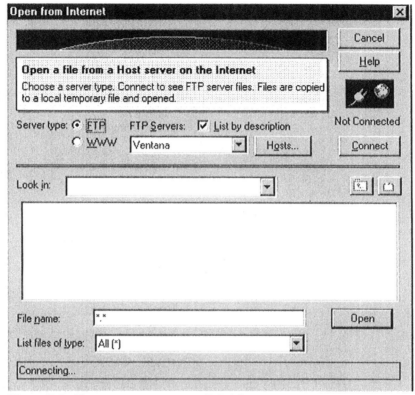

Figure 7-5: Choose your server type (FTP) here.

5. In the FTP Servers list box, click the server you want. The example uses Ventana. (If you have no servers listed, see the section "Setting Up FTP Connections" to see how to set them up. You can click the Hosts button and set up servers from this dialog box. The steps are the same as in the section "Setting Up FTP Connections" in this chapter.)

6. Click the Connect button. 1-2-3 connects you with the host, which displays a directory of files, as shown in Figure 7-6.

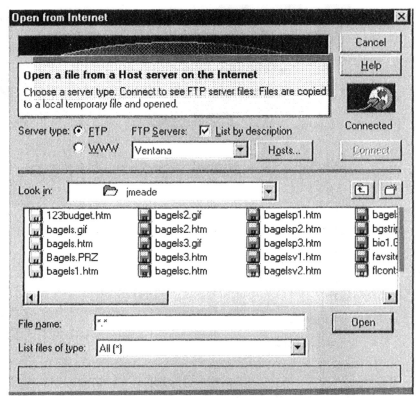

Figure 7-6: Once you connect, you see a directory of files.

7. If necessary, select the type of file you want in the box labeled List files of type.

8. Click the file you want to open. The example uses sales_results.123.

9. Click Open. 1-2-3 copies the file to a local temporary file and opens it. (The original file, on the server, is not affected.) As Figure 7-7 shows, the file appears in 1-2-3, where you can then save it as your own if you wish.

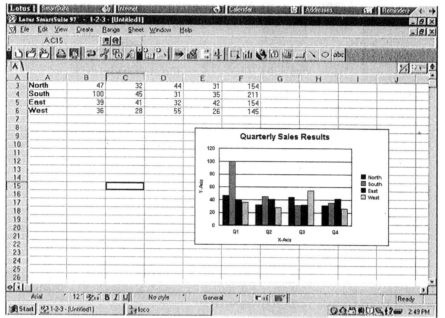

Figure 7-7: The file appears in 1-2-3 on your local computer, where you can save it under a new name if you like.

Keeping a Record When You Open Files From the Internet

You can record the date, time, and the full path you used to copy a file from the Internet:

1. Start Word Pro (or Freelance, 1-2-3, or Approach). Click File, then Internet, and then FTP Connection Setup.

2. In the FTP Connection Setup box (Figure 7-2), click Capture record of Open from Internet. The record then appears in the document's description in various places (such as the Open dialog box).

Opening an Internet Document From a Web Site

You don't have to open files just from FTP sites, you can also open them from Web sites (sites whose Internet address begins with "http://www").

Tip

When you access a home page by opening it as described in this section, you aren't just browsing the Web. You are copying the document to your computer.

Here's what you do:

1. Start your SmartCenter program. This example uses Word Pro.

2. From the File menu, click Open.

3. In the Open dialog box, click Internet. (Or, you can accomplish steps 1 through 3 by clicking the Open Document from the Internet SmartIcon.)

4. In the Browse from Internet dialog box, click WWW. The Browse from Internet dialog box displays the File Name list box, as shown in Figure 7-8.

5. In the File Name box, select a recent file if you have one listed. Or type in a URL. For instance, you could type in http://www.vmedia.com to open a copy of the Ventana Home page.

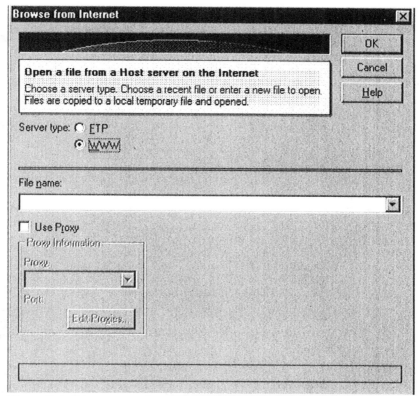

Figure 7-8: Select or type in a World Wide Web page you want to open.

6. Click OK. The HTML Import/Export Options dialog box comes up, shown in Figure 7-9. You may want to make some selections. For instance, you may want to deselect Download Graphics from the Internet. Then click OK.

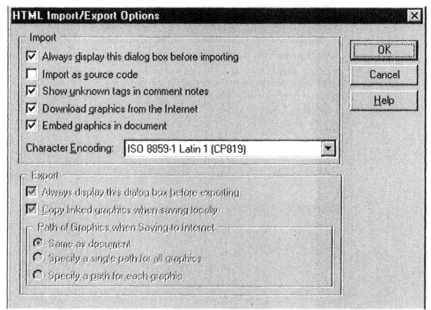

Figure 7-9: You can choose not to download graphics and make other choices here.

Word Pro (or whichever program you're using) imports the Web Page to a temporary file. If you wish, you can save it on your own computer by clicking the Save SmartIcon and completing the Save As dialog box. If you don't want to save the temporary file, click the X in the top right corner of the document to close it.

Embedding a Browser on a Notepad Page

In this chapter you've seen how to copy and save files from the Internet from within SmartSuite programs. Organizer offers a related capability— the ability to use your browser without leaving Notepad.

In the Organizer Notepad, you can embed a browser on a Notepad page. The connection is an *OLE* (Object Linking and Embedding) connection, and you can then go to the browser by clicking its icon on the Notepad page.

Here's how to set it up:

1. Start Organizer, and click the Notepad tab.

2. Double-click the Notepad Contents page to create a new page. (Or just click on an existing page, if you have one.) Type a title for the page if you like. (I used the title Lotus Home.) In the Create Page box, click OK.

3. Click the Notepad page to put the cursor on the page.

4. From the Create menu, choose Object.

5. In the Object Type list box of the Create Object dialog box, select Netscape Hypertext Document, as shown in Figure 7-10.

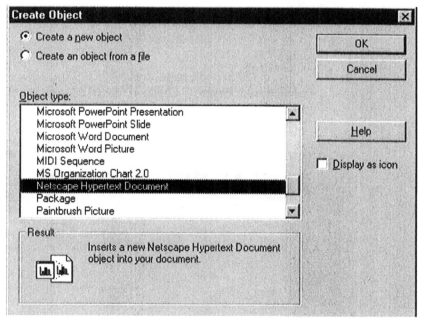

Figure 7-10: Select Netscape Hypertext Document as the object type.

6. Select Display as icon, so that an object will appear on the Notepad page to represent the object.

7. Click the Change Icon button. In the Change Icon dialog box (Figure 7-11), in the Label box, type in the label you want. (I used "Lotus Home Page.") Click OK.

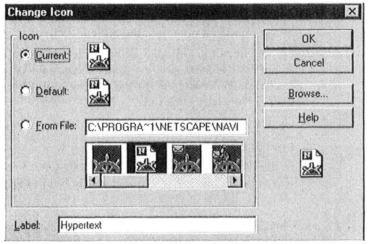

Figure 7-11: Type in the label you want for the icon.

8. Click OK.

9. Click the Notebook page, and press F2. Your changes to the page get entered. Figure 7-12 shows the page with the embedded object on it.

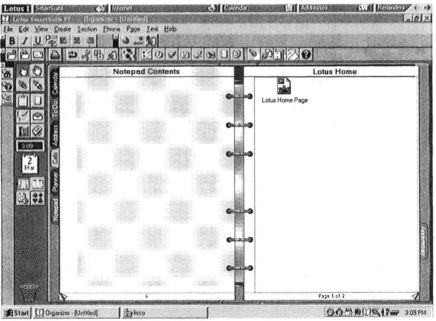

Figure 7-12: The embedded object appears on the Notepad page.

Now, you can set up the object so that it goes to Lotus Home Page:

1. Double click the object. The Navigator browser comes up, showing no location.

2. Type in the address for whatever location you want to go to, such as the Lotus Home Page—http://www.lotus.com.

3. If you want to type other material on the Notepad page, just minimize the browser, click on the page, and type your material.

4. When you are done, close Organizer.

Saving Documents to the Internet (Uploading)

The steps for saving a document to an Internet computer are quite similar to those for opening one from the Internet. Saving to the Internet is useful when you want to share a document with others—often other members of your team who may review it or enhance it in various ways. (Chapter 14 talks about the SmartSuite team tools those people may apply to the document.)

You can save a file to the Internet from 1-2-3, Word Pro, Freelance, or Approach (which I think of as the primary applications in SmartSuite. Organizer and SmartCenter are specialty items.) For this example, I used Freelance. Certainly people have many occasions to place their Freelance presentations on the Web, either as a way to distribute them in general, or to share them with team members for review.

Putting a document on the Internet for others to download is not the same as publishing a Web page. To work with a document you have saved to the Web, people download a copy and use it on their own computers. To work with a Web site, people connect with that site and read the page on the Internet computer. The Web page often contains links you can click on to move to other Web pages.

To upload a document to the Internet:

1. Start the application (Freelance here). On the Welcome screen, you could choose any SmartMaster, content topic, and look. I chose the Business Plan content topic and the 1997 look. Choose OK.

2. For Select a Content Page, select any page you want. For the example, I chose Business Plan Title Page. Click OK. Click in the block labeled Click Here to type business name, and type a name—Babette's Bagels, for the example. You have a sample file, and you can save it to the Internet.

3. Click the SmartIcon for Save a File to an FTP Server. (You could, of course, use menus instead.) The Save to Internet dialog box comes up, shown in Figure 7-13.

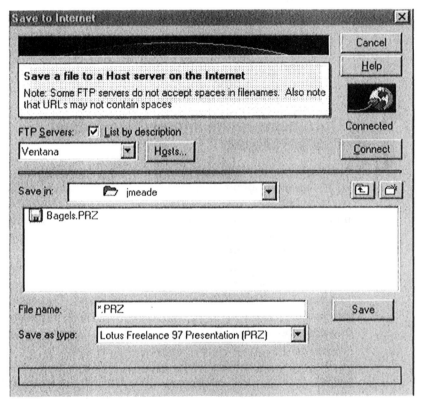

Figure 7-13: Use this dialog box to save to the Internet.

4. From the FTP Servers box, select a computer to save to. (If you don't have any Internet computers listed, click the Hosts button and type in the description and address for one or more computers. See "Setting Up FTP Connections" earlier in this chapter for an explanation). For the example, I used the Ventana computer that I set up earlier.

5. Click the Connect button to connect with the Internet computer.

6. In the Save in box, choose a folder, if you wish.

7. In the File Name box, type a name for the presentation. I used bagels.PRZ.

8. In the Save as Type box, select a file type for the presentation you're going to save. Figure 7-14 shows the list of file types you can choose. The example keeps the .PRZ format. (If you choose .HTM as your file type, a dialog box of additional options comes up. Chapter 8 talks about publishing a page as a Web page.)

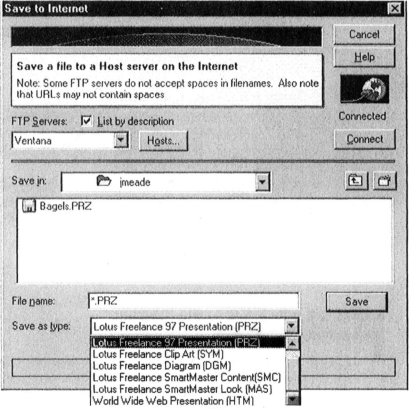

Figure 7-14: Choose one of these file types.

9. Click Save. If you have write permission to the host computer, you save your Freelance presentation to the computer.

Warning

You have to have permission to upload to an FTP site. Usually you get the permission from the administrator of the site. Most FTP sites are used for downloading files (no special permission required), not uploading them.

When you're done, you may want to save the file to your local disk as well. In Freelance, click File, then Save As, and save the file with the name bagels.PRZ. Close the file, and exit from Freelance.

Autoconnecting to Save Files to the Internet

If you save files to the same Internet computer most of the time, you can set up your Internet connections so that you automatically save to that computer:

1. Start Word Pro (or Freelance, 1-2-3, or Approach), and click File, then Internet, then FTP Connection Setup.

2. In the FTP Connection Setup box (Figure 7-2), click Auto Connect Save to Internet and specify the server you want to save to. Whenever you choose "Save a file to an FTP server," you automatically log in to the server you've specified.

Setting Up Live Links to the Internet

A *URL* (Uniform Resource Locator) is a Web address of the form http://www.address.com. Plans call for Lotus to allow you to link to a URL from any SmartSuite application. At the moment, Word Pro and 1-2-3 have the ability to allow you to connect to a Web site by clicking in a document. In Word Pro, you can click on a link in the document to connect with an Internet site. In 1-2-3, you can click on a button in a spreadsheet to connect directly with a Web page.

Setting Up a Link in Word Pro

When you're creating a document in Word Pro, you can set up a live link to any Internet URL. People reading the document on their computer can then double-click the link to open a destination document. The benefit? If someone is keeping the Internet document up-to-date with current information, then those who click the live link get the benefit of that up-to-date information.

Here's how to create a link to a URL in a Word Pro document:

1. Start Word Pro and create a blank document. Save it, if you wish. I saved mine as Ventana_link. I also typed in some initial text, "Some people may want to know about the." Now you're ready for the link.

2. Place the cursor where you want to put the link in the document— after the word "the" in Figure 7-15.

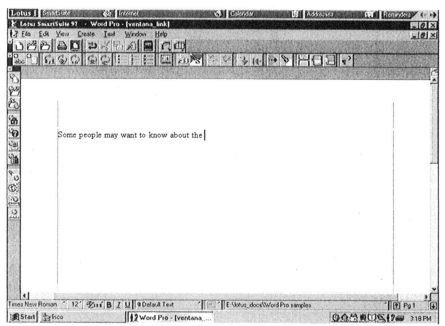

Figure 7-15: Put the cursor where you want to make the link.

3. From the Create menu, choose Click Here Block.

4. In the Create Click Here Block dialog box, choose Follow a Link from the Behavior list box, as shown in Figure 7-16.

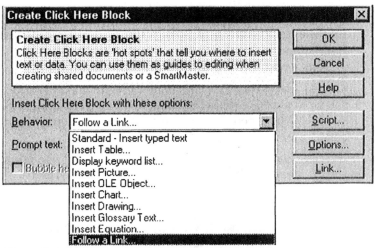

Figure 7-16: Choose Follow a Link.

5. Click the Link button.

6. In the Click Here Link box, Figure 7-17, click the Internet button, so you can put in the URL.

7. In the Browse from Internet dialog box, Figure 7-18, click on your Server type (FTP for the example), and select the server. For the example, I used the server that Ventana set up at the beginning of this chapter. In the File Name box, type *.* and press Enter so you can see all the files. Then click bagels.htm.

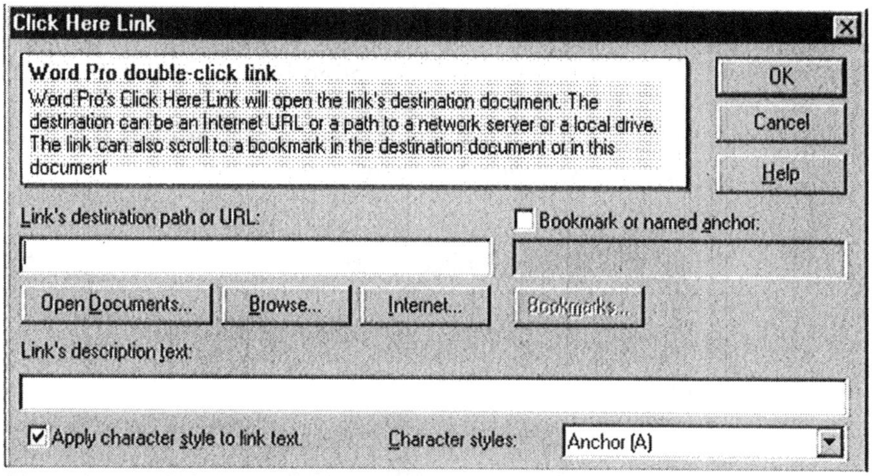

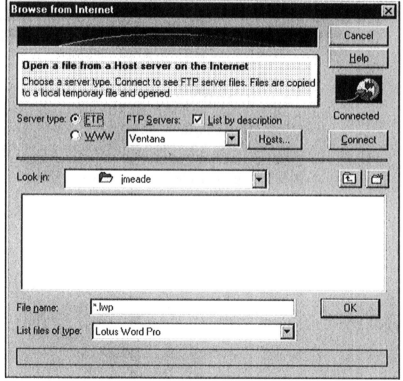

Figure 7-17: Click the Internet button.

Figure 7-18: Select your server type here.

8. Click OK.

9. In the Link's Description Text box in the Click Here Link dialog box, type the text you want people to see in your document, telling them about the link, such as **our new acquisition** for the example. See Figure 7-19.

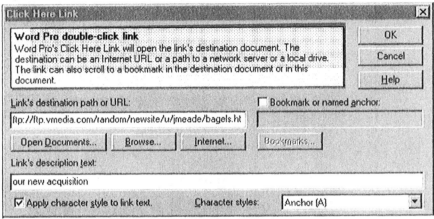

Figure 7-19: Type the text you want people to click on.

10. Click OK. You return to the Click Here Block dialog box.

11. Click OK again. The text appears in blue and underlined in your document. See Figure 7-20. You have just created a live link to the net. Whenever anyone double clicks on the underlined text, they go to the location you've set up on the Internet (the Freelance presentation screen in my example).

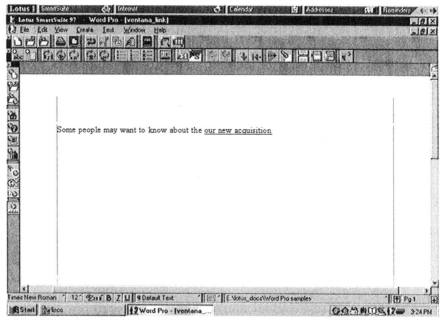

Figure 7-20: The link appears in the document.

Tip

Creating links to the Net in Word Pro is pretty fancy. Sometimes you may choose to work in a smaller, more manageable universe, though. You can create links to locations in the current document or in other SmartSuite documents, instead of to documents on the Internet. Instead of clicking on Internet in the Click Here Link box, Figure 7-17, click on Open Documents to link to a document you have open (including the current one) or on Browse to choose another document to link to.

Creating a 1-2-3 Button Link to the Web

In 1-2-3, you can put a button on the page that is linked to an Internet page. Any time someone clicks the button, they connect with that Internet page.

Here's how to do it:

1. Start 1-2-3. Just for the fun of it, choose a SmartMaster in the Welcome to 1-2-3 dialog box. For the example, I used Create a Personal Budget. Click OK. I saved the sample worksheet as budget.

2. If you don't have them showing already, display the Internet SmartIcons. (To display them, click the button at the left of the SmartIcon bar at the top, then click Internet Tools.)

3. Click the SmartIcon labeled "Create a Button with a Link to a URL." The Create a Link Button dialog box comes up.

4. In the Button Text box, type in text as you want it to appear on the button. I use **Financial Center**.

5. In the Link to box, type the URL for the Web page. I used www.tfc.com—a source of financial information. Figure 7-21 shows the completed dialog box.

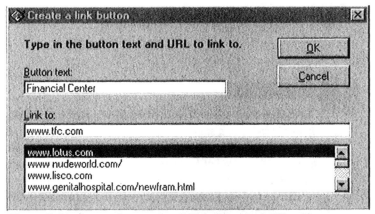

Figure 7-21: A sample completed dialog box looks like this.

6. Click OK.

7. Click the sheet where you want to have the button. The button appears on the spreadsheet, as shown in Figure 7-22. To go to the Web page, just click the button. 1-2-3 starts up your browser and goes to the specified Web page. Cool.

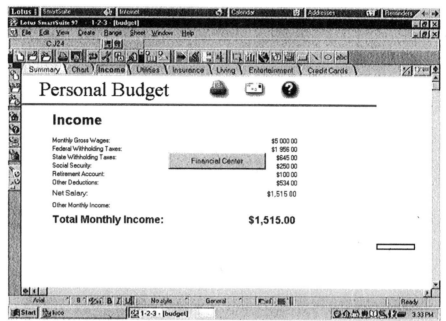

Figure 7-22: Click the button to go to a Web page.

Moving On

Downloading and uploading files is certainly a useful way for people to exchange information. Setting up live links within a document is an even more direct form of interaction, because people don't even have to leave the current document to go to an Internet site. And, if you know you often want to go to a Web site when working in a particular worksheet, why not set up a button with a link to the site?

An even more interactive way to make information available, though, is to publish not only files but also home pages on the Net. You can do that with Word Pro, as we'll explain in the next chapter. We'll also talk about how to publish documents from 1-2-3, Freelance, and Approach.

8

Putting Pages on the Web

When it comes to the Internet, SmartSuite aims to be "the total package," which is quite admirable for what looks on the surface to be a collection of desktop programs. Chapters 6 and 7 have shown what SmartSuite can do for searching, sharing, and linking on the Net. SmartSuite can also hold its head up high when it comes to publishing on the Net—creating Web pages or otherwise putting documents on the Net for others to enjoy.

Publishing a page to the World Wide Web is more fun than just putting a file on the Web for others to copy, as I have explained in Chapter 7, "Sharing & Linking on the Internet." When you put up a Web page, people connect with that page and read it right there on the Internet. (They don't have to download it to their computer and open it in a program on their own computer.) If you have links in the Web page, people can click them to go to other Web pages.

Word Pro is the king of Web-page makers in SmartSuite. When you combine its SmartMasters with its built-in design features, you have all the power you could want in creating Web pages. Though the other SmartSuite programs do not offer as much as Word Pro for publishing to the Net, Freelance, 1-2-3, and Approach nevertheless also have respectable Web publishing tools. You can publish Freelance, 1-2-3, and Approach documents in HTML format (Hypertext Markup Language, the programming language for Web pages) for others to download.

Publishing Pages to the Web With Word Pro

No mere word processor, Word Pro is quite the Web page maker as well. It offers something that pure Web page programs don't offer, too, because you can use its spell checker, Thesaurus, frame features, and all its high-powered word processing features. The easiest way to make a Web page, though, and to be sure that you have laid it out well, is to use a SmartMaster.

Finding a Nice Web Page SmartMaster

When you create a Web page with a SmartMaster, all you have to do is personalize it. It's a "fill-in-the-blanks" exercise. Also, there may be some extra pictures and text on the page, and you may choose to delete that. Later, you may choose to modify the look, and I talk about that in this chapter, in the section "Jazzing Up Your Page." Thanks to the SmartMaster, though, you can look professional without really straining at it. Here's what to do:

1. Start Word Pro your favorite way. (I usually click its icon in SuiteStart, because that takes just one click.)

2. In the Welcome to Lotus Word Pro dialog box, click the Create a New Document from a SmartMaster tab.

3. Click Browse for More Files. The dialog box displays two list boxes: Select a Type of SmartMaster and Select a Look. See Figure 8-1.

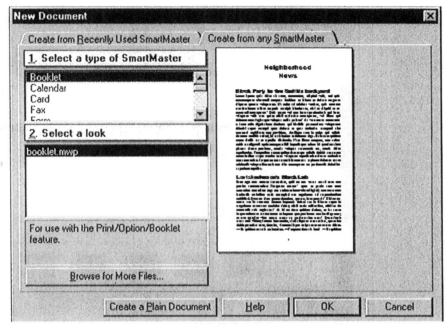

Figure 8-1: There are lots of Internet SmartMasters to choose from. Any of the SmartMasters will work just fine as a Web page, of course.

Tip

You can preview your SmartMaster in the box on the right side of the dialog box. You can shop through all the possibilities without ever leaving the dialog box. Although you can't get a complete idea of the look of a page because the previews are too small, you can get a pretty good idea.

4. Choose a Web page. If you click Internet - Corporate, you see one set of Internet SmartMasters. If you click Internet - Personal, you see another collection (the latter being, of course, warmer and more informal). For the example, I chose Internet - Personal in the type box, and home1.mwp in the look box.

5. Click OK.

A nifty, fully designed Web Page appears in Word Pro, ready for you to add your own special flavor. See Figure 8-2.

Figure 8-2: Thanks to SmartMasters, you're almost done before you start.

Naming Your Web Page

The name you give your Web page is the name that others see at the top of their browser when they display your page. When someone links to your page, they use your Web page name in the linking URL.

Here's how to name your Web page:

1. Display the document for the Web page. (The example uses the Web page just created from a SmartMaster.)

2. Click the block labeled "Click here to type home page title," and type a title. I type the words "Jeff's Insights." (If you're not using a SmartMaster, click the Heading1 paragraph style in the Status bar at the bottom and type in your title.)

   Now you're ready to put the title on the divider tab for the document.

3. Double-click the divider tab, and type the title of the Web page—
"Jeff's Insights" for the example.

Tip

If the divider tab isn't showing, click the icon at the top of the scroll bar on the right to display it. The icon looks like a series of tabs. Or, click the View menu, then Set View Preferences, and then Show Divider tabs.

Saving the Page Locally

When you have it the way you want it, you are going to publish the page to the Internet. It's a good idea to save any document regularly as you go along, though, in the format you will use on the Internet—HTML.

To save the page locally:

1. Click the Save SmartIcon (an arrow pointing into a folder).

2. In the Save As dialog box, type a name for the document. I use "Jeff's Insights"—the same name I'll be using later, but this time for a name on the local computer.

3. Click the arrow at the right of the Save as Type list box. The choice of file types displays, shown in Figure 8-3.

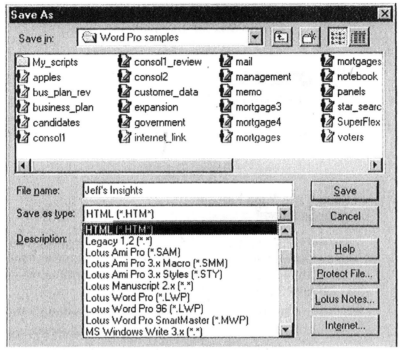

Figure 8-3: Choose HTML file type.

4. If you like, type in a description and choose a folder. Then click the Save button. The HTML Import/Export options box comes up, shown in Figure 8-4.

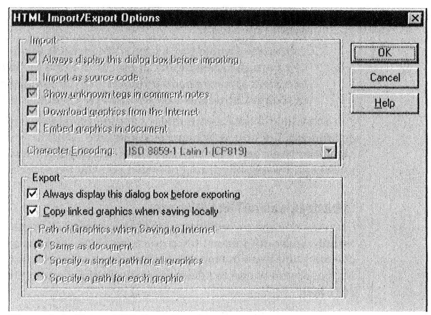

Figure 8-4: Choose HTML options here.

5. Click OK. You have saved the document in HTML format.

Putting Your Own Words on the Page

Once you've saved the page in HTML format, you've done the nitty gritty work of creating a Web page. Of course, unless you put in some text of your own, you aren't really offering anything to anyone who comes to your page. Although adding text and modifying the page is a Word Pro activity, I'll go over it briefly here.

Adding Text

To add text, click on any of the Click Here blocks, then type. Click here blocks are placeholders in SmartSuite SmartMasters. When you create a document based on a SmartMaster, the click here blocks contain text that prompts you as to what to do. For instance, a click here block could say "Click here to type in a Title."

You might want to type in the introduction. Here's how:

1. Click the block labeled "Click here to type an introduction to your home page."

2. Type some sample text. I type, "My friends tell me I have excellent insights. Some think I'm psychic. I don't really think so, but I do seem to have good intuition. Here are some of my latest thoughts. I bring this up-to-date every month or so."

You would follow the same steps to put in text elsewhere in the sample document. Click on a click here block and type in text. If you're making a real Web page, you'll probably put tons of attention into just doing that—weeks and weeks of figuring out what you want to tell the world.

Deleting Unwanted Text & Pictures

You may be used to deleting in Word Pro already. Chances are, you'll want to take out some of the pictures and Click Here blocks. Later in the chapter you'll see how to add various design features of your own. Suppose you wanted to delete the picture at the bottom that says Send Me Mail:

1. Right-click the element you want to delete, the Send Me Mail frame for the example.

2. Click Delete Frame.

3. In this example, select the remaining text, and press the Del key.

Tip

As you attempt to delete various ingredients of the SmartMaster, you may run into a number of possibilities. What you're deleting may be part of a table. Or it may be a frame. Or it may be a Click Here block. In general, if you right-click, select, and press Delete, you can get rid of whatever you want. If you make a mistake, click the Undo SmartIcon, or choose Undo from the Edit menu.

Previewing the Page in a Browser

You can preview your HTML file in an Internet Browser. After all, publishing to the Net is a commitment. Before you make your work so completely public, you may want to take a close look at how it will look to others. (The page may look different from in Word Pro, because the browser has some control on the appearance of the page.) To preview your page:

1. If you don't have the Internet authoring tools showing already, click the Internet SmartIcon for Show/Hide Web Authoring Tools. The Web Tools appear at the top of the page, shown in Figure 8-5.

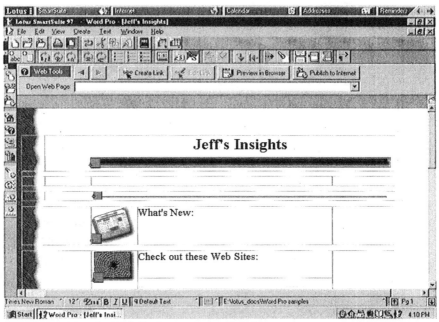

Figure 8-5: Use the Web Tools to preview in a browser.

2. Click Preview in Browser. Word Pro launches your browser and shows the Web page in it. Click the icon of a box in the top right of the browser to maximize it. Figure 8-6 shows the sample Web page in the Netscape Navigator browser.

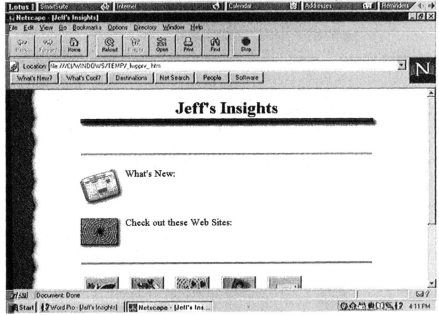

Figure 8-6: The sample page looks like this in Netscape Navigator.

    3. Click the X in the top right of the browser to close it.

Jazzing Up Your Page

Internet SmartMasters are probably the way to go for most of us, at least at the outset in creating a Web page. Why not enjoy the advantages of all that the professional designers put into the Web page?

However, professional designers are just people, too. They put lines, pictures, and background color on the page. As you get used to designing Web pages, you're likely to want to do those things yourself. And you can.

Adding a Horizontal Line

You can use the regular Word Pro menus at the top to add a horizontal line to your Web page. Lines are a time-honored way to separate the parts of a page from one another. Here's how to add a horizontal line:

    1. If the Web Tools aren't displayed already, click the Show/Hide Web Authoring Tools SmartIcon to display them.

2. Click in the document where you want to put the line. (Word Pro only allows you to put the line on a blank line in the document.) On the sample page, I clicked below the rest of the sample material, in a blank area at the bottom.

3. Click the Create menu, then Horizontal Line. The line appears in the document.

Adding a Link

You can also use the Web tools to set up links on your Web page. Links are a great service to the users who come to your page, helping them connect directly to pages similar to your own.

Suppose you wanted to set up a link to the Lotus Home Page:

1. Be sure the Internet tools are showing. If they aren't, click the SmartIcon for Show/Hide Web Authoring tools.

2. Select the text or the graphic that will appear as the link. For the example, I clicked in the section labeled "Check out these Web Sites," type in Lotus Home Page, and select the text.

3. Click the Create Link button in the Web Tools bar. The Create Link dialog box comes up. See Figure 8-7.

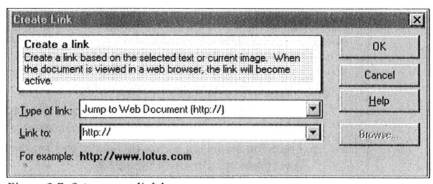

Figure 8-7: Set up your link here.

4. Select a type of link, though the suggested one is most probable—Jump to Web Document (http://).

Tip

You may want to be sure your filename has no spaces in it. Microsoft Internet Explorer works fine with file names that have spaces in them, but Netscape Navigator does not recognize names with spaces in them.

5. In the Link to box, type the destination; for the example, http://www.lotus.com.

6. Click OK.

The text now appears in blue and underlined on your page. When a user clicks it from an Internet browser, the linked page comes up.

Tip

To change a link once you've set it up, click on the link in your HTML document. Then click the Edit Link button in the Web Tools bar. The Edit Link dialog box comes up, which looks just like the Create Link box, shown in Figure 8-7. Make your changes, and click OK.

Importing a Picture

Word Pro is great at handling pictures, and, of course, pictures are valuable on any Web page. (Word Pro has clip art stored in the directory c:\wordpro\graphics, if you have installed the program on your C: drive.)

Here's how to import a picture in Word Pro:

1. Put the cursor where you want to place the image. I put the cursor on a blank part of the screen in the sample Web page.

2. From File menu, click Import Picture. The Import Picture dialog box comes up, shown in Figure 8-8.

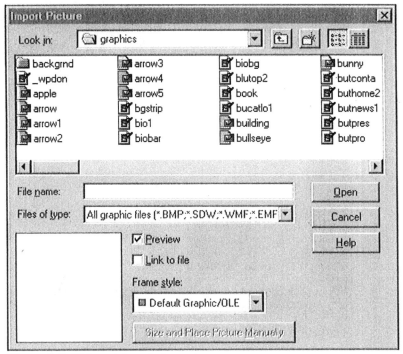

Figure 8-8: Pick a picture to import.

3. Double-click the picture you want. I double-clicked "apple." The apple appears on the page inside a frame. See Figure 8-9.

Tip

You can import pictures from any source. In the Import Picture dialog box, navigate to the directory containing the picture you want. Select the file containing the picture, and click Open.

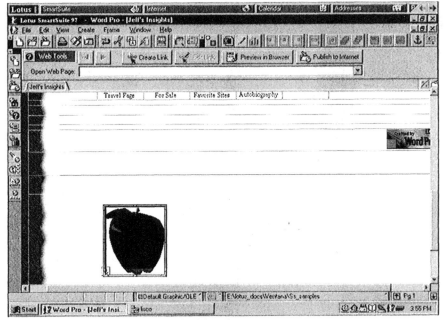

Figure 8-9: The picture appears inside a frame.

Changing the Wallpaper or Background Color

Use the Lotus InfoBox to change the background color or the wallpaper of a Web page. Background color is quite useful on Web pages, because color gives a page a certain mood. Also, color can just be fun. Many individuals seem to like a black background—as a stark contrast to usual backgrounds. You can get clever and show muted images in the background. The choices are about as numerous as if you were painting walls or putting up wallpaper in your home.

Here's how to change the background color or wallpaper in a Word Pro document:

1. For the example, I created a new, plain document in Word Pro. Click anywhere on the page to put the insertion point there.

2. Right-click, and click Page Properties. The Lotus InfoBox comes up.

3. Click the tab for "Color, pattern, and line style." A number of choices come up, as shown in Figure 8-10.

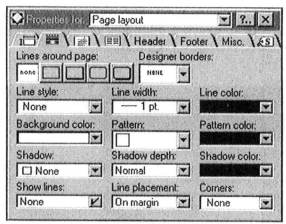

Figure 8-10: Choose page background color here.

4. Click the arrow beneath the Background color list box, and click on a color.

5. Click on the arrow for Pattern, and select a pattern.

Tip

As you try out colors and patterns in the InfoBox, the results show up automatically in the document. You can experiment until you find what you want, without ever leaving the InfoBox.

You can leave the InfoBox open as you continue to work. If you want to close it, click the X in the top right of the InfoBox.

Publishing the Page to the Internet

To publish to the Internet, follow the same steps described in Chapter 7 in the section "Saving Documents to the Net." Chapter 7 also describes how to get set up for saving to the Internet. Here is a quick summary of the steps to publish your page to the Internet:

1. For a Web page, be sure you've saved the document as an HTML file.

2. Click the SmartIcon for Publish as Web Page(s).

3. Click OK in the Publish as Web Page dialog box (or, if you wish, click "Do not show me this message again"). The Save to Internet dialog box comes up. See Figure 8-11.

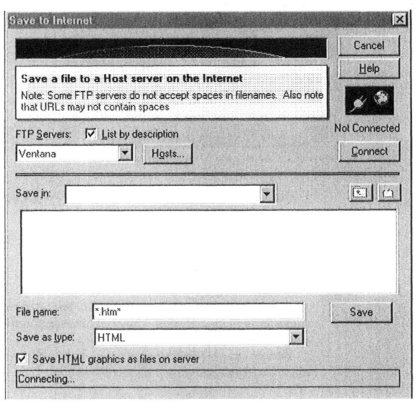

Figure 8-11: Choose your Internet server and name the file here.

4. Type in a name for the file. I used jeff.htm.

5. Click Save. The HTML Import/Export Options dialog box comes up. Click OK. If you have the privileges on the server, Word Pro saves your document on the Internet.

Publishing Your Freelance Presentation to the Web

Freelance doesn't offer Web authoring tools like those in Word Pro that allow you to do things like set up links to Internet URLs. When you create a Web page, users can go to that page and read it on the Internet server. But Freelance does have admirable capabilities for saving a presentation to the Net that people can then download and run on their own computers.

In Chapter 7, I talked about posting a Freelance .PRZ file to the Web so that you could share it with others. Your team members would then download the file to their computers and open it from Freelance.

You can also save a Freelance presentation as HTM files (the kind that Internet documents use). Files with the extension .HTM are actually HTML files. File extensions are 3 characters, so Freelance drops the L from HTML when saving it. Suppose you wanted to save the file "bagels" from the previous chapter in HTML format. Here's what you do:

1. Click its icon in SuiteStart to start Freelance. Click File, then Open, click the presentation you want to open, and then click Open again. The example uses a file named "bagels."

2. Display the Internet SmartIcons if they aren't showing already. (Click the arrow to the left of the Universal SmartIcon bar, then be sure that Internet Tools is selected.)

3. Click the Publish as Web pages SmartIcon (a globe with a page in front of it). A dialog box labeled "Publish as Web Page(s) Instructions" comes up. See Figure 8-12.

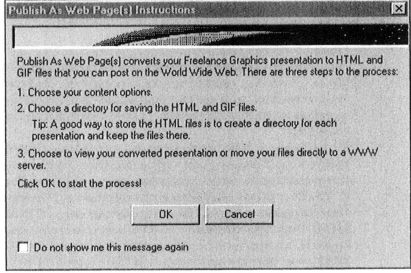

Figure 8-12: Instructions for Web Publishing comes up.

4. Click OK.

5. The Publish as Web Page(s) Options dialog box comes up. See Figure 8-13.

6. Once you choose your options, click OK. For the example, I accepted the suggested options (Lotus Home Page page button, table of contents links, and speaker notes).

7. The Publish as Web Page(s) dialog box comes up. Type in the file name, or click it in the list so that it appears in the File Name box. Choose a directory for the presentation, if you wish. Be sure that the Save as Type box lists World Wide Web Presentation (HTM).

8. Click Save.

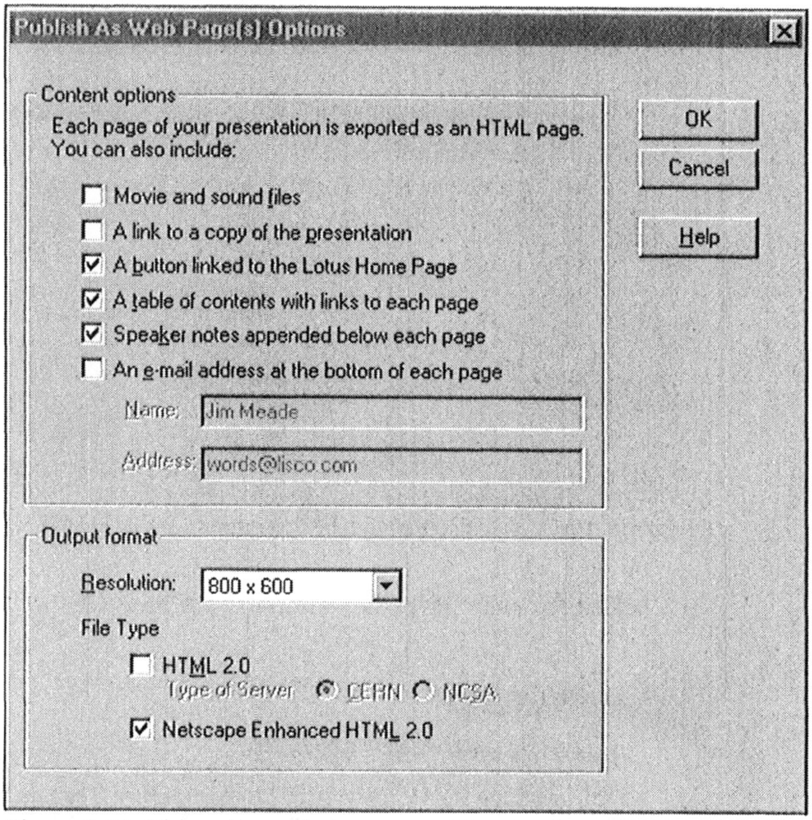

Figure 8-13: Choose the options you want for your Internet presentation.

In a separate directory, Freelance saves each page of the presentation as an HTML file, and the dialog box in Figure 8-14 comes up.

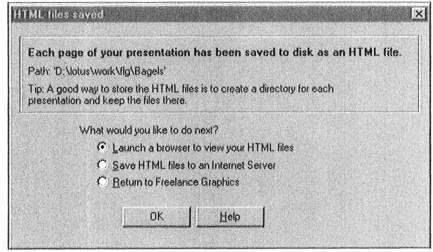

Figure 8-14: This box confirms that you have saved in HTML format.

9. Click OK to view the presentation in your browser.

Tip

> *To save to a server, here's what to do:*
>
> 1. *Click Save HTML files to an Internet Server. The Save to Internet dialog box comes up and asks you to choose a server.*
>
> 2. *For my example, I chose Ventana.*
>
> 3. *A dialog box comes up and asks "Would you like to connect to Ventana now?" I clicked Yes.*
>
> 4. *My local computer connects with the Internet computer. I clicked Save, and Freelance saves the presentation pages to the Web. (As explained in Chapter 7, you have to have Write privileges before you can save a file to the Internet computer.)*

Publish as Web Page Options

Freelance gives useful capabilties for streamlining a presentation you save to the Web. Here is a brief explanation of each option:

Movie and sound files. If you have put media or sound files into your presentation, you can specify that they be included in the Web presentation. Then, if the person running the presentation has Freelance Graphics, he or she can launch a Freelance Screen Show from the Web and have the Screen Show include sound or movies.

Link to a copy of the presentation. The saved presentation will be linked to a copy of the presentation in the same directory where you save the presentation.

A button to the presentation saved to the Web. (When you link to a copy of your presentation, Freelance adds this button.) If users click the button, they jump to the Lotus Home Page on the Web.

A button linked to the Lotus Home Page. The saved presentation will include a button that links to the Lotus Home Page.

A table of contents with links to each presentation page. If you choose this, the table of contents page will list all of the presentation pages and give links to those pages (each page will then have a link back to the table of contents).

Speaker notes appended below each page. If you had Speaker Notes in your presentation, they will appear at the bottom of the HTM page that corresponds to the page on which they appeared in the presentation.

An e-mail address at the bottom of each page. If you fill in your name and Internet address, Freelance will append them to every page in the presentation. A mail icon and navigation buttons will appear at the top of each page.

Publishing Your Spreadsheet to the Web

You can share a spreadsheet on an FTP site or WWW site in the same way as you share a document from any of the other SmartSuite programs, as I explain in Chapter 7. From within 1-2-3, you would click the Internet SmartIcon labeled "Save a File to the Internet," choose a host, and follow the rest of the steps set out in Chapter 7. You could choose to save the file as a Lotus 1-2-3 Workbook, as a SmartMaster, or as a text file. But you can't save it as an HTML file. However, you can save a range to the Internet in HTML format, as I explain in the next section.

Publishing a 1-2-3 Range to the Internet

You can publish a range from a spreadsheet to the Internet as a table in HTML format. Here's how:

1. Click the 1-2-3 icon in SuiteStart or use some other method to launch 1-2-3.

2. Click the Open an Existing File SmartIcon to open a document in 1-2-3. Select the worksheet you want, and click Open. The sample uses the document "budget" from Chapter 7. Or, you can create a new Workbook using the Create a Personal Budget SmartMaster.

3. Complete some data in the worksheet. For the example, click the Income tab, click in the column containing figures, and type in sample figures. Figure 8-15 shows a sample 1-2-3 range to be used in this example.

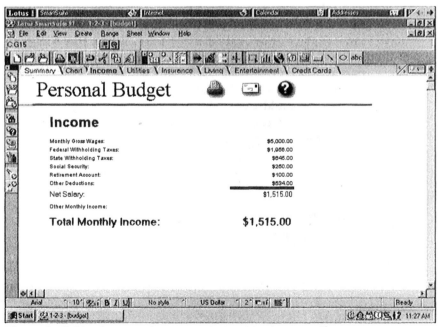

Figure 8-15: Here's a sample range to be used in the example.

4. Be sure the Internet SmartIcons are displayed, and click the SmartIcon for Publish a Range to the Internet. The Publish a Range to the Internet dialog box comes up. See Figure 8-16.

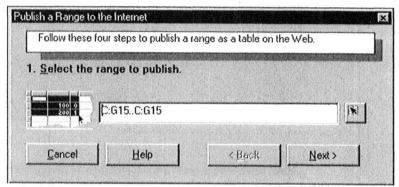

Figure 8-16: Select a range to publish.

5. Type in the range to publish.

Tip

The easiest way to select a range is with the Range Selector. Click the button to the right of the range in the dialog box, then drag across the cells you want to select.

6. Click Next. The Assistant asks you to format the table as it will appear on the Web. For the example, I selected Show Table Title and type in the title "Income." I also selected Show Cell Borders and Make Columns Equal Width. As you make a selection, a preview in the dialog box shows the effect of the choice. Figure 8-17 shows my completed box.

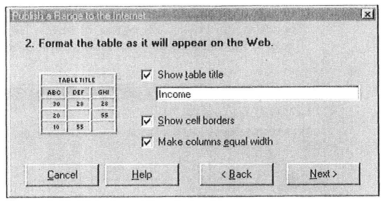

Figure 8-17: Make formatting choices here.

7. Click Next. The Assistant asks you to "Format the page as it will appear on the Web" (as opposed to formatting the table in the previous step). You can type in a Page title, Table description, a line below the description, the editor's name, and an e-mail address. Figure 8-18 shows a sample box.

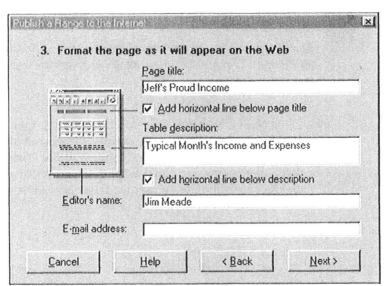

Figure 8-18: Put in your instructions for formatting the page.

8. Click Next. The Assistant gives you the opportunity to preview the page in your Web browser. See Figure 8-19.

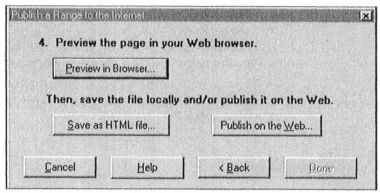

Figure 8-19: You can select the option to preview the page in your Web browser, then save it locally and/or to the Web.

9. Click the Preview in Browser button to preview the table. Your browser launches, and the table displays as it will appear as an Internet document. See Figure 8-20.

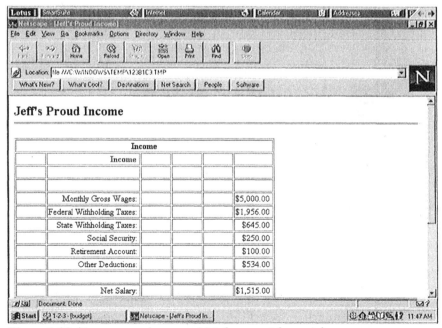

Figure 8-20: You can preview your Net document in your browser.

10. Close or Minimize your browser to return to the Lotus Assistant. To save the file locally, click the Save as HTML File button. The Save File As dialog box comes up, with the file type listed as HTML files. Type in a name and click Save. Freelance saves the file.

11. Click Done in the "Publish a Range to the Internet" box when you're finished saving your range as an HTML file, and, if you're done with it, exit 1-2-3.

Tip

To save to the Internet, click the Publish on the Web button. Follow these steps:

1. *In the Save to Internet dialog box, be sure the FTP server you want is selected.*

2. *If you are not connected to the server, click the Connect button.*

3. *In the File name box, type in a name, if you like. I typed 123budget. Htm. 1-2-3 saves the range to the Internet computer and returns to the Publish a Range to the Internet box.*

See Chapter 7 for a full discussion of saving a file to the Internet.

Putting Approach Views on the Web

You can save Approach views to the Internet in .APT format. Others can then open the file from the Internet and work with it on their computers in read-only format.

Of course, people often want to be free to make changes. They can do so. Just choose File, then Save As, then type in a new name for the file. Then you can work with the data as much as you wish.

In Approach, you don't store data. Rather, you store views through which you look at the data stored in an associated database file. Approach has the following kinds of views: form (used to look at one record at a time), report, form letter, mailing labels, worksheet, crosstab, chart, and envelope. In general, a view is the basic document you use in Approach. In Word Pro, you speak of documents. In 1-2-3, you work with spreadsheets. In Freelance, you create presentations. In Approach, you work with views.

If you create a new Approach file using a SmartMaster such as the Internet World Wide Web sites database (discussed in Chapter 6), the file comes with a number of predefined views. This chapter works with such views.

Here's how to place an Approach view on the Web:

1. Click the Approach icon in SuiteStart to start Approach. Create a new file or open an existing one. For the example, I opened the file surfnet.APR, created in Chapter 6. Click OK.

2. Be sure that the view tabs are showing. Click View, then Show View tabs.

3. Display the view you want to save. For the example, I clicked the Find by URL tab.

4. From the File menu, choose Internet, then Save to Internet. In the Save to Internet dialog box, Figure 8-21, choose either Current View Only, or All of the Views. For the example, I chose All of the views.

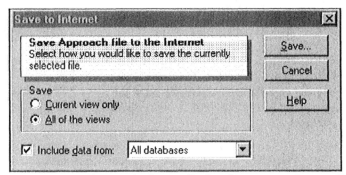

Figure 8-21: Choose whether to display the current view or all views.

5. Click to select how much data you want to save: All Databases, Found Set, Current Record, or Blank Databases. For the example, I chose Current Record.

6. Click the Save button.

7. The Save to Internet dialog box comes up, shown in Figure 8-22.

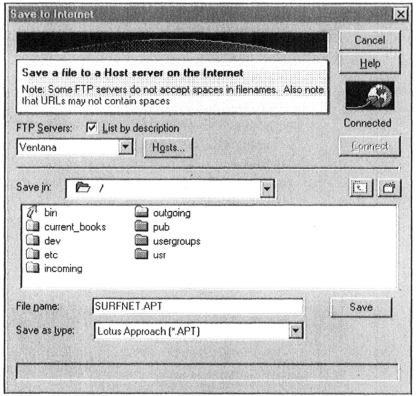

Figure 8-22: Here's the familiar "Save to Internet" dialog box, as seen in Approach.

8. From the FTP Servers box, select a host server.

9. Click Connect.

10. Select the folder you want to save to on the server.

11. Type in a file name for the APT file. The example uses the name SURFNET.APT.

12. In the Save as type box, select Lotus Approach (APT).

13. Click Save. Approach saves the file to the directory you've selected on the Internet. (You have to have permission to save the file to the Internet computer. Though permission is often automatic for downloading files, you usually have to make arrangements with the system administrator before you can upload files as in this example.)

Putting a View on the Web in HTML Format

You can also save Approach views as Web pages on the Net in HTML format. Here's what to do:

1. From the File menu, click Internet, then Publish as Web Page(s). The Save to Internet dialog box comes up.

2. Select the FTP Server you want to use. Be sure that the file name and type are the ones you want—for this example, SURFNET.HTM for the filename and HTML file (*.HTM) as the type.

3. Click Save. An HTML Preferences dialog box comes up. Click OK.

Approach saves the file on the Internet in HTML format. Others can then read the file with their browsers.

Moving On

Thanks to the Internet, you can now make information available to millions. In Word Pro, you can create full-featured Web pages. In 1-2-3, Approach, and Freelance, you can save files in HTML format that others can read inside their Web browsers.

The Internet is at the heart of SmartSuite, as it is at the heart of computing in the late 90s.

Just as much at the heart of SmartSuite, though, is using SmartSuite programs together. Chapter 4 showed one example of using SmartSuite programs together—1-2-3 and Freelance. The next chapter resumes this type of discussion, and shows you how to use 1-2-3 and Word Pro together.

PART THREE

Mixing SmartSuite Applications

9

Combining 1-2-3 & Word Pro

Word Pro and 1-2-3 are both giants among programs. Many a person spends all day every workday in one or the other without a thought of needing anything more. If you begin to need 1-2-3 capabilities while using Word Pro, well, you can create tables in Word Pro. Though few people use 1-2-3 as a word processor, it can certainly handle text very well. As long as you're working in rows and columns, you can be content using just 1-2-3.

However, when you begin to combine them, you gain freedom and power you may not have expected. Sure, you can create a table in Word Pro. But you can create better ones in 1-2-3. If it's as easy to combine 1-2-3 with Word Pro as to work in either program separately, why not do it? And now, it is easy to combine these two "heavyweights" of software programs.

In this chapter, you see how to copy a table from Word Pro to 1-2-3 by dragging and dropping it. Then, you turn right around and see how to copy one in the other direction (1-2-3 to Word Pro) by dragging and dropping. You see how to embed a workbook in Word Pro, which means that you have the full power of the 1-2-3 workbook as you work in Word Pro. And (my personal favorite, because it keeps your Word Pro data current), you see how to link a 1-2-3 range to a Word Pro document. Linking means that any change to the 1-2-3 range shows up right away in Word Pro.

Using Word Pro and 1-2-3 together is very similar to using 1-2-3 and Freelance together, as discussed in Chapter 4. So, if you have gone through Chapter 4, you'll feel familiar with some of what you see here.

Copying a Table From Word Pro to 1-2-3

Word Pro makes great tables. It's hard to dispute that. Here are a few examples of things you can do with Word Pro tables. In a Word Pro table cell you can put text, pictures, even equations. And you can put some formulas in there, too. You can put a table in the midst of document text, inside a frame, inside a column, or in a header or footer. You can drag the sides of columns to make them the width you want. You can drag and drop cells.

For all their power and beauty, though, Word Pro tables are still tables in a word processor. They aren't spreadsheets. 1-2-3, though, is a spreadsheet program. It can do about everything Word Pro tables can do with cells. But it has power not available in Word Pro. For instance, Word Pro does come with a list of built-in functions—about six of them. 1-2-3, being a true spreadsheet, offers hundreds. 1-2-3 has features like What-if Table, Backsolver, and Inverted Matrixes—advanced capabilities used by experienced spreadsheet users, statisticians, and mathematicians.

The point is, 1-2-3 is a mature spreadsheet product whose sole purpose in life is to create full-featured tables. If Word Pro tables don't suit your purposes on some occasions, you may want to use 1-2-3 for a table started in Word Pro.

To get the power of a spreadsheet for your Word Pro table, you can use SmartSuite and copy the Word Pro table into 1-2-3.

Creating the Word Pro Table

To start, you have to have a Word Pro table to work with. Then, you can copy it to 1-2-3 and continue to work.

Suppose, for instance, you wanted to know the monthly payments for a $75,000 mortgage at a number of different interest rates. You could do the whole table in Word Pro. But it might take a while, and you might end up pulling out your calculator to help now and then.

If you copied the table into 1-2-3, though, you could apply functions to it that are not available in Word Pro. In this example, you could apply the function for calculating payments. In fact, you could create a What-if Table in 1-2-3 (not yet available in Word Pro, though—the way things are changing so fast, it probably will be in a coming version of Word Pro).

Here's how to create the Word Pro table:

1. Start Word Pro your favorite way. For instance, you could click the Win 95 Start menu, click Programs, locate Lotus Word Pro 97, and click it. Click the Create Plain Document button. A blank document comes up.

2. Click Create, then Table.

3. In the Create Table dialog box, shown in Figure 9-1, click the arrows to the right of the box to set 3 as the Number of Columns and 7 as the Number of Rows. Click OK.

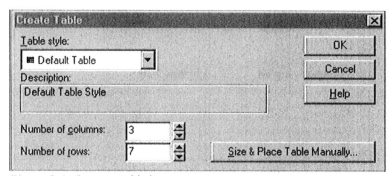

Figure 9-1: Create a table here.

4. Click in each cell and type in the data. I labeled the first column Mortgage Amount, the second Interest Rate, and the third Monthly Payment. In the first cell under mortgage amount, I put $75,000.00. For interest rate, I listed these rates: 7.5%, 8%, 8.5%, 9%, 9.5%, and 10%. I left the amounts in the Monthly Payment column blank.

   You don't have to format the table for this example to work.

   a. For the example, I labeled each column and selected and clicked the B in the status bar at the bottom to bold the heads.

   b. I dragged across the cells containing numbers, right clicked, clicked Text Properties, and, in the Properties InfoBox, clicked the Alignment tab, then clicked the button for right alignment (a picture of right-aligned lines).

c. I selected the number for mortgage amount (75,000).

    d. In the Properties InfoBox, I clicked Table Cell in the list box at the top.

    e. I clicked the # tab, then clicked Currency on the left and U.S. Dollar on the right.

    f. I selected the interest rates, clicked Table Cell in the InfoBox, clicked the #tab, and clicked Number as the Format category and Percent as the Current Format. I left the Monthly Payment column blank (because 1-2-3 is going to fill that in.) Then I clicked the X at the top right of the InfoBox to close it. Figure 9-2 shows the completed Word Pro table.

5. When you have the table the way you want it, you may want to save it. (You don't have to save it to be able to copy the data.) I clicked the Save SmartIcon and saved mine as "mortgages."

Mortgage Amount	Interest Rate	Monthly Payment
$75,000.00	7.5%	
	8%	
	8.5%	
	9%	
	9.5%	
	10%	

Figure 9-2: Here's a sample table I plan to copy to 1-2-3.

Starting 1-2-3

Now, you start 1-2-3, if you don't have it running already:

1. Start 1-2-3 your favorite way. Perhaps click the 1-2-3 icon in SuiteStart (at the right side of the Win 95 Taskbar).

2. In the Welcome to 1-2-3 dialog box, click Create a Blank Workbook.

Selecting the Table in Word Pro

In Word Pro, there's a difference between selecting all the cells in the table and selecting the entire table. If you want to copy the entire table, follow these steps to select it:

1. Click the Word Pro button on the Win 95 Taskbar to return to Word Pro.

2. Click anywhere inside the table.

3. From the Table menu, choose Select, then Entire Table. Word Pro selects the table. Figure 9-3 shows the selected table.

Mortgage Amount	Interest Rate	Monthly Payment
$75,000.00	7.5%	
	8%	
	8.5%	
	9%	
	9.5%	
	10%	

Figure 9-3: Your selected table looks like this.

Dragging the Word Pro Table to 1-2-3

The secret to dragging a table is to watch the shape of the mouse pointer. Here's what to do:

1. Place the mouse pointer on the border of the table.

2. When the mouse pointer changes to the shape of a hand, hold down the mouse button and drag the table.

3. Drag the table to the 1-2-3 button in the Win 95 Taskbar at the bottom. Hold down the mouse button. (If you release the mouse button on top of the Taskbar button, you get an error message.)

4. Now that 1-2-3 is active, continue to hold down the mouse button, and drag the table to where you want it to appear in 1-2-3. For the example, I put the table at the top left of the spreadsheet.

5. Release the mouse button. The table now appears in 1-2-3, where you can use spreadsheet capabilities on it if you wish. Figure 9-4 shows the table as it initially appears. (Some of the formatting is lost.)

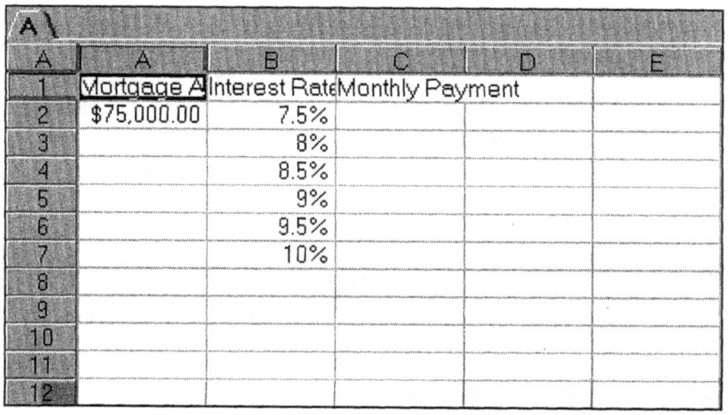

Figure 9-4: The copied table at first looks like this in 1-2-3.

6. You may then want to format the data. For the example, I dragged across the column labels and clicked the B at the bottom to bold the column titles. I used a shortcut to fit the cell contents to the column. I positioned the mouse pointer between the column heads at the top (the rows labeled A, B, and so on). When it changed to a double arrow, I double-clicked.

7. If you like, save the spreadsheet. Click the Save SmartIcon, type in a name for the workbook, and click Save. I saved mine as "mortgage." Figure 9-5 shows the table after I saved and formatted it.

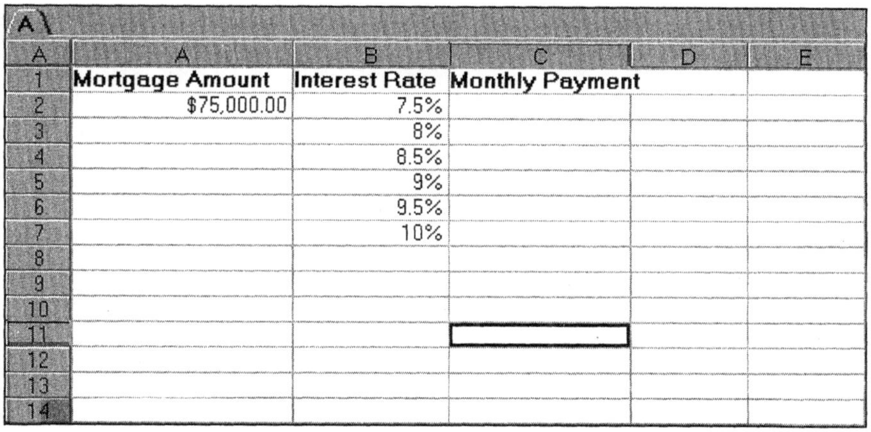

Figure 9-5: This table is now ready for you to work on it in 1-2-3.

Creating the What-if Table in 1-2-3

Once you have the Word Pro table in 1-2-3, you can do things with it that perhaps you can't do in Word Pro. For this example, I created a What-if Table to fill in the mortgage amounts in the "Monthly Payment" column. This example has nothing directly to do with copying between the programs. It's just a good example of why you might want to copy from Word Pro to 1-2-3.

Here's how to create the What-if Table:

1. Select the range of cells from B3:B7 and drag it downward to create a blank cell at B3.

2. Click the cell where you want the @function to appear: Cell A:C3 in the example.

3. Click the @Function selector (the button just above the SmartIcons at the top), and click List All. A list of 1-2-3 @functions appears. See Figure 9-6.

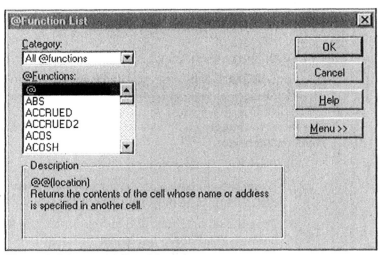

Figure 9-6: You see a list of functions.

4. Choose the function you want. For the example I used PMT. Click OK.

5. Complete the function in the spreadsheet. See the contents box in Figure 9-7 (at the top, next to the @Function selector) to see the formula for calculating monthly payments.

	A	B	C	D	E
1	Mortgage Amount	Interest Rate	Monthly Payment		
2	$75,000.00	7.5%	$524.41		
3		8%			
4		8.5%			
5		9%			
6		9.5%			
7		10%			

A:C2   @PMT(75000,B2/12,30*12)

Figure 9-7: The contents box shows the formula for calculating monthly payments.

6. Click Range, then Analyze, then What-if Table.

7. In the What-if Table box, use the range selector (the arrow icon to the right of the text box) to put in your Table range and Input cell 1. Figure 9-8 shows a completed What-if Table Assistant.

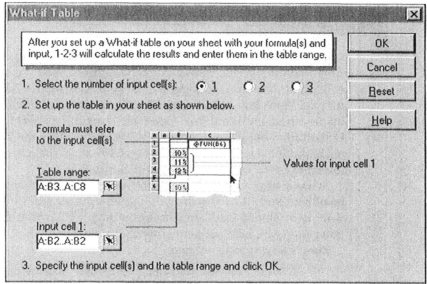

Figure 9-8: Complete the dialog box like this.

8. Click OK. 1-2-3 puts in the values for the Monthly Payments.

9. If necessary, right-click column C, then click Range Properties. Click the # tab in the Lotus InfoBox, and click Currency for Category and US Dollar for Current format. Click the X at the top to close the InfoBox. Figure 9-9 shows the completed table, with the monthly payments now filled in.

	A	B	C	D
1	**Mortgage Amount**	**Interest Rate**	**Monthly Payment**	
2	$75,000.00	7.5%		
3			$524.41	
4		8%	$550.32	
5		8.5%	$576.69	
6		9%	$603.47	
7		9.5%	$630.64	
8		10%	$658.18	
9				
10				
11				
12				

Figure 9-9: 1-2-3 completes the table for you, filling in monthly payments.

Copying a Range From 1-2-3 to Word Pro

Copying from 1-2-3 to Word Pro is almost the same simple drag-and-drop operation as just shown for copying from Word Pro to 1-2-3; however, there are some differences. Instead of copying the 1-2-3 cell contents into the Word Pro table, SmartSuite places the 1-2-3 range as an object inside a frame in Word Pro. The object is an OLE (Object Linking and Embedding) object. You can then resize and position the object as you wish, but the data is not actually Word Pro data. The object remains linked to 1-2-3. The example should clarify this.

What if, after you created your What-if Table, you wanted to use the results in Word Pro? Perhaps you're preparing a report in Word Pro and want to be able to use Word Pro formatting. Well, with drag and drop, you can copy a 1-2-3 range to a Word Pro document.

Here's how to copy a range:

1. If Word Pro isn't running, click its icon in SuiteStart to start it. Open or create a document where you want to place the 1-2-3 range. I used a new, blank document.

2. Click the 1-2-3 icon in SuiteStart to start it if it's not already running. (For the example, I used the workbook "mortgage" created in the previous section.)

3. Open the workbook and display the sheet that has the range you plan to copy. The example uses the sheet shown in Figure 9-9.

4. Select the range you want to copy—A1:C8 in the example, shown in Figure 9-10.

	A	B	C	D
1	Mortgage Amount	Interest Rate	Monthly Payment	
2	$75,000.00	7.5%		
3			$524.41	
4		8%	$550.32	
5		8.5%	$576.69	
6		9%	$603.47	
7		9.5%	$630.64	
8		10%	$658.18	
9				
10				
11				

Figure 9-10: Select the 1-2-3 range you want to copy to Word Pro.

5. Drag the range to the Word Pro button in the Windows Taskbar. Don't release the mouse button.

Tip

To drag a range, put the cursor at the top of the range and wait for it to take the shape of a hand. When you drag the range to the Taskbar, remember to hold down the button. If you release the mouse button on top of the Taskbar button while dragging a range, you see an error message that tells you to continue to hold down the mouse button to make Word Pro active.

6. Word Pro becomes active. Drag the range to where you want it in the Word Pro document, then release the mouse button. The range appears in a frame in Word Pro, as shown in Figure 9-11.

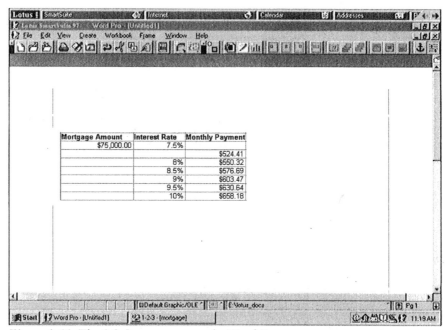

Mortgage Amount	Interest Rate	Monthly Payment
$75,000.00	7.5%	
		$524.41
	8%	$550.32
	8.5%	$576.69
	9%	$603.47
	9.5%	$630.64
	10%	$658.18

Figure 9-11: The 1-2-3 range appears in Word Pro.

The range is an object on top of the sheet—not a part of an existing table, should you happen to drag the range into an existing table. (When you drag from Word Pro into 1-2-3, the data becomes part of 1-2-3.) The range doesn't overwrite any data you have in Word Pro; it just sits of top of it. It is an OLE object. You can drag its corners and sides to resize it, and you can drag the entire object. When you double-click it to work on the data, you are actually working with the linked data in 1-2-3.

Tip

To reposition the range, place the cursor anywhere on the frame. (Be sure it is in the shape of a hand.) Then drag it to a new location.

Resizing 1-2-3 Objects

You can't just drag the corner to resize the frame, as you often can with Windows objects. One way to resize the frame is to use the menus. Here's how:

1. From the Frame menu, choose Graphics Scaling. The InfoBox for Frame comes up. See Figure 9-12.

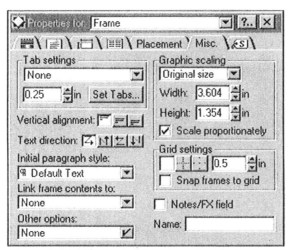

Figure 9-12: Use the InfoBox to resize the frame.

2. Click the Size and Margin tab (third in from the left) and use the arrows next to the Width and Height text boxes to change the dimensions. Figure 9-13 shows the Size and Margin tab.

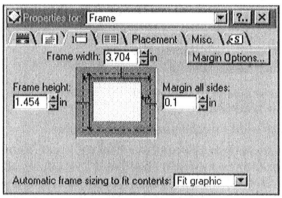

Figure 9-13: Change frame dimensions here.

Embedding a 1-2-3 Workbook in Word Pro

There is a step beyond copying a range from 1-2-3 to Word Pro, as explained in the previous section. You can embed a complete 1-2-3 workbook in Word Pro.

What if you want to keep the power of 1-2-3 for your table but have the table reside in Word Pro? Perhaps you're preparing a report with data that requires the power of a spreadsheet. You can embed the 1-2-3 data into a Word Pro document. The 1-2-3 workbook then becomes a part of the Word Pro document.

Copying the Table in 1-2-3

If you want to edit the data in the workbook, you can literally use 1-2-3 from within Word Pro. Here's what to do:

1. Start 1-2-3 if it's not running already.

2. Open the workbook you want to embed. For the example, I used the "mortgage" workbook from earlier in the chapter.

3. Select the data you want to embed. For the example, I again selected the whole table, as shown earlier in Figure 9-10.

4. Click Edit, then Copy.

The data is in the Win 95 Clipboard, ready for you to copy it into Word Pro. Now, though, you don't just copy it. You embed it.

Starting Word Pro & Pasting the Data

Once you have copied the data from 1-2-3 to the Clipboard, you're ready to embed the workbook in Word Pro:

1. Start Word Pro, if it's not running already.

2. Create or open a document where you want to embed the 1-2-3 data. (For the example, I had Word Pro running already.) I clicked the Create a New Document SmartIcon to create a new document. I typed in some brief text, and saved the document as "mortgage3." Figure 9-14 shows the document before I embedded the workbook.

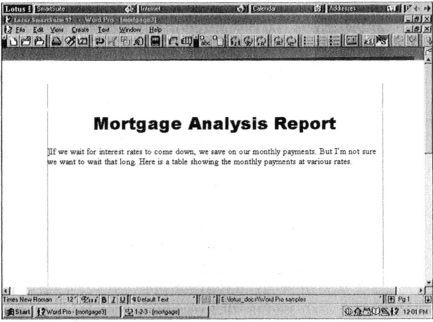

Figure 9-14: A Word Pro document awaiting an embedded workbook.

3. Place the cursor where you want the embedded data to appear.

4. Click Edit, then Paste Special.

5. In the Paste Special dialog box (Figure 9-15), be sure that Paste is selected. From the As box, select "Lotus 1-2-3 97 Workbook Object." Click OK.

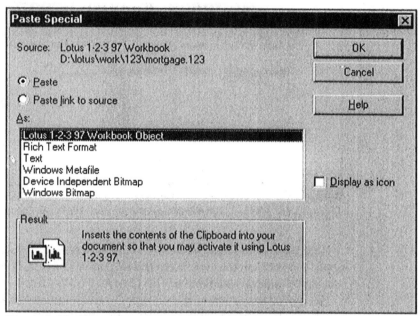

Figure 9-15: Select "Paste" and "Lotus 1-2-3 97 Workbook Object."

The 1-2-3 workbook is embedded in the Word Pro document. See Figure 9-16.

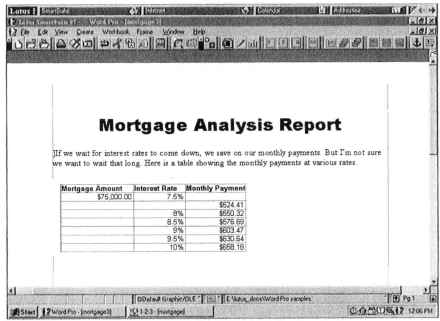

Figure 9-16: The 1-2-3 workbook appears in the Word Pro document.

You have embedded the entire 1-2-3 workbook, not just the selected data. That means that you have the full power of 1-2-3. If you want to use an @function available in 1-2-3 but not in Word Pro, you can do so.

To reposition or resize the workbook, follow the instructions in the section Resizing 1-2-3 Objects, where I discuss copying a 1-2-3 range to a Word Pro document.

Editing Data in the Embedded Workbook

To edit the data in the embedded workbook, follow these steps:

1. Double-click inside the frame. The table takes on the appearance of a 1-2-3 worksheet. See Figure 9-17.

2. Click a cell and edit, just as you would in any 1-2-3 worksheet.

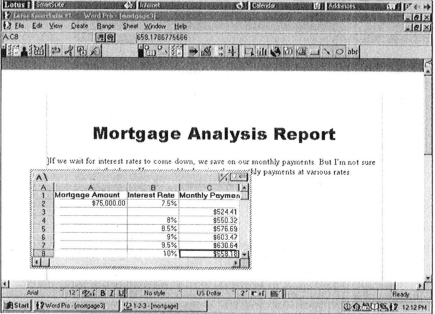

Figure 9-17: The table is embedded 1-2-3.

When you're finished editing, click in Word Pro anywhere outside the workbook frame.

Fancy though the embedded workbook may be, it still doesn't solve a problem many face when working with 1-2-3 and Word Pro together. What if you want changes in the 1-2-3 range to be reflected automatically in Word Pro? You can link the range and the Word Pro table, as the next section explains.

Linking a Range From 1-2-3 to Word Pro

Embedding 1-2-3 data in Word Pro, as just explained, is fine for data that you don't change too often. However, what if you have 1-2-3 data that you're updating frequently and you want to use Word Pro to present the data? You can *link* the 1-2-3 range to your Word Pro document. Then, any changes in the 1-2-3 data automatically show up in the Word Pro document. (I think that's pretty neat.)

For the example, I used the sample tables I've been using throughout the chapter.

Copying the Data in 1-2-3

To copy and link the data, here's what you do:

1. If 1-2-3 is not running already, click its icon in SuiteStart or use another method to start it.

2. Create or open a workbook and display the range you want to link. For the example, I again used the "mortgage" worksheet.

3. Select the range you want to link. For the example, I again used A1:C8.

4. From the Edit menu, choose Copy. You have placed the range in the Win 95 clipboard and are ready to link it to Word Pro.

Setting Up the Link in Word Pro

The steps in Word Pro are almost identical with those for copying or embedding. But you make an additional choice in the Paste Special dialog box. Here's what you do to set up the link in WordPro:

1. If Word Pro is not already running, click its icon in SuiteStart or use another method to start it.

2. Create or open the document you want to link to. For the example, I created a document named Mortgage4 that will display current monthly mortgage payments. See Figure 9-18.

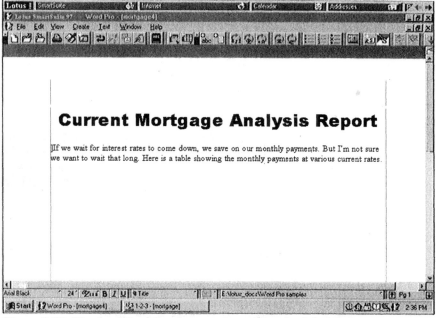

Figure 9-18: Here's a Word Pro document awaiting the 1-2-3 link.

3. Click in the Word Pro document where you want to have the linked data appear.

4. From the Edit menu, choose Paste Special. The Paste Special dialog box comes up, shown earlier in Figure 9-15.

5. Select Paste link to Source.

6. In the As box, click 1-2-3 97 Workbook Object, then click OK.

   The 1-2-3 data appears in a frame in the Word Pro document, as when you copy or embed a range. Figure 9-19 shows the linked data in Word Pro. There is an important difference, though. This time, if you change anything in 1-2-3, it automatically changes in Word Pro.

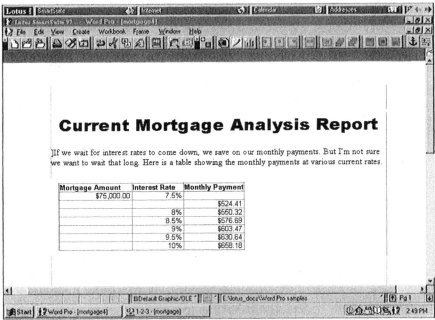

Figure 9-19: Your linked data looks like this in Word Pro.

Testing the Link

To test the link, change something in 1-2-3 and see if the change shows up in Word Pro. Suppose interest rates suddenly dropped dramatically. Figure 9-20 shows the 1-2-3 spreadsheet where I have changed the interest rates in column B and the monthly payments in column C.

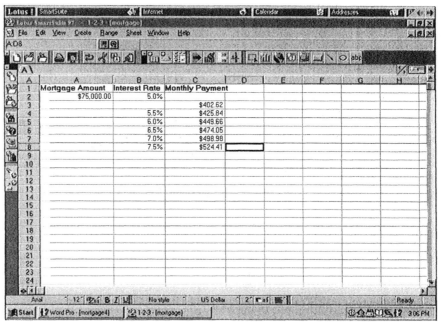

Figure 9-20: This worksheet has changed values from previous versions of the worksheet in this chapter.

If you click on the Word Pro button in the Win 95 Taskbar, you see that the changed 1-2-3 values show up in Word Pro. See Figure 9-21.

People have a tendency to keep their data in 1-2-3. And they have a tendency to prepare written reports about the data using Word Pro. Linking is the ideal way to make certain that Word Pro always reflects the latest data in 1-2-3.

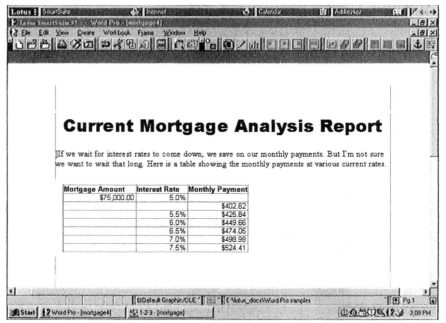

Figure 9-21: In a linked document, changes in 1-2-3 show up immediately in Word Pro.

Moving On

1-2-3 and Word Pro are sister programs. They have one another in mind as they work. You can use each for what it is best at without having to overlook the other. If you want to copy a table from Word Pro to 1-2-3 (where you can analyze its data to death), you can do that readily. If you want to copy a range or a worksheet from 1-2-3 to Word Pro, hey, no problem. To copy, you can drag and drop. To set up links, you use Paste Special.

Word Pro and 1-2-3 also have nice, open relationships with the other members of the suite. In the next chapter we'll look at how you might use Word Pro together with Freelance or Organizer.

10

Combining Word Pro With Other SmartSuite Programs

S martSuite users may, by inclination, be spreadsheet users first and foremost. Lotus, after all, began as the maker of what was at the time the world's most famous spreadsheet. Say what you will, though, most people tend to spend most of their working time using their word processors. Even the Lotus audience finds itself using Lotus Word Pro for hours at a time.

If Word Pro is your "main squeeze" (as the old saying goes), you can call in materials from the other suite members as the need arises. In Chapter 9, I've already talked about bringing 1-2-3 material into Word Pro (and vice versa). In this chapter, I talk about bringing nifty Freelance graphic materials and tables into Word Pro and about using Word Pro with Organizer.

There is a particularly good reason for using Word Pro as your home base as you work. You can use Word Pro as a notebook that holds documents from your other SmartSuite applications: 1-2-3, Freelance, and Approach. It can hold documents from any Windows 95 application that supports Object Linking and Embedding (and that's most applications). Once you've set up the links, you start in Word Pro and, from within Word Pro, automatically switch to a document in the appropriate sister application.

In this chapter you find out about using Freelance with Word Pro and about using Word Pro with Freelance. You find out about using Word Pro with Organizer, and—probably best of all—about using Word Pro as a notebook.

Using Freelance Material in Word Pro

Word Pro and Freelance share the same reciprocity as Word Pro and 1-2-3 (which I talked about in Chapter 9).

What you choose to copy to Word Pro may be different if you're using Freelance than if you're using 1-2-3. Rather than copying a complex 1-2-3 table, you may want to copy a Freelance graphic (clip art, a drawing, or a diagram). Should you happen to have a Freelance table you want to copy to Word Pro, you can do that, too. And you can copy in the other direction—from Word Pro to Freelance.

Copying a Graphic From Freelance to Word Pro

Freelance puts its SmartSuite companion programs to shame when it comes to creating, such things as pictures of computer equipment, or Gantt diagrams, even fancy tables. It's only fitting that Freelance would excel at such visual matters—it's a graphics program.

The comparison with graphics in 1-2-3 or Word Pro is worth mentioning, though, because the spreadsheet program and the word processing program do offer graphics of their own. Before the era of suites, one might have justifiably decided to stick with one's current program (1-2-3 or Word Pro) to create a graphic instead of using Freelance.

Such narrowness is no longer the right choice, though. In the new SmartSuite, if you want visual material to use in your word processor or spreadsheet, you don't have to accept any second-rate substitutes. You can go straight to Freelance for the real deal, then copy the graphic into your other program.

Creating a Freelance Presentation

Suppose you are writing a document about government in Word Pro and want to bring in some suitable graphics from Freelance. Here's what you'd do:

1. Start Freelance your favorite way. Perhaps click the Win 95 Start button, highlight Programs, highlight Lotus SmartSuite, then click Lotus Freelance Graphics 97. The Welcome to Freelance Graphics dialog box comes up.

2. For the example, click the tab labeled Create a New Presentation Using a SmartMaster.

3. In the Select a Content Topic list box, select [No content topic].

4. In the Select a Look box, select Blank. (For the example, the topic and look don't matter.) Click OK.

5. The New Page dialog box comes up. For the example, click Bullets & Clip Art, as shown in Figure 10-1. Then click OK.

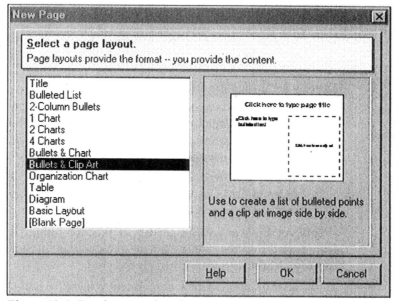

Figure 10-1: For the example I chose a page layout that uses clip art.

6. It's a good idea to save the presentation often. I save mine right away. Click the Save SmartIcon, type in a name for the presentation in the Save As box (I used the name "government"), and click Save.

Figure 10-2 shows the new presentation with the "Bullets & Clip Art" page displayed.

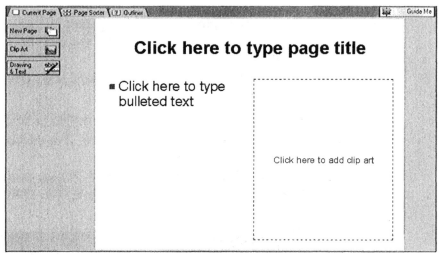

Figure 10-2: Here's a sample page awaiting a cool Freelance graphic.

Selecting & Copying the Graphic in Freelance

Chances are, if you have occasion to turn to Freelance for a graphic, you will be taking a graphic from an existing presentation. For the example, though, I created a sample graphic, which I then copied. Here's how to create and copy the graphic:

1. In the "government" presentation just created, click on Click Here to Add Clip Art. A dialog box comes up labeled Add Clip Art or Diagram to the Page as shown in Figure 10-3.

Now you have at your fingertips a collection of high quality clip art, nicely sorted into the categories you're most likely to want. In the View box on the right, be sure Clip Art is selected.

2. In the Category box, click the down arrow, and click the category you want. For the example, I clicked Agenda.

3. Click any box in the "notebook," then use the scroll arrows or the keyboard arrow keys to move among the pictures. For the example, I clicked "Man at Table (7 of 7)." See Figure 10-4.

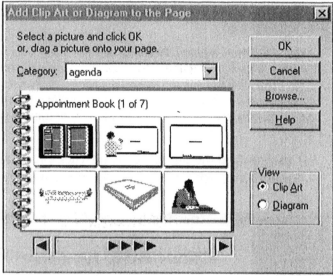

Figure 10-3: Choose the clip art you want here.

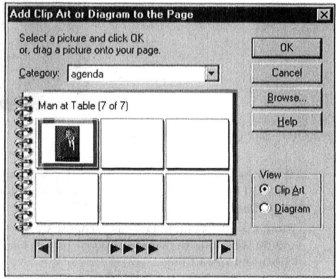

Figure 10-4: Shop around and choose a graphic you like.

Tip

You're not limited just to Freelance clip art. If you wish, click the Browse button in the Clip Art dialog box, and choose Clip Art from anywhere. After you click Browse, the Browse dialog box comes up. From there, you can even click the Internet button and retrieve clip art from the Internet. I don't do it here, but you would locate the art you want, then click Open.

4. Once you find the clip art you want, click OK. The clip art appears on the page, see Figure 10-5. Now you're ready to copy it.

Figure 10-5: Your clip art appears on the page.

5. When the clip art comes onto the page, the art is already selected. If you are working with an existing graphic and the art isn't already selected, click it to select it.

6. From the Edit menu in Freelance, choose Copy. A copy of the graphic goes into the Win 95 clipboard. You're ready to paste the clip art into Word Pro.

Pasting the Graphic Into Word Pro

Often, you'll have Word Pro running already when you want to paste. For the example, I used Word Pro for the first time in this chapter. Here's what to do:

1. Start Word Pro. (Perhaps click the SmartSuite drawer in SmartCenter, then double-click the Lotus Word Pro icon.) In the Welcome to Lotus Word pro dialog box, click the Create a Plain Document button.

2. Click where you want the clip art to appear in the document. For the example, I typed a title and some sample text, and saved the example as "government." Figure 10-6 shows the example before I pasted in the clip art.

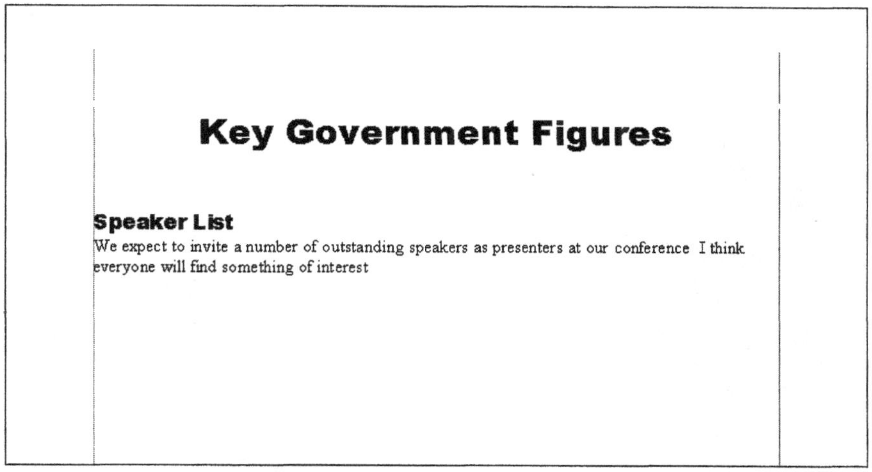

Key Government Figures

Speaker List
We expect to invite a number of outstanding speakers as presenters at our conference. I think everyone will find something of interest

Figure 10-6: Here's a Word Pro document awaiting clip art.

3. From the Edit menu, click Paste. The clip art appears in the document, as shown in Figure 10-7.

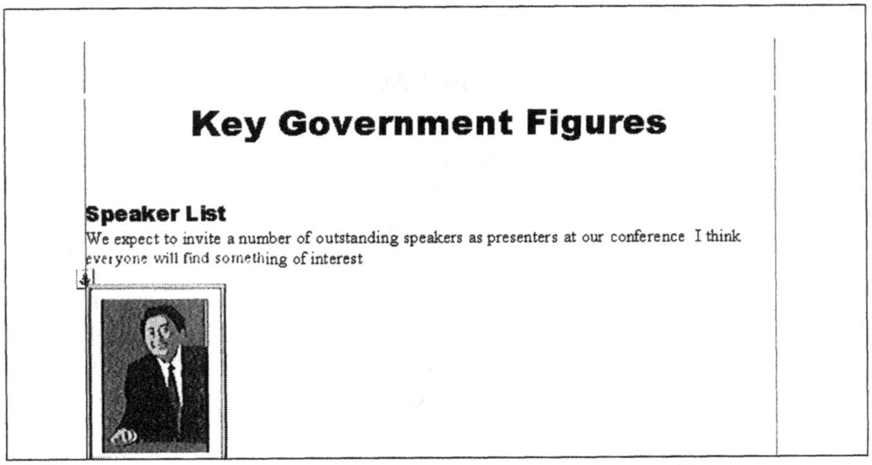

Figure 10-7: Here's a Word Pro document sporting Freelance clip art.

Dragging & Dropping Graphics

If you prefer to drag and drop the clip art, in Freelance click and drag the clip art to the Word Pro button on the Windows 95 Taskbar. Hold down the button. Word Pro will open. In Word Pro, click where you want the clip art to appear. The clip art shows up there, just as when you use the menus—pretty nifty. See Chapter 9 for more discussion of dragging and dropping between SmartSuite programs.

Tip

The Word Pro frame with the copied clip art doesn't overwrite any text. It's an OLE object on top of the document. It's linked to the source document. If you want to resize the frame, select it, and choose Frame, then Graphics Scaling, and use the InfoBox. See Chapter 9 for more details. (The process is the same as for copied 1-2-3 objects.)

Copying a Table From Freelance to Word Pro

Copying a table from Freelance to Word Pro is the same as dragging one from 1-2-3 to Word Pro, as explained in Chapter 9.

Freelance's strength in tables, as you might expect, is in making things look good. Freelance doesn't offer any @functions, the way 1-2-3 does. Even Word Pro has a few mathematical functions. A table is most likely to end up in Freelance because someone wanted to present the information well. In Freelance, you have more capability than in the other SmartSuite programs in adding color to the table, putting in fancy bullets, creating borders to cells or to the table.

When you copy the table to Word Pro, it retains its Freelance formatting. One reason to copy a Freelance table to Word Pro, then, would be to display a table that looks the best that it can look.

It also might happen that someone from your team shows a table that you like in a presentation, and you ask to copy the table to Word Pro.

In the example, I created a nice-looking table using a SmartMaster, then copy it to Word Pro.

Creating a Nifty Table in Freelance

Often, you'll have existing tables in Freelance that you may want to copy. For the example, I created a table using a Freelance SmartMaster. Here's how I created the table to copy:

1. Click the Freelance icon in SuiteStart to start Freelance.

2. In the Welcome to Lotus Freelance Graphics dialog box, go to the Select a Content Topic box, and click Business Plan, as shown in Figure 10-8. Then click OK.

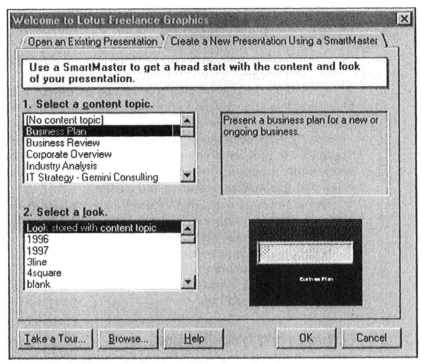

Figure 10-8: Choose the Business Plan SmartMaster.

3. In the New Page dialog box, select the topic for Total Funding Required, as shown in Figure 10-9. Click OK.

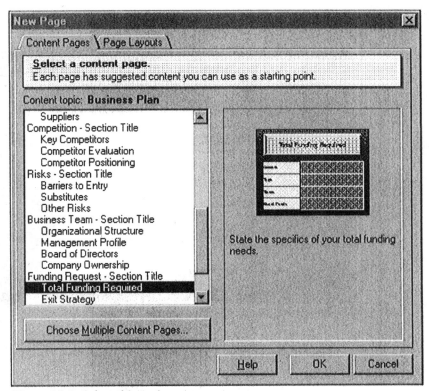

Figure 10-9: Select this topic.

4. For the example, complete the table. Double-click inside the
   table. Type in your entry in the right column. Press the down
   arrow or click in the cell for the next entry you want to type.

Figure 10-10 shows a sample table.

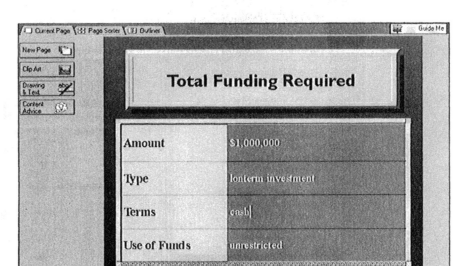

Figure 10-10: You can create a sample Freelance table like this.

Now that you have a sample table, you are ready to copy it to Word Pro.

Dragging the Table From Freelance to Word Pro

If you did the previous example in this chapter, you probably have Word Pro open already. If you don't, click the Word Pro button in SuiteStart to start it. If you want to drag something from Freelance to Word Pro, you have to have Word Pro running.

With both programs running and displaying the documents you want to use, you're ready to copy the table. Here's what to do:

1. Click the Freelance button on the Win 95 Taskbar to move to Freelance, if you're not there already.

2. Click to select the table. (If you have been typing in the table, you may need to click outside it first, then click it once to select it.) When you have the table selected, handles appear on all four sides.

Figure 10-11 shows the selected table.

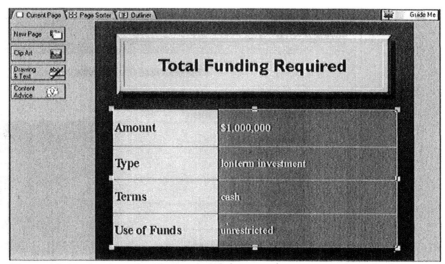

Figure 10-11: A selected table in Freelance has handles on all four sides.

3. Drag the table to the Word Pro button in the Windows taskbar. Don't release the mouse button.

Tip

When you drag in Freelance, you don't have to wait for the pointer to take the shape of a hand. And you don't have to click on one of the sides. Just click anywhere on the selected table, and drag. The pointer takes the shape of a hand as you drag.

4. Word Pro becomes the active program. Drag to the position in the document where you want to copy the table, then release the mouse button.

Figure 10-12 shows the table in Word Pro.

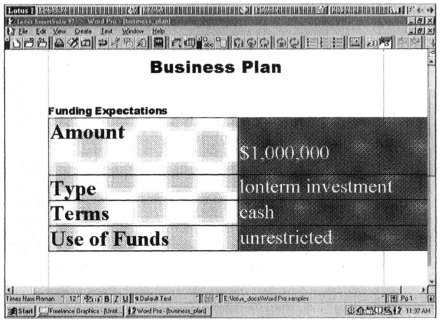

Figure 10-12: The copied table appears in Word Pro.

Resizing the Freelance Object in Word Pro

As for the copied graphic described earlier in this chapter, the table copied from Freelance becomes an OLE object on top of the document. It isn't the same as a table you create inside Word Pro. You can select it and drag it to a new location if you wish.

To change its size, here's what to do:

1. Click Table.

2. Click Size Row/Column.

3. Click the tab for Width and Height, and make your changes. Figure 10-13 shows the Word Pro InfoBox with the Width and Height tab displayed.

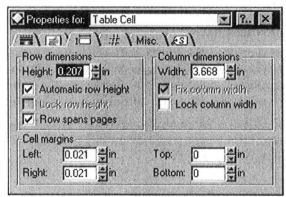

Figure 10-13: Change the width and height of the Word Pro tables columns and rows here.

When you're done, you may want to save and close the documents.

Converting a Word Pro Outline to a Freelance Presentation With Present It!

Tip

Converting an outline, as explained here, involves Lotus' BASIC-like scripting language, LotusScript. Scripting is programming. This topic, then, may be more advanced than, say, just dragging and dropping a table. You don't have to write programming code to run the script.

Sometimes SmartSuite programs offer advanced capabilities in the form of scripts you can execute on your own. Chapter 17 talks about LotusScript and how you might create scripts of your own.

Present It! is an existing script you can use to convert a Word Pro outline to a Freelance presentation. If, like many people, you work primarily in Word Pro and just turn to Freelance for special occasions, you may well choose to create your outline in Word Pro.

Creating the Outline in Word Pro

Here's how to create the outline:

1. Start Word Pro. For the example, click the Create from Any SmartMaster tab, then, in the Select a Type of SmartMaster box, click Outline. Click OK. (You don't have to use the Outline SmartMaster to create an outline. I used it here for convenience.)

2. In the blank document that comes up, type in your outline. Figure 10-14 shows a sample outline I've created. I saved it with the name "expansion."

Expansion Plans

I. Geographical Expansion

    A. New England

    B. The South

II. Economic Expansion

    A. Increased sales of basic items

    1. Growth through investment management

Figure 10-14: Here's a sample Word Pro outline to convert to a Freelance Presentation.

Running the Present It! Script

With the outline in place, you're ready to run the Present It! script:

1. Drag across the entire outline to select it.

2. From the Edit menu, click Script & Macros, then Run.

3. In the Run Script dialog box (Figure 10-15), be sure that Run Script Saved in Another File is selected.

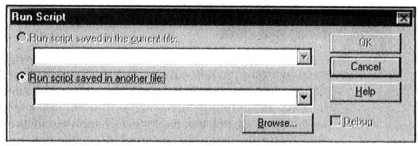

Figure 10-15: Select "Run script saved in another file."

4. Click the Browse button. In the Files of Type box, select ASCII Script Files, and double-click the scripts folder in the Look in box at the top.

5. Select the file prsit.lss (Figure 10-16), and click Open.

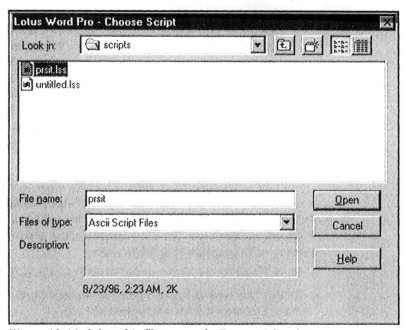

Figure 10-16: Select this file to run the Present It! script.

6. In the Run Script dialog box, click OK. Freelance will start and display your outline as a presentation.

Using Word Pro Material in Freelance

You can use Copy and Paste (or drag and drop) to copy graphics or tables from Word Pro to Freelance. To copy a graphic from Word Pro to Freelance, you select it and drag it. If you prefer, you can use Copy and Paste. Once the graphic is in Freelance, you can resize it or move it around. Best of all, you can use Freelance tools to enhance it.

Freelance is the true graphics program, so you may not have too many occasions to copy graphics from your word processor to the program that specializes in graphics—Freelance Graphics. However, you might have an existing graphic in Word Pro, and you might want to copy it to Freelance to use it in a Screen show or to enhance it with Freelance drawing tools.

Copying a Graphic From Word Pro Into Freelance

Word Pro does come with a clip art collection of its own. (To check out the clip art, from the File menu, choose Import Picture, and look over the graphics in the Import Picture dialog box.) Freelance's art is more elaborate, but you might have clip art in Word Pro that is just what you want. (That has often happened to me.) Or you may have developed a graphic with Word Pro drawing tools that you'd now like to use in Freelance. Here's how to copy a graphic from Word Pro to Freelance.

Starting Word Pro & Creating the Sample Graphic

Often, you'll be working with existing graphics when you want to copy them to Freelance. Maybe you have a logo in Word Pro that you want to copy. Perhaps you have spent weeks developing a diagram and want to have it appear in Freelance. For the example in this chapter, I used a SmartMaster with graphics in it. Here's how:

1. Start Word Pro by clicking the Word Pro icon in SuiteStart.

2. In the Welcome to Lotus Word Pro dialog box, click the Create a New Document from a SmartMaster tab.

3. Click the Browse for More Files button.

4. In the Select a type of SmartMaster box, click Internet - Personal.

5. In the Select a look box, click kidpg1.mwp. (I used the SmartMaster because it has some neat graphics to copy.)

Figure 10-17 shows the completed New Document dialog box.

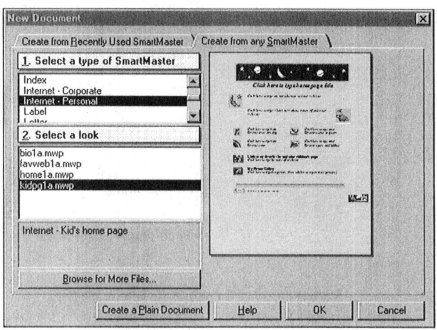

Figure 10-17: Here's the SmartMaster I used for the example.

6. Click OK.

Figure 10-18 shows Word Pro with the page displayed.

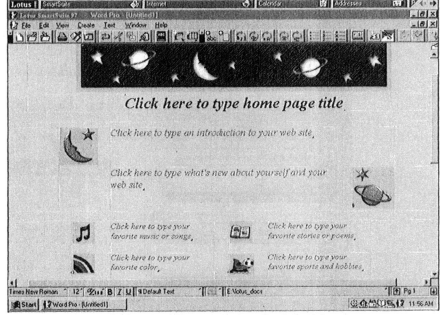

Figure 10-18: Here's the Word Pro page using the SmartMaster.

Starting Freelance & Preparing To Receive the Copy

To copy to Freelance, it must be running and the page must be displayed that you want to copy to. Here's what to do:

1. Start Freelance Graphics by clicking the Freelance icon in SuiteStart.

2. In the Welcome to Lotus Freelance Graphics dialog box, you could create a new presentation. For the example, I clicked the tab labeled Open an Existing Presentation, and I clicked the presentation "competitors" from earlier in the chapter. Then I clicked OK.

3. Click the New Page button.

4. In the New Page dialog box, click the Page Layouts tab, then click Basic Layout in the Select a Page Layout box, and click OK. A new blank page opens.

5. For the example, I clicked where it says Click Here to Type Page Title and typed "Where to start." Then I clicked outside the Click Here block.

Figure 10-19 shows the Freelance page awaiting a graphic.

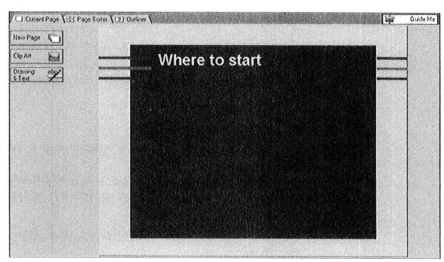

Figure 10-19: This Freelance page will receive the Word Pro graphic.

Copying the Graphic to Freelance

To copy the graphic, you'll select the graphic in Word Pro and drag it to Freelance. Here's what to do:

1. Click the Word Pro button in the taskbar to move to Word Pro.

2. In Word Pro, double-click on the picture of a house, next to the words My Picture Gallery so that you are inside the frame. (You can use any picture you want.)

3. From the Edit menu, choose Copy.

4. Click the Freelance button on the taskbar. In Freelance, click on the page where you want the graphic to appear.

5. From the Freelance Edit menu, choose Paste. The picture appears on the Freelance Page.

Tip

You can also use drag and drop to copy the picture. In Word Pro, click the frame containing the picture to select it. With the pointer in the shape of a hand, drag to the Freelance button on the taskbar. Hold down the button, then release it on the Freelance page. The graphic now appears in Freelance, where you may want to move it and enhance it.

Enhancing the Graphic in Freelance

Once you have the graphic in Freelance, you can apply Freelance's powerful drawing tools to it.

For the example, I dragged the picture to a different location on the page, and dragged the corner to enlarge it. Here's how I enhanced the graphic:

1. I clicked the Drawing & Text button to open the drawing and text Toolbars.

2. I clicked the icon labeled abc, then dragged on the page to create a text box, and typed in the text. (In the example, I used "First, go to people's homes.") Then I clicked outside the text box.

Figure 10-20 shows the Freelance page with the Word Pro graphic on it.

Figure 10-20: Word Pro graphics can be useful in Freelance.

Copying a Table From Word Pro Into Freelance

There could be a number of reasons for copying a table from Word Pro to Freelance, beginning with the most obvious reason—you might want to use a table you've created in Word Pro in a Freelance presentation (just as you might similarly use a 1-2-3 table).

Starting Word Pro & Creating a Sample Table

Word Pro has excellent table capabilities. Regular Word Pro users might find themselves creating tables there simply because there's no real need most of the time to create them in 1-2-3 or Freelance. Here's how to create a sample table:

1. To start Word Pro, click the Word Pro icon in SuiteStart.

2. In the Welcome to Lotus Word Pro dialog box, click Create a Plain document.

3. Type the title you want. (For the example, I typed a title at the top—Management Team, and pressed Enter.)

4. To create the table, click the Create menu, then click Table. In the Create Table dialog box (Figure 10-21), click the arrows next to Number of Columns to change them to "4." Leave the number of rows as is (4), or change them to 4 if necessary.

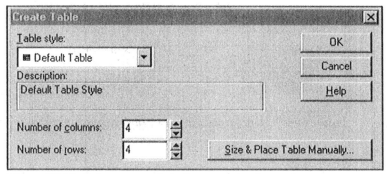

Figure 10-21: Set your number of rows and columns here.

5. Click OK. A blank table appears on the page, with the cursor in the first cell. See Figure 10-22.

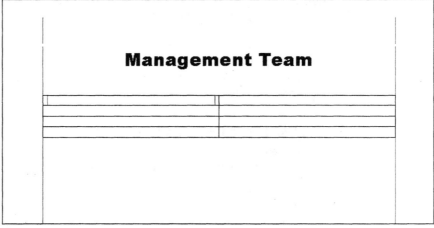

Figure 10-22: Your blank table looks like this.

6. Complete the table. Type data in the cells. Click on a cell to move to it, or use the keyboard arrow keys to navigate. When you're done, you can click outside the table.

Figure 10-23 shows my sample table. I then saved the table as "management."

Management Team	
President	Joseph Perkins
Chief Financial Officer	Marie Perez
Chief Operations Officer	Ling Wu
VP of Marketing	David Hawkins

Figure 10-23: Here's a sample table, ready to be transported to Freelance.

Starting Freelance & Preparing to Receive the Copy

You have to have Freelance open and the page ready to receive the copy:

1. Start Freelance by clicking the Freelance icon in SuiteStart.

2. You could create a new presentation or, as I do, open an existing one. I clicked the tab labeled Open an Existing Presentation, then clicked the file named "competitors," and clicked OK.

3. I clicked the New Page button. In the Select a Page Layout box, I clicked Table, and clicked OK. A blank page comes up.

4. I clicked in the click-here block labeled Click Here to Type Page Title. I typed in a title — "Management Team"—and clicked OK. Then I clicked outside the click-here block.

Figure 10-24 shows the Freelance page awaiting a table.

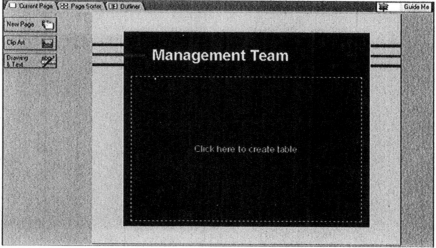

Figure 10-24: Here's a Freelance page awaiting a table.

Copying the Table to Freelance

You can use drag and drop to copy the Word Pro table to Freelance. Here's how:

1. First, click the Word Pro button in the taskbar to make Word Pro the active program.

2. To select the whole table, first click inside the table. Then, from the Table menu, click Select, then Entire Table.

3. Position the cursor at the border of the table so that it takes the shape of a hand.

4. Drag the table to the Freelance button on the taskbar. Hold down the button until Freelance becomes active.

5. Position the cursor over the area labeled Click Here to Create Table, and release the mouse button. A copy of the Word Pro table appears in Freelance.

6. Click outside the table to deselect it.

Figure 10-25 shows the Freelance page with the Word Pro table on it.

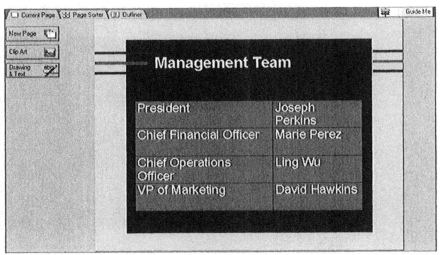

Figure 10-25: The Word Pro table appears in Freelance.

Enhancing the Word Pro Table in Freelance

Once you have the table in Freelance, you can use Freelance's advanced artistic capabilities to dress it up. Here is one small example:

1. Click the table to select it.

2. Right-click, and click Table Properties to bring up the Lotus InfoBox.

3. With the AZ tab displayed (Font, Attribute, and Color), in the Font name box, click Book Antiqua.

4. In the Text shadow box, click the arrow for the list box, and click Below right.

5. In the Depth box, click the arrow for the list box, and click Deep.

Figure 10-26 shows the page with the InfoBox open and the changes displayed in the table.

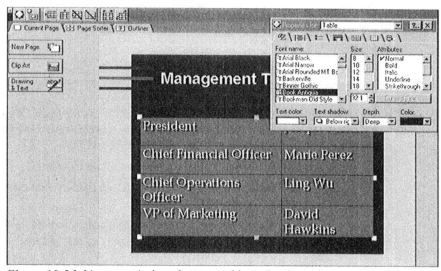

Figure 10-26: You can nicely enhance a table in Freelance.

Putting Word Pro & Organizer Together

Word Pro and Organizer are both likely to become "staple" programs for SmartSuite users. You're likely to keep track of your time and your frequently-used addresses in Organizer. And you may spend a good part of each day preparing documents in Word Pro. Because you're likely to spend a good bit of time in both programs, you'll probably end up wanting to use something from Organizer in Word Pro. This section looks at one such possibility—copying Organizer addresses into Word Pro.

If you get into the habit of keeping your addresses in Organizer, you may end up wanting to use those addresses together with Word Pro to perform a mail merge. That is, you would create a form letter in Word

Pro, and you would use Organizer to supply addresses for the form letter. Chapter 13 talks about using Word Pro with a number of other programs, including Organizer, to perform mail merges. If you want to use an Organizer address in Word Pro, you can readily copy from the one to the other.

If you become a true Organizer devotee, all the addresses you ever need will end up in the Organizer address book. Occasionally, you'll want those addresses in other programs. If you want them in Word Pro, the copying is automatic.

Getting Set Up in Word Pro

The only real requirement in Word Pro for copying an Organizer address is that Word Pro must be running. You don't have to be in any special part of the document. To get set up in Word Pro:

1. Click the Word Pro icon in SuiteStart to start it.

2. In the Welcome to Lotus Word Pro dialog box, click Create a Plain Document.

3. For the example, I typed in some sample text leading up to the address and saved the document as star_search.

Figure 10-27 shows the document awaiting an Organizer address.

Star Search

Those who are seeking employment as movie stars may find this agency a good place to start:

Figure 10-27: This Word Pro document is awaiting an Organizer address.

Copying the Address From Organizer

You cannot just drag and use keyboard shortcuts for copying. You need to do a special copy for the address you want to copy to Word Pro. Here's what you do:

1. Click its icon in SuiteStart to start Organizer.

2. Click File, then Open, and, in the Open dialog box, click the file that has the address you want. Click the Open button.

3. Click the Address tab.

4. Click the address record you want to copy. Figure 10-28 shows a sample address.

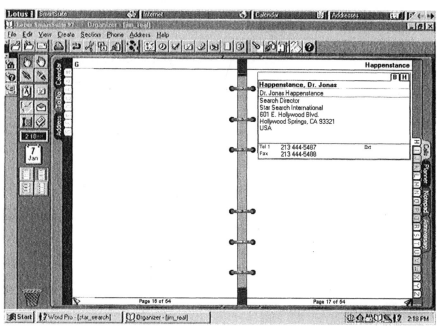

Figure 10-28: Here's an Organizer address to copy.

5. From the Edit menu, choose Copy Special.

6. From the Copy Special dialog box (Figure 10-29), choose Full Address (Default). Click OK.

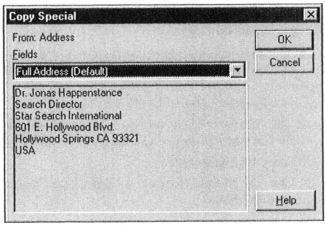

Figure 10-29: Choose Full Address.

7. Click the Word Pro button in the taskbar to switch to Word Pro. Put the cursor where you want to paste the address.

8. From the Edit menu, click Paste. The address appears neatly in the document. See Figure 10-30.

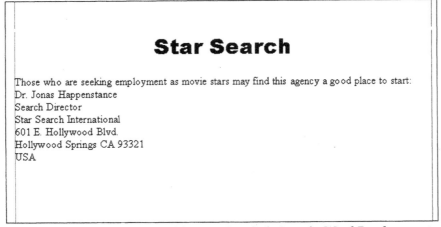

Figure 10-30: The Organizer address copies nicely into the Word Pro document.

Using Word Pro as a Control Center

You can use Word Pro as a place to gather lots of useful documents. You create Word Pro *divisions*, and use OLE to link the contents of those divisions to documents in other applications. The applications don't have to be SmartSuite applications either.

Suppose you're creating a business plan. You can store an overview in a regular Word Pro division, a 1-2-3 spreadsheet of projected profits in another division, a Freelance Presentation for potential investors in another, and a Microsoft Word document listing principal officers in another.

Starting Word Pro & Displaying Divider Tabs

First, start Word Pro and be sure that the divider tabs are showing at the top. The divider tabs show the divisions you have in your Word Pro document. Click on a tab to move to a division (or, in the control center analogy I'm using in this chapter, to operate the controls in the control center).

Here's how to start Word Pro and display the divider tabs:

1. Click the Word Pro icon in SuiteStart or use another method to start Word Pro.

2. In the Welcome to Lotus Word Pro box, you can choose a SmartMaster if you like. For the example, I clicked the Create a New Document from a SmartMaster tab, and clicked Browse for More Files.

3. In the Create from any SmartMaster tab, I clicked Miscellaneous for the type and busplan.mwp for the look. Click OK. See Figure 10-31.

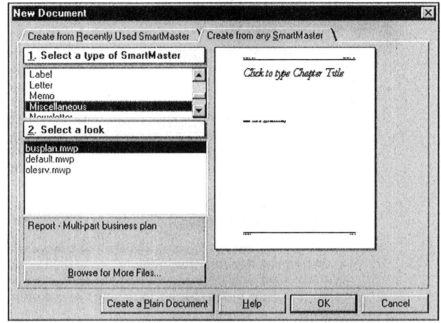

Figure 10-31: I chose a business plan SmartMaster.

4. If divider tabs are not displayed, click the icon at the top of the scroll bar to display them.

Figure 10-32 shows the sample document with the divider tabs displayed.

Figure 10-32: The sample document has multiple divisions with their tabs displayed at the top.

Creating a Word Pro OLE Division

The key to using Word Pro as a notebook is setting up divisions linked to the documents you want. You create divisions that use OLE (Microsoft's Object Linking and Embedding). Here's how:

1. In Word Pro, click the Create menu, then click Division.

2. In the Create Division dialog box (Figure 10-33), click the Create OLE Division button.

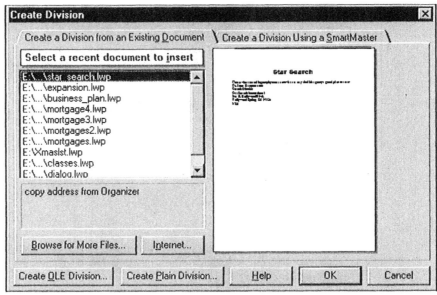

Figure 10-33: Click the Create OLE Division tab.

3. In the Insert OLE Division box (Figure 10-34), decide where you want the division to appear. I clicked the After Current Division button. Click OK.

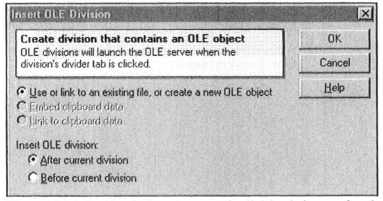

Figure 10-34: Decide whether you want the division before or after the current one.

4. In the Create Object box, select Create an object from a file, as shown in Figure 10-35.

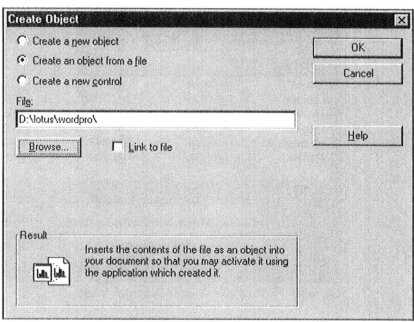

Figure 10-35: Select Create an object from a file.

5. Select "Link to file." Then, any changes in the source application will automatically appear in the Word Pro document.

6. To locate the document you want to link, click the Browse button. In the Browse box, shown in Figure 10-36, navigate to the file you want to link. For the example, I used a sample workbook

called sales_results, which I created in Chapter 4. (You can use any example you want, from any application.) Click the file you want, and click OK.

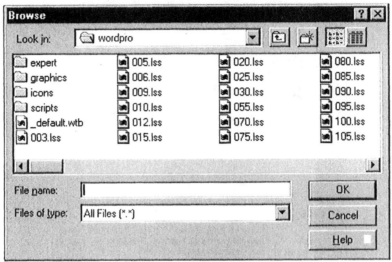

Figure 10-36: Navigate to the file you want to link.

7. In the Create Object dialog box, click OK.

The linked document appears in its source application—1-2-3 in this example.

Figure 10-37 shows the linked document, displayed in 1-2-3.

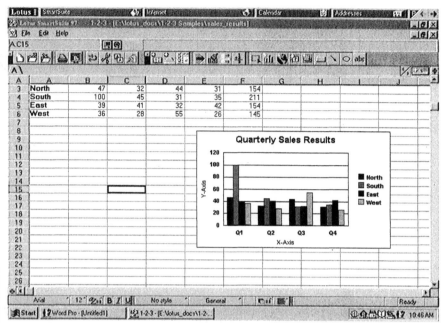

Figure 10-37: The linked document displays in its source application.

Returning to Word Pro

The linked document is actually a division within Word Pro. You can't tell it immediately, because you simply see the linked application itself.

Tip

> *You can use the Win 95 Taskbar to navigate among applications you have placed in Word Pro divisions. Simply click on the buttons for the applications as you usually would. You can also return to Word Pro by clicking the Word Pro button in the Taskbar.*

To return to Word Pro, click the X at the top right of the Title bar to close the application (1-2-3 in the example). You return to the application, and the new division displays after the current division, with the name "Division," as shown in Figure 10-38.

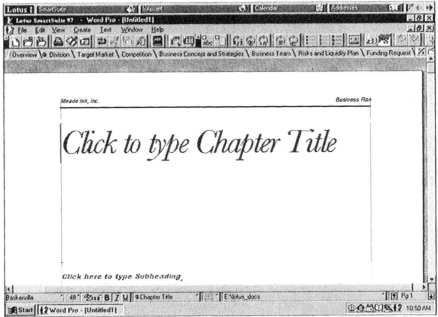

Figure 10-38: The new division displays in Word Pro, with the name "Division."

Tip

You'd probably rather have a meaningful name for the division, instead of just the name "Division." To rename the division, right-click the divider tab, click Division Properties and, in the Division Properties dialog box (Figure 10-39), type in a new name. I typed the name "Sales." Click OK.

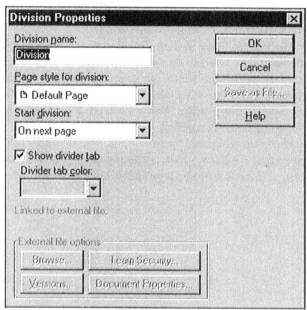

Figure 10-39: Type in a new name here.

Displaying the Linked File

You can set up as many divider tabs as you want containing OLE links. Like the drawers in SmartCenter (Chapter 2), the Word Pro linked divider tabs are a great way to get organized.

Once you have your tab or tabs, you simply click on them to display their contents. When you click the tab, the linked application starts (if it's not running already), and the document displays.

Moving On

If Word Pro is your home base during your day in the office (as it is for many people), you don't have to feel restricted any more if you want to use the powerful capabilities of other programs. You can readily link Word Pro with Freelance, as I have shown in this chapter. And you can truly make Word Pro your home base by putting linked documents into divisions in Word Pro.

You may be less likely to have Freelance as your main program, instead of Word Pro or 1-2-3. If you're a design artist, though, then Freelance may be your main home. Or, if you've been spending weeks on a presentation, you may develop a short-term attachment to Freelance and see it as your main program. You've seen in this chapter how to use Freelance material in Word Pro.

Two powerful programs you may also want to use together are 1-2-3 and Approach. 1-2-3 is a great spreadsheet but just a so-so database program . . . until its friend Approach teams up with it.

PART FOUR

More Mixing SmartSuite Applications

Approaching 1-2-3

1-2-3 is probably the king of the programs in SmartSuite. After all, it's the first Lotus program and the one that gave the company its name. Lotus Approach, though, has specialties that 1-2-3 doesn't equal. Approach, first and foremost, is a *relational* database program, and 1-2-3 creates only flat databases. If you want to have the advantages of a database program where you can share information across several different tables of information, you have to use Approach. In SmartSuite, you can readily create an Approach database from 1-2-3 data, then have Approach capabilities at your disposal.

Approach is good at other things, too, besides being a relational database. It is outstanding at creating mailing labels. It's the cat's meow at forms and reports. And, as its *piece de resistance*, it can create dynamic crosstabs for allowing you to get varying views of data that has three or more variables.

This chapter shows all these ways to take advantage of the power of Approach for your 1-2-3 data. These two programs are sisters in the best sense of the term—they help each other out. Approach, in particular, lends its expertise to its "big sister" 1-2-3.

Making Approach Mailing Labels From 1-2-3 Data

If you keep your addresses in 1-2-3, now you can still get the benefit of Lotus Approach mailing labels.

Mailing labels aren't most people's favorite thing to create. People love to *use* them. They're great time-savers once they exist. But making them can be painstaking.

In the SmartSuite family, Approach is the mailing label specialist, as only befits a program whose purpose in life is to handle data (such as names and addresses). Yet many people maintain their data in 1-2-3. It's so easy just to type information into the rows and columns of the spreadsheet. You can have the best of both worlds—you can keep your data in 1-2-3, but you can create Approach mailing labels when the need arises.

Creating an Address Database in 1-2-3

Creating a database of addresses in 1-2-3 is simple; just start up the program, set up the columns, and type in the data. Let's try it, step by step:

1. Click the SmartSuite drawer in SmartCenter, then double-click the Lotus 1-2-3 icon.

2. In the Welcome to 1-2-3 dialog box, click the Create a Blank Workbook button. 1-2-3 starts, showing a blank worksheet in a blank workbook.

3. Type in column labels and sample data. Click in cell A1 and type **Cust-ID**.

4. Press the right arrow key. In cell B1, type **Company Name**. Press the right arrow key again, and type the next column head **First Name**. Then type the additional column heads **Last Name**, **Street**, **City**, **State**, **Zip**, and **Phone**.

5. Drag across the column labels to select them, then click the B button at the bottom to bold them.

6. For any column that is too narrow to read the column head, place the cursor between the columns, next to the column letter, at the top of the column. When the pointer becomes a double-arrow, double-click. The column becomes the correct width to display the data.

7. Type in data for each row. For instance, for row two I typed 66213 for Cust-ID. For Company Name, I typed Phoenix Pumps. Press the right arrow key on the keypad after each entry, and type in the information. Figure 11-1 shows my sample database.

8. Click the Save SmartIcon (an arrow pointing into a folder), and save the workbook. I saved mine as "customers."

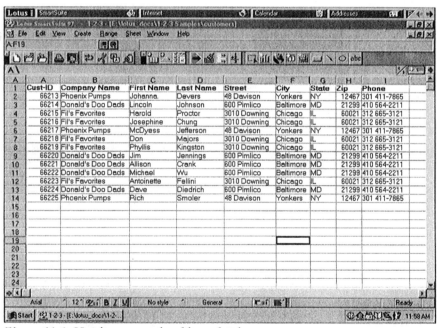

Figure 11-1: Here's my sample address database.

You don't have to leave 1-2-3 to create the Approach mailing labels. (Approach, as I have noted, is a most aware and willing assistant to its sister program.) Here's what to do:

1. From within the spreadsheet "customers" created in the previous section, click anywhere inside the 1-2-3 database to place the cursor inside it.

2. Click the Create menu, then Database.

3. Click Mailing Labels. The mailing label dialog box comes up. 1-2-3 selects the entire table and puts the address of the range in the box. See Figure 11-2. (If you want to change the range, click the selection arrow next to the text box, and drag over the cells you want.)

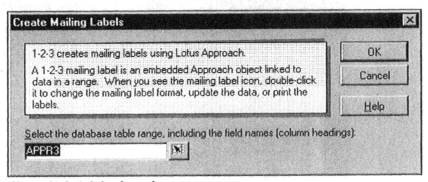

Figure 11-2: 1-2-3 selects the range.

4. Click OK.

5. Click in the spreadsheet where you want the mailing labels icon to appear. Any blank area will do. For the example, I clicked on cell B16. 1-2-3 starts the Mailing Label Assistant, shown in Figure 11-3. (You may have to be patient. It sometimes takes a while for the assistant to appear.) Use the assistant to design your labels.

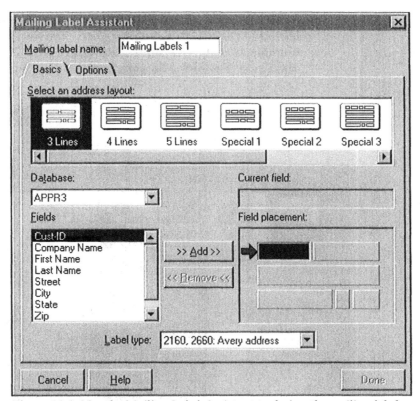

Figure 11-3: Use the Mailing Label Assistant to design the mailing labels.

Working With the Address Assistant in 1-2-3?

Now, you are still in 1-2-3, but you can use the Mailing Label Assistant to help you prepare Approach mailing labels. (SmartSuite allows 1-2-3 and Approach to appear almost as a single program here.)

In the Address Assistant, choose a format for the label, choose the range to include, and set up the fields the way you want them to appear on the label. Here's how:

1. Click the Basics tab if it's not clicked already.

2. For database, accept the default—APPR3 for the example.

3. In the Fields box, click the information you want to appear on the label, and click the Add button to place it on the label. For the example, I clicked First Name, Last Name, Street, City, State, and Zip. Figure 11-4 shows the completed Mailing Label Assistant.

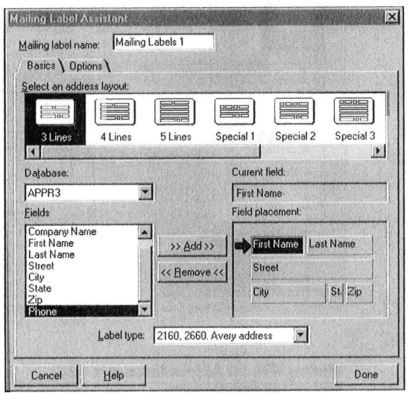

Figure 11-4: Place the fields you want onto the mailing label.

4. Use the Label type list box to choose the type of label. For the example, I accepted the default—2160, 2660: Avery address.

5. Click Done.

1-2-3 places a mailing label icon in your sheet. Figure 11-5 shows the label as it first appears—an Approach window displaying the labels. Approach has actually started, though you have not left 1-2-3 and have not started Approach. It starts automatically.

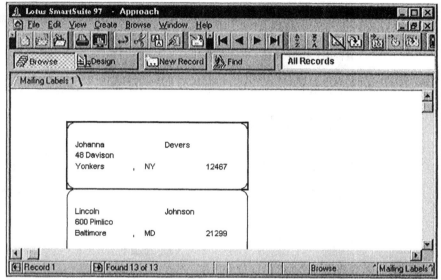

Figure 11-5: The mailing labels display in an Approach window.

Tip

You can readily switch to Approach to work on your mailing labels without leaving 1-2-3 by having the mailing labels display as an icon in 1-2-3. To make the Approach window appear as an icon, click either the minimize button or the close button in the top right of the Approach window. To display the window from the icon, double-click the icon. Figure 11-6 shows the 1-2-3 database with the Approach Mailing Labels as an icon.

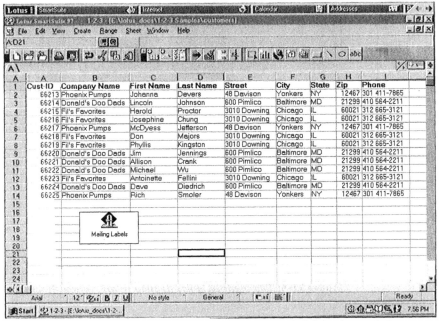

Figure 11-6: Approach is an icon labeled "Mailing Labels" in the worksheet.

Printing the Mailing Labels in Approach

To print the mailing labels, use Approach commands. Though you don't have to leave 1-2-3 to get to Approach, you use Approach menus and commands to print the labels. Here's what to do:

1. Double-click the Mailing Labels icon to display the Approach window.

2. In the Approach window, click the Print SmartIcon (a picture of a printer). (Or, you can click File. Then you can choose either Print or, if you prefer, Print Preview.)

3. To return to 1-2-3, close or minimize the window, or click File, then "Exit & Return to Lotus 1-2-3."

Modifying Data in the Form

Once you have your embedded Approach object for your mailing labels, you may want to change the mailing label format (an Approach format) or update the data (which is in 1-2-3).

To make changes to the mailing label format, double-click the mailing label icon, which actually places you in Approach. For instance, you might want to change Mailing Label properties like so:

1. Click Mailing Label in the Approach menu.

2. Click Mailing Label Properties. A Lotus InfoBox comes up, shown in Figure 11-7. You can change a number of properties for the labels in the box, including the margins.

Changes you make in the Approach form appear in the 1-2-3 database table.

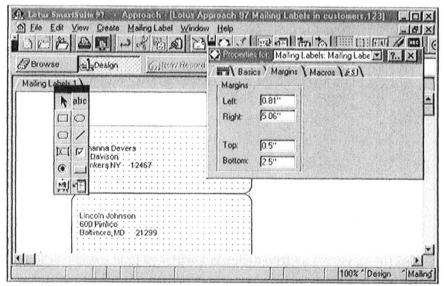

Figure 11-7: Use the InfoBox in Approach to change mailing label properties.

Warning

If you add a row or column to the table in 1-2-3, you have to repeat the steps for creating the Approach mailing labels described in the section "Working with the Address Assistant in 1-2-3." As you create the labels in the Address Assistant, you have to redefine the range containing the table so that it includes the new row or column.

Creating an Approach Database From 1-2-3 Data

In SmartSuite, you can now readily use 1-2-3 data to create Approach databases, which then have all the database power of Approach.

Many people may be in the habit of keeping databases in 1-2-3, because it's so easy to type data into rows and columns. In Approach, though, you can do much more with data than create views. You can readily redesign databases by adding or taking away fields. You can create special views of the data. You can create reports.

To create the Approach database, you start and work from within Approach. Here's how to create an Approach database using 1-2-3 data:

1. Click the Approach icon in SuiteStart to start Approach.

2. In the Welcome dialog box, click Cancel.

3. From the File menu, click Open.

4. In the Open dialog box, navigate to the workbook that contains the data for your Approach database.

5. In the Files of type box, select Lotus 1-2-3 (*.123, *.WK*).

6. Select the workbook containing the data. Figure 11-8 shows the Open dialog box with a sample workbook selected.

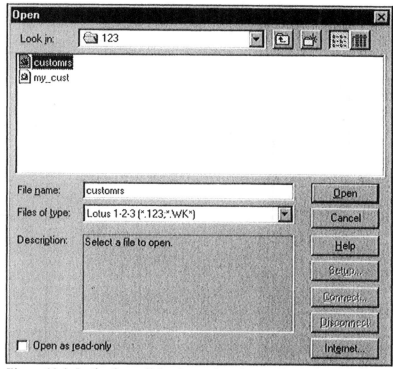

Figure 11-8: In the Open dialog box, select the workbook containing the data you want to convert.

7. Click the Open button.

8. In the Select Range box, Figure 11-9, select the sheet or the named range you want to use, and click OK.

   The New dialog box comes up.

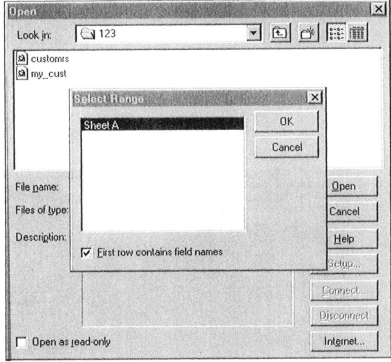

Figure 11-9: Select the sheet or the named range you want to use.

9. In the New dialog box, specify the name of the Approach database. I used the name "my_customers." See Figure 11-10. Click Create.

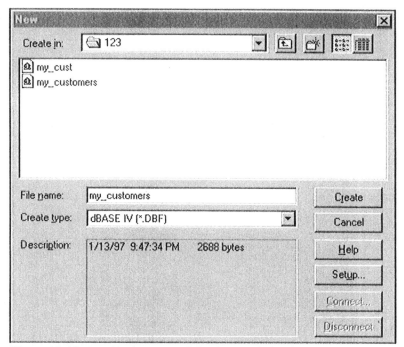

Figure 11-10: Specify the name of the Approach database.

Approach creates an Approach database with 1-2-3 column headings as field names. See Figure 11-11.

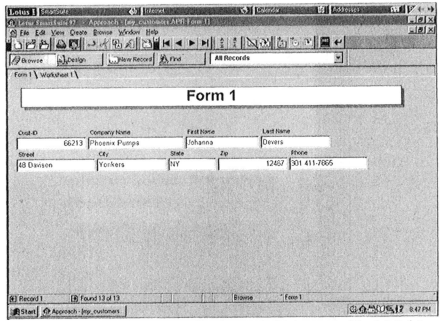

Figure 11-11: Approach creates a nifty Approach database out of the 1-2-3 data.

Linking 1-2-3 Data to an Approach Database

You can link 1-2-3 data to an Approach database. Then, any change you make to the Approach .APR file automatically shows up in the 1-2-3 workbook.

Opening the Workbook With the Data

For this example, I linked the "customers" worksheet in 1-2-3 with Approach:

1. Click the 1-2-3 icon in SuiteStart to start 1-2-3.

2. In the Welcome to 1-2-3 dialog box, click the Create a Blank Workbook button.

Once you're in 1-2-3, use the usual procedures to open a worksheet. (If you don't have an existing workbook you want to use, follow the steps in section "Creating an Address Database in 1-2-3" earlier in this chapter to create one.)

3. For this example, I clicked the File menu, then clicked the "customers" workbook from the list of recent files at the bottom. (You can also click the Open SmartIcon and navigate to the workbook you want.)

4. To link with Approach, use named ranges. Be sure the 1-2-3 data you want to link is a named range. For the example, I dragged across the column heads and the data in the customer list, then clicked the 1-2-3 Range menu. I clicked Name in the Name dialog box; in the Name text box, I typed the name **customers** for the range, then clicked OK.

Linking the 1-2-3 Data in Approach

In Approach, you start the program and open a 1-2-3 workbook much as you did in the section "Creating an Approach Database From 1-2-3 Data" earlier in this chapter:

1. Click the Approach icon in SuiteStart to start Approach.

2. In the Welcome dialog box, click Cancel.

3. From the File menu, click Open.

4. In the Open dialog box, navigate to the workbook that contains the data for your Approach database.

5. In the Files of type box, select 1-2-3 Ranges (*).

6. Locate the folder containing the range you want to link, and double-click the folder. A list of ranges appears.

7. Click the range you want to link. Figure 11-12 shows the Approach Open dialog box with the Range selected.

8. Click Open.

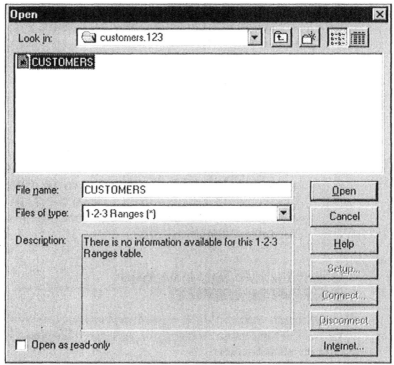

Figure 11-12: Click the range you want to link.

Approach establishes the link with the 1-2-3 range and displays the first record. The worksheet appears in another tab, labeled Worksheet 1 in this example.

Saving the Approach File

You save the Approach file in the usual way. If you open it again, 1-2-3 will start automatically and display the linked file. If you modify data in the Approach form, the changes appear in your 1-2-3 workbook. Similarly, changes to the 1-2-3 data show up in the Approach form the next time you open the Approach form.

To save the Approach file:

1. Click the Save SmartIcon (an arrow pointing into a folder).

2. In the Save dialog box, type a name in the File name box. I typed the name "linked customers."

3. Click Save.

Creating an Approach Form Using 1-2-3 Data

You can readily convert 1-2-3 data into an Approach form. Rows and columns (that is, what you get in 1-2-3) are okay for viewing information. Sometimes you have to squint a little and you may have to think. But you can read the information. However, spreadsheet rows and columns—even when nicely formatted—really can't compete with an Approach form for readability. In an Approach form you can readily see the field names and easily identify the contents of each field in the record. Approach specializes in forms, so of course its forms surpass those of 1-2-3.

Also, it's easier and more accurate to enter data into an Approach form than into the 1-2-3 rows and columns.

Creating the Form in Approach

You can display a 1-2-3 list and turn it into an Approach database. Once you have the workbook displayed, Approach does the work of creating the form. Just follow these steps:

1. Click the SmartSuite drawer in SmartCenter, then double-click the Lotus 1-2-3 icon.

2. In the Welcome to 1-2-3 dialog box, click the workbook you want in the list of Recently Used Workbooks, and click OK. (For the example, I used the workbook "customers.")

3. Click anywhere inside the range and, from the menu, click Create, then Database, then Form.

4. In the Create Form dialog box, confirm that the range selected is the one you want.

5. Click OK.

6. Click where you want the icon for the form to appear in the 1-2-3 worksheet. I clicked in cell C16. The Form Assistant comes up, shown in Figure 11-13. The Form Assistant creates the form using Lotus Approach, but you just continue working in 1-2-3. Behind the scenes, 1-2-3 uses Approach to create the form.

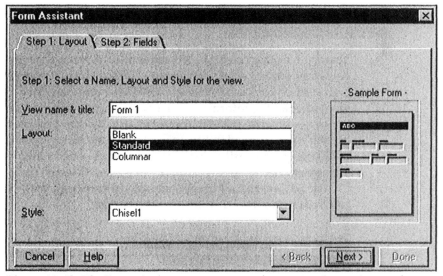

Figure 11-13: The Form Assistant creates your form using Lotus Approach.

7. In the View name & title field, type in a name. Press Tab or click in another field to move to it. For Layout and Style, I accepted the choices recommended automatically.

8. Click Next. The Fields tab displays. Hold down Ctrl and click the fields you want in the Fields box. For the example, I clicked Company Name, First Name, Last Name, and Phone.

9. Click the Add button. The fields appear in the list of "Fields to place on view," as shown in Figure 11-14.

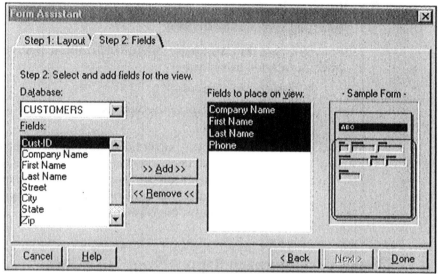

Figure 11-14: Select the fields you want on the form.

10. Click the Done button. The Approach form appears on your 1-2-3 worksheet.

Like the icon for Approach mailing labels discussed earlier in this chapter, the Approach form is an object on top of the worksheet—not actual cells on the worksheet. The Approach form doesn't overwrite 1-2-3 data.

You can, however, modify data in the Approach form and the changes will appear in the 1-2-3 database table. If you change the data in the 1-2-3 table, the changes show up in the Approach form when you activate it.

Warning

If you add rows or columns to the 1-2-3 range, they don't show up in the Approach form unless you follow the steps to recreate the form..

Viewing the Form

Once you have the Approach form in 1-2-3, follow these steps to view different records in the form:

1. Double-click the form.

2. Press PgDn to display the next record or PgUp to display the previous record.

3. To modify the form, such as changing its size, you can click and drag the form on the worksheet. For the example, I dragged a corner inward to shrink the form. Then I clicked on the form so that the cursor took the shape of a hand and dragged it to the lower left corner of the worksheet.

Creating an Approach Report From 1-2-3 Data

You can also readily create Approach reports using 1-2-3 without leaving 1-2-3. The steps are similar to those for creating a form.

Approach reports have outstanding formatting. It's easy to read the title, identify the column heads, and see the information laid out on the report. The next section explains how to display 1-2-3 data in an Approach report.

Opening a Worksheet

If you don't have it running already, start 1-2-3 in one of the usual ways. To open a worksheet:

1. Click its icon in SuiteStart to start 1-2-3.

2. In the Welcome to 1-2-3 dialog box, be sure the tab is displayed for Open an Existing Workbook. In the list of Recently Used Workbooks, click "customers."

3. Click OK.

Creating the Report

To create the report, you use the 1-2-3 menus:

1. Click anywhere inside the range for the report.

2. Click Create, then Database, then Report. The Create Report dialog box comes up.

3. If it is not selected automatically, use the selector arrow to select the range you want to include in the report. Figure 11-15 shows my Create Report dialog box. Click OK.

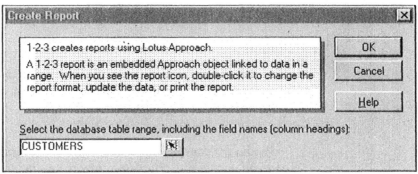

Figure 11-15: In this dialog box, select the range for the report.

4. Click in the sheet where you want the data object to display. I clicked in a blank area at cell C16.

The Report Assistant comes up, as shown in Figure 11-16.

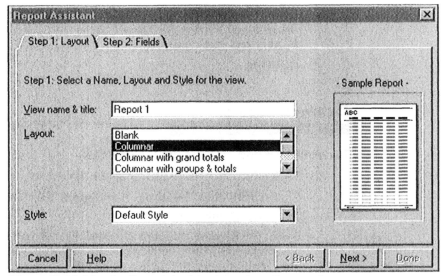

Figure 11-16: Use the Report Assistant to set up the report.

Tip

The Form Assistant is Lotus Approach, but you don't have to leave 1-2-3 to use it. The Report Assistant is similar to the Form Assistant. You can name the report there, design the layout, and choose the fields to include.

Suppose, for the example, you wanted a report showing just company names and city. Here's how to use the Report Assistant:

5. In the View name & title field, type in a name for the report. I typed "locations."

6. You can select a layout and style if you like. I accepted the default (those that appear automatically in the program).

Tip

If you want to try out various layouts or styles, click each one, and see a preview in the Sample Report box on the right.

7. Click Next. The Fields tab displays.

8. Hold down Ctrl, and in the Fields box, click each field you want to display in the report. For the example, I clicked Company Name, City, and State.

9. Click the Add button to place the fields on the view. Figure 11-17 shows the completed Fields tab. Click the Done button. An icon for the report appears in 1-2-3, as shown in Figure 11-18.

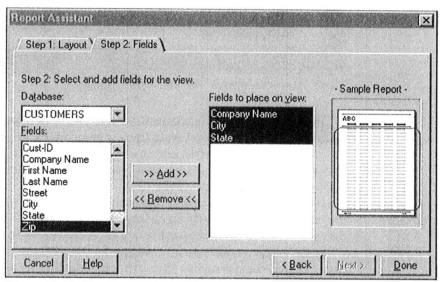

Figure 11-17: Here is my completed Fields tab.

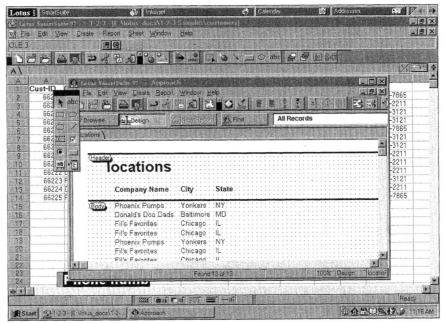

Figure 11-18: An icon for the report appears in 1-2-3.

The Approach report works just like the one for Mailing Labels from earlier in the chapter. If you want to view or print the report from 1-2-3, double-click the Approach icon in the worksheet. To return to 1-2-3, close or exit Approach. (For instance, you can click the exit icon—an X—in the top right of the Approach window.)

If you make changes to the Approach report, the changes appear in the 1-2-3 database table. If you change the data in the 1-2-3 table, the changes show up in the Approach report when you activate the report.

However, if you add a row or column to the 1-2-3 database table, you have to go through the steps to create a new Approach report containing the new range.

Creating an Approach Dynamic Crosstab

You can create Approach *dynamic crosstabs* with 1-2-3 data. Dynamic crosstabs are a great way to analyze data with three or more variables. Suppose, you wanted to analyze sales by region, by product, and by time of the year, and you wanted to see the effect on, region and product if you changed the time of year. In a dynamic crosstab, you can change one variable and see the effect on the other variables.

Crosstabs are pretty cool, and again, as for Forms and Reports, they are an Approach specialty. If 1-2-3 couldn't create them by cooperating with Approach, it would probably have to offer them on its own. By working together with Approach, though, 1-2-3 can offer you the sophistication of the Approach dynamic cross tabs from within 1-2-3.

Creating the Crosstab

You use 1-2-3 menus to start the Crosstab assistant. Then, Lotus Approach guides you as you use the assistant—even though you never leave 1-2-3.

To create the crosstab:

1. Click the SmartSuite drawer in SmartCenter, then double-click the Lotus 1-2-3 icon.

2. In the Welcome to 1-2-3 dialog box, click the workbook you want to use. (Otherwise, click Create a Blank Workbook button and create a new workbook, as explained in the mailing labels section at the start of this chapter.) For the example, I continued to use the customers database I created at the beginning of this chapter.

Warning

To create an Approach dynamic crosstab, you must work with a database table with at least two rows and three columns.

3. To have the assistant select your range automatically, click anywhere inside the range for the report.

4. On the menus, click Create, then Database, then Dynamic Crosstab. The Dynamic Crosstab dialog box comes up.

5. If it is not selected automatically, use the selector arrow to select the range you want to include in the report. Figure 11-19 shows my Dynamic Crosstab dialog box. Click OK.

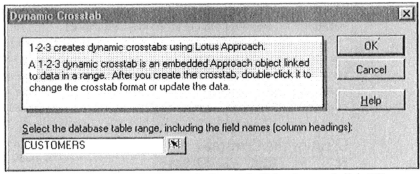

Figure 11-19: Complete the Dynamic Crosstab dialog box and click OK.

6. Click in the sheet where you want the dynamic crosstab to appear. I clicked in cell E17. 1-2-3 starts the Crosstab Assistant.

   In the Crosstab Assistant (Figure 11-20), you choose the rows, columns, and values for the crosstab much as in previous assistants discussed in this chapter.

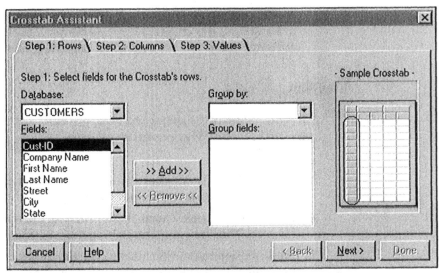

Figure 11-20: Use the Crosstab Assistant to set up the crosstab.

7. In the Fields box, hold down Ctrl and click the fields you want to include, then click the Add button. For the example, I clicked First Name and Last Name. Click Next.

8. In the Columns tab, hold down Ctrl and Company Name, City, and State in the Fields box, and click the Add button. Click the Next button.

9. Select a field for the summary. I used Company Name. In the Values tab, click Company Name in the Fields box, and click the Add. Accept "Count" in the box for "Calculate the."

10. Click the Done button.

1-2-3 places the dynamic crosstab in the sheet. See Figure 11-21.

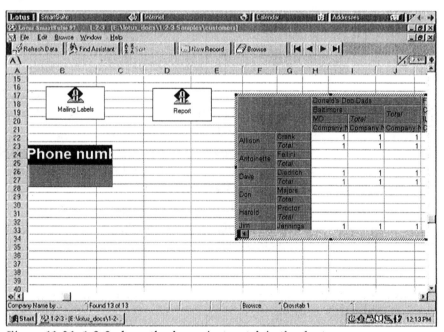

Figure 11-21: 1-2-3 places the dynamic crosstab in the sheet.

Warning

You can't modify the data in the crosstab. You can drag the crosstab object to a new location if you wish.

As with other Approach objects discussed in this chapter, if you change the 1-2-3 database table, the changes show up automatically in the crosstab when you activate it. If you add a row or column to the 1-2-3 database table, though, you have to recreate the crosstab to reflect the changes.

Creating an Approach-based Query Table in 1-2-3

A *query table* is the SmartSuite 97 way to sort or find specific records in a database table. Theoretically, you could create a 1-2-3 query table without ever realizing you were using Approach as well. However, a 1-2-3 database table does use its companion program, Approach, to create the table. The steps are similar to those for the other Approach activities I've described in this chapter.

Creating the Query Table

As with the other examples in the chapter, use an existing 1-2-3 data table as the basis for the query table. To create the query table:

1. Click the 1-2-3 icon in SuiteStart.

2. In the Welcome to 1-2-3 dialog box, click the workbook you want to use. For the example, I used the customers database used throughout this chapter.

3. Click anywhere inside the range for the report.

4. On the menus, click Create, then Database, then Query Table. The Query Table assistant comes up. See Figure 11-22.

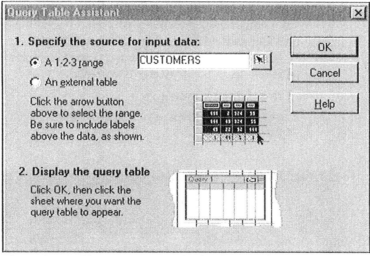

Figure 11-22: Choose your range in the Query Table Assistant.

5. You can use the selector arrow to select the range you want to include in the query table. For the example, I used the Customers range, already selected. Click OK.

6. Click in the 1-2-3 worksheet where you want the Query Table to display. I clicked in cell C30. The Worksheet Assistant comes up, shown in Figure 11-23.

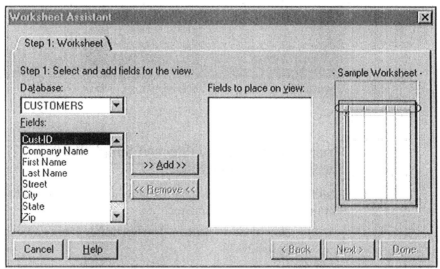

Figure 11-23: Use the Worksheet Assistant to select the fields for the view.

7. As in other examples in this chapter, hold down Ctrl and click the fields in the Fields box you want to include. For the example, I clicked all fields, then clicked the Add button.

   When you have the fields you want to include in the Query table, you can display it in the worksheet.

8. Click the Done button.

   The Query Table displays in the worksheet, as shown in Figure 11-24.

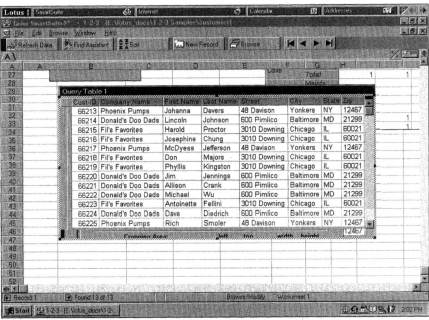

Figure 11-24: The Query Table displays in the worksheet.

Trying Out the Query Table—A Simple Sort

Use the buttons just below the menus on the worksheet to use the Query Table. For instance, to sort records:

1. Click the Sort button. The Sort dialog box comes up, shown in Figure 11-25.

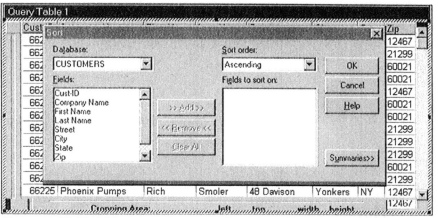

Figure 11-25: Use this to set up a sort in the query table.

2. As in other examples in the chapter, click the fields you want to sort by in the Fields box, then click the Add button. For the example, I used Last Name.

3. Click OK. The table sorts the data. Figure 11-26 shows the Query Table sorted by last name.

Cust-ID	Company Name	First Name	Last Name	Street	City	State	Zip
66216	Fil's Favorites	Josephine	Chung	3010 Downing	Chicago	IL	60021
66221	Donald's Doo Dads	Allison	Crank	600 Pimlico	Baltimore	MD	21299
66213	Phoenix Pumps	Johanna	Devers	48 Davison	Yonkers	NY	12467
66224	Donald's Doo Dads	Dave	Diedrich	600 Pimlico	Baltimore	MD	21299
66223	Fil's Favorites	Antoinette	Fellini	3010 Downing	Chicago	IL	60021
66217	Phoenix Pumps	McDyess	Jefferson	48 Davison	Yonkers	NY	12467
66220	Donald's Doo Dads	Jim	Jennings	600 Pimlico	Baltimore	MD	21299
66214	Donald's Doo Dads	Lincoln	Johnson	600 Pimlico	Baltimore	MD	21299
66219	Fil's Favorites	Phyllis	Kingston	3010 Downing	Chicago	IL	60021
66218	Fil's Favorites	Don	Majors	3010 Downing	Chicago	IL	60021
66215	Fil's Favorites	Harold	Proctor	3010 Downing	Chicago	IL	60021
66225	Phoenix Pumps	Rich	Smoler	48 Davison	Yonkers	NY	12467
66222	Donald's Doo Dads	Michael	Wu	600 Pimlico	Baltimore	MD	21299

Figure 11-26: Here's the data in the query table sorted by last name.

To return to 1-2-3, click outside the Query Table. As with other examples in this chapter, the query table is an object on top of 1-2-3. You can resize it or drag it. To remove it, click it once to select it, then press the Del key.

Tip

To display only the title bar of the Query Table, click the minimize icon (a rectangle) in the top right of the Query Table title bar.

Moving On

Lotus 1-2-3 and Lotus Approach have a wonderful symbiosis. Recognizing the powerful database capabilities in Approach, 1-2-3 doesn't try to equal them. It simply taps into them. Want to create high-quality mailing labels for your 1-2-3 database? Use 1-2-3 together with Approach. Likewise, you can use 1-2-3 and Approach together to create databases, forms, reports, dynamic crosstabs, and query tables.

Word Pro, for the most part, doesn't need the kind of database connections that 1-2-3 has with Approach. However, in one notable instance, Word Pro does need to link with databases—when providing information to complete a form letter used in a mail merge. The next chapter shows how to mix Word Pro with a variety of different databases to perform a mail merge.

12

Using SmartSuite to Supply Word Pro With Data

Word Pro is the place to write letters in SmartSuite. There's no question about that. Word Pro has all the tools for writing—great SmartMasters, all the editing tools, spell checker, grammar checker, Thesaurus.

When it comes to combining a Word Pro letter with data, though, the power of SmartSuite comes into play. When you perform a mail merge, you combine a Word Pro merge document (that is, usually the letter you're sending) with data stored somewhere else. The merge letter contains text (such as, "Please buy what we're selling"). It also contains codes for data you want to put in (such as codes for names and addresses of people you'll be mailing to). The merge letter is a form letter with codes that becomes a number of personalized letters when merged with the list of names and addresses.

Once you have the codes in place, you can merge them with data from a number of sources. Usually, you set up the codes by working with a particular database so you can be sure your codes exactly match the data fields. (If you call for "first name," you have to be sure your database has a field called "first name.")

You can store data in Word Pro and use a Word Pro table for your merge letter. You are much more likely, though, to store an address database somewhere else—in 1-2-3, Organizer, or Approach.

Creating a Word Pro Merge Document

You can use all the tools in Word Pro to create the best-looking letter you can. You can type the letter first and put in the merge fields later. However, you can put in merge fields simultaneously as you create the letter. Then you can be sure the letter reads the way you want it to.

In this section, I create a single letter to use in the other sections of this chapter as I consider merging data from a variety of databases. To create the letter:

1. Start Word Pro in one of the usual ways, such as clicking its icon in SmartStart.

2. In the Welcome box, you can choose any SmartMaster or none at all. For the example, I clicked the tab for Create a New Document from a SmartMaster, then clicked the Browse for More Files button.

3. In the New Document dialog box, choose a type of SmartMaster and a look. For the example, I clicked Letter as the type and letter3.mwp as the look. Figure 12-1 shows my completed New Document dialog box. Click OK.

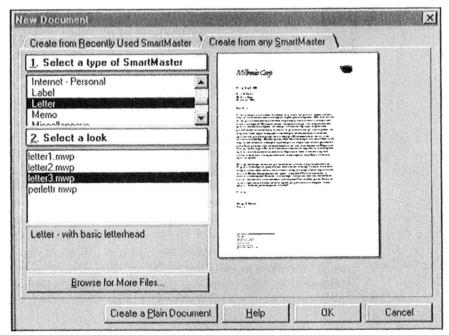

Figure 12-1: Choose a type and a look.

4. If you wish, type in a company name and supply a logo. I selected the company name and typed in the new name "SuperFlex Back Massage, Inc." I clicked on the block that says "Click here to insert your Logo," clicked on a picture file in the Import Picture box, and clicked Open.

5. Click the Save SmartIcon and save the file as SuperFlex.

Figure 12-2 shows my sample file. (You can just as easily work with a blank document for your example. I used the SmartMaster and the logo for the fun of it.)

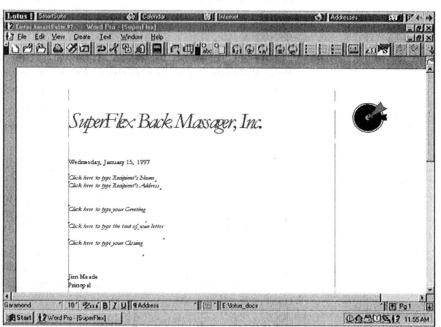

Figure 12-2: Here's my sample file for creating a merge document.

Merging a 1-2-3 Address List

You can use a number of sources for your address database. For this section of the chapter, I used the 1-2-3 address database I created in Chapter 11. You have to have the 1-2-3 database table in place before you can insert merge fields into the merge document.

Creating the 1-2-3 Database

For the example, I used the 1-2-3 database "customers," which I had used throughout Chapter 11.

Here's how to create the database of addresses in 1-2-3:

1. Click the SmartSuite drawer in SmartCenter, then double-click the Lotus 1-2-3 icon.

2. In the Welcome to 1-2-3 dialog box, click the Create a Blank Workbook button. 1-2-3 starts, showing a blank worksheet in a blank workbook.

3. Type in column labels and sample data. Click in cell A1 and type **Cust-ID**.

4. Press the right arrow key. In cell B1, type in **Company Name**. Press the right arrow key again and type in the next column head **First Name**. Then type in these additional column heads **Last Name**, **Street**, **City**, **State**, **Zip**, and **Phone**.

5. Drag across the column labels to select them, then click the B button at the bottom to bold them.

6. For any column that is too narrow to read the column head, place the cursor between the columns at the top of the column, next to the column letter. When the pointer becomes a double-arrow, double-click. The column becomes the correct width to display the data.

7. Type in data for each row. For instance, for row two I typed 66213 for Cust-ID. For Company Name, I typed Phoenix Pumps. Press the right arrow key on the keypad after each entry, and type in the information.

8. Click the Save SmartIcon (an arrow pointing into a folder), and saved the workbook. I saved mine as "customers."

For the examples in this chapter, I created a second sheet in the customers workbook, copied and pasted the address database into it, and resized the columns to fit the data as I did when making the original. Figure 12-3 shows my sample 1-2-3 address database.

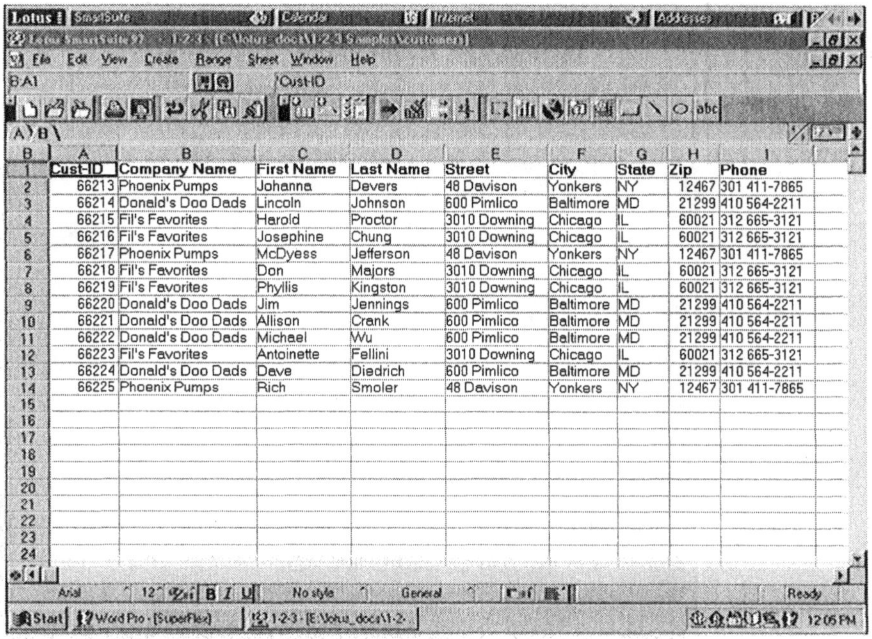

Cust-ID	Company Name	First Name	Last Name	Street	City	State	Zip	Phone
66213	Phoenix Pumps	Johanna	Devers	48 Davison	Yonkers	NY	12467	301 411-7865
66214	Donald's Doo Dads	Lincoln	Johnson	600 Pimlico	Baltimore	MD	21299	410 564-2211
66215	Fil's Favorites	Harold	Proctor	3010 Downing	Chicago	IL	60021	312 665-3121
66216	Fil's Favorites	Josephine	Chung	3010 Downing	Chicago	IL	60021	312 665-3121
66217	Phoenix Pumps	McDyess	Jefferson	48 Davison	Yonkers	NY	12467	301 411-7865
66218	Fil's Favorites	Don	Majors	3010 Downing	Chicago	IL	60021	312 665-3121
66219	Fil's Favorites	Phyllis	Kingston	3010 Downing	Chicago	IL	60021	312 665-3121
66220	Donald's Doo Dads	Jim	Jennings	600 Pimlico	Baltimore	MD	21299	410 564-2211
66221	Donald's Doo Dads	Allison	Crank	600 Pimlico	Baltimore	MD	21299	410 564-2211
66222	Donald's Doo Dads	Michael	Wu	600 Pimlico	Baltimore	MD	21299	410 564-2211
66223	Fil's Favorites	Antoinette	Fellini	3010 Downing	Chicago	IL	60021	312 665-3121
66224	Donald's Doo Dads	Dave	Diedrich	600 Pimlico	Baltimore	MD	21299	410 564-2211
66225	Phoenix Pumps	Rich	Smoler	48 Davison	Yonkers	NY	12467	301 411-7865

Figure 12-3: You can use a 1-2-3 database for your merge records.

Warning

You should not have the database open when you perform the merge. If you are using an existing database, do not start 1-2-3 and open the workbook containing the database. If you have just created it, click the Exit button in the top right (an X) to exit from 1-2-3.

Selecting the Database in Word Pro

Once you have your database of addresses in place and the document in Word Pro that you want to use as the merge document, you can put merge fields into the letter from the 1-2-3 database. Here's what to do:

1. If you aren't in Word Pro already, click its button in the Taskbar to return to Word Pro.

2. In the merge document ("SuperFlex" in the example), click Text, then Merge, then Letter.

The Mail Merge Assistant comes up, shown in Figure 12-4.

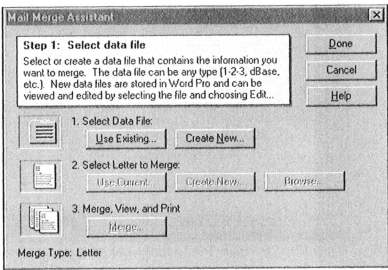

Figure 12-4: Use the Mail Merge Assistant to choose the data file for the merge.

3. Under Select Data File, click the Use Existing button.

4. In the Browse box, from the "Files of type" box, select Lotus 1-2-3 97 (*.123) or Lotus 1-2-3 (*.W*). I selected Lotus 1-2-3 97 (*.123).

5. In the Look in box, locate the folder containing the workbook with the database table you want for the merge. I selected "customers." Figure 12-5 shows my completed dialog box. Click Open.

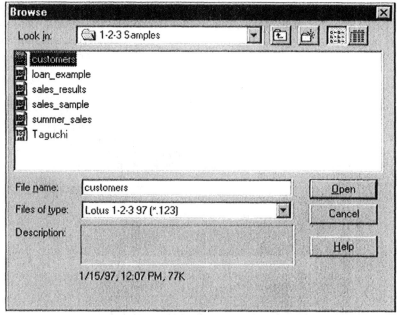

Figure 12-5: Locate the workbook you want for the merge, and click Open.

6. In the 123 Choose Range dialog box, click the radio button for Entire File, Worksheet, or Range. For the example, I clicked Range and accepted the range "customers," as shown in Figure 12-6. Click OK.

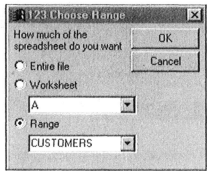

Figure 12-6: I clicked Range and accepted the range "customers."

7. A "Merge Data File Fields" dialog box (Figure 12-7) comes up. If field names are in the first record of the data file (as they are for the example), click OK. The Mail Merge Assistant returns, ready for Step 2—select document and insert.

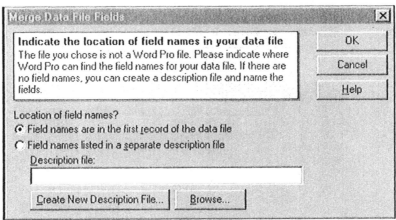

Figure 12-7: Choose merge fields here, and click OK.

8. Select the Word Pro document to contain the merge fields. For the example, click the Use Current button.

The Merge Assistant now becomes a bar at the top of the page, as shown in Figure 12-8. You use this bar to add the merge fields to your letter.

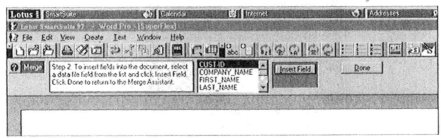

Figure 12-8: Use the Merge Assistant at the top to merge fields into your letter.

Merging With Other Databases

Merging with any other database is almost identical with merging with a 1-2-3 database. Instead of selecting a 1-2-3 database in the Browse box in Step 4, you select an Approach, Word Pro, or Organizer database of addresses.

Figure 12-9 shows the Browse dialog box, used to choose the database for the merge. To work with another type of database—not the 1-2-3 database used in Merging a 1-2-3 Address List—choose the file type you want in the Browse dialog box. Then choose the file name you want in the File name box.

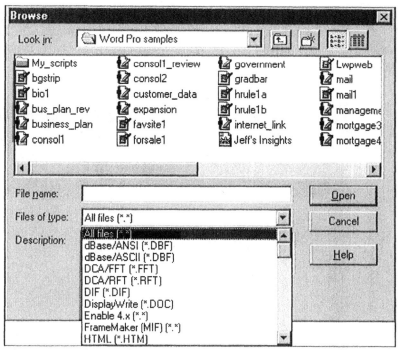

Figure 12-9: Choose a file type here.

Typing the Letter & Putting in Merge Fields

With the Merge bar at the top of the screen, you can have the fun of typing your letter in the usual way in Word Pro, yet putting in live merge fields wherever you want them.

Warning

Merge fields are Word Pro power fields. You have to put them in using the Merge bar. You can't just duplicate the symbols for the merge fields using the keyboard. Such imitation merge fields won't work.

For the example, these are my steps in creating the merge letter:

1. Click where it says "Click here to type Recipient's Name."
2. Click First_Name in the Merge bar, then click the Insert Field button. The merge field appears in the letter, as shown in Figure 12-10.

Figure 12-10: The merge field appears in the letter.

3. Press the space bar, then click Last_Name in the Merge bar, and click the Insert Field button to place the field in the letter.

Tip

To place any punctuation marks, spaces, or line breaks between fields in a merge document you have to add them yourself just as when you type any document.

4. Click where it says "Click here to type Recipient's Address," and insert merge fields for the rest of the address. You can use the scroll arrows in the Merge bar to show additional fields. Figure 12-11 shows the letter with the completed address.

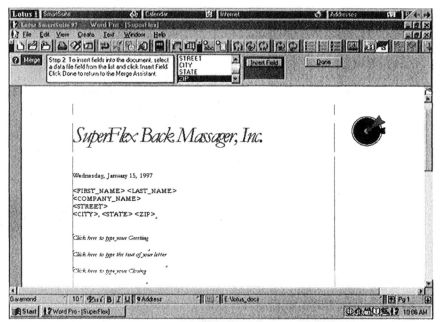

Figure 12-11: Here's the merge letter with merge fields inserted for name and address.

Tip

The "click here" blocks have nothing to do with inserting merge fields. You can just as readily insert merge fields into a document with no click here blocks. Just position the cursor where you want it, then insert the field.

5. Type text and, where needed, insert merge fields into the remainder of the letter. Figure 12-12 shows a completed sample letter.

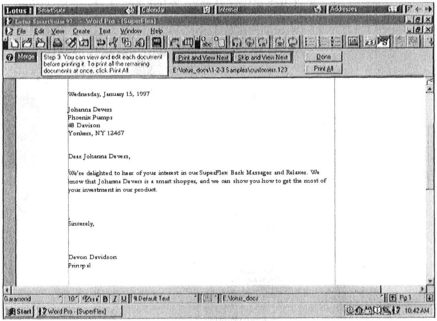

Figure 12-12: Here's my completed sample letter.

Performing the Merge

As with so many tasks in life, the setup is everything. Once you have set up your merge as described in the preceding sections, then carrying out the merge is a simple enough matter:

1. Click the Done button in the Merge bar. The Mail Merge Assistant returns, displaying Step 3, as shown in Figure 12-13. Notice

the check marks in the icons that indicate that steps 1 and 2 are completed.

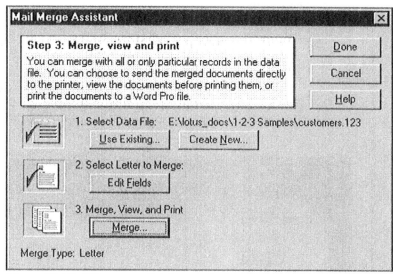

Figure 12-13: When you click Done, the Mail Merge Assistant returns.

2. In step 3, labeled "Merge, View, and Print," click the Merge button. The Merge, View and Print dialog box comes up. See Figure 12-14.

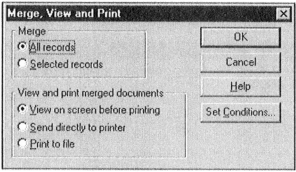

Figure 12-14: Choose whether to merge all or selected records, and whether to view them on screen, print directly to a printer, or print to a file.

You have several options in the Merge, View and Print box. You can merge all records or just the ones you select. You can view on screen before printing (often a good idea, at least the first time you print a merge document), send them directly to a printer, or print to a file.

3. For the example, I accepted the defaults in the Merge, View and Print box. If they are not already clicked, click the radio buttons for All Records and View on screen before printing. Click OK.

   Word Pro displays the first letter in the merge and displays the Merge bar at the top. See Figure 12-15. If you notice anything you want to correct, you can use Word Pro editing to do so.

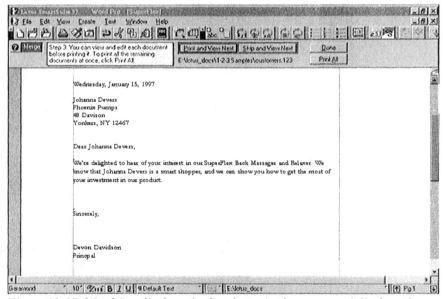

Figure 12-15: Word Pro displays the first letter in the merge and displays the Merge bar at the top.

Setting Merge Conditions

Mail merge power users may even want to print only records that meet specific conditions. To see how to set conditions, click the Set Conditions button in the Merge, View and Print box. If you want to just look over the options but not set any conditions, click the Cancel button to return to the Merge, View and Print box.

4. In the Merge bar, you can click the button for Print and View Next (if you want to print the current letter and check the next one), the button for Skip and View Next (if you want not to print the current one and then view the next), or (most commonly) the button for Print All.

5. For the example, I clicked Done in the Merge bar. The original merge letter displays.

Ordinarily, you might then close the document or exit Word Pro. For this chapter, though, I left the Word Pro merge document open as I looked at the possibilities for merging the document with other databases besides the 1-2-3 database used so far.

Moving On

Mail merges are great time-savers. Judging from the number of personalized mass mailings each of us receives each day, mail merges are a way of life in the modern world.

You never know for sure where the database for your merge might reside. You can use a Word Pro database, but you might just as well have data in 1-2-3, Approach, or Organizer. In SmartSuite, you can readily perform a mail merge using data from any of those databases.

Mail merges are for printed mail. Often in SmartSuite, though, you'll want to send electronic mail from within any of the SmartSuite programs. The next chapter looks at how to do just that.

13

Sending & Routing E-mail

SmartSuite has not just you in mind but your entire team. It has sophisticated ways for you to work together with others on your team. To be able to work with others, of course, you have to be able to send them your stuff, and the heart of sending and routing things to others is mail.

SmartSuite programs work directly with your mail application, and you don't even have to switch to the mail application to get things done. You work right from within the application.

You can start e-mail from within any of the main SmartSuite programs—1-2-3, Word Pro, Approach, or Freelance. Once you start the mail application, the choices are the same no matter which SmartSuite program you started in. The example in this chapter shows e-mail started from 1-2-3.

Sending Mail From 1-2-3

You don't even have to leave 1-2-3 to compose your mail messages. In addition to the messages, you can send a workbook or a picture of a range. And you can decide whether to send to everyone at once or to route them to a series of users one at a time.

Starting 1-2-3 & Creating a Workbook

First, you start 1-2-3 in one of the usual ways and display the workbook you want to send. Here's how I do it for the example:

1. Click its icon in SuiteStart to start 1-2-3. The Welcome screen comes up.

2. You can either open an existing workbook, create a new one using a SmartMaster, or create a blank one. For the example, I clicked the tab for Create a New Workbook Using a SmartMaster. In the list box for SmartMaster templates, I clicked "Create a Territory Sales Plan," as shown in Figure 13-1. Click OK.

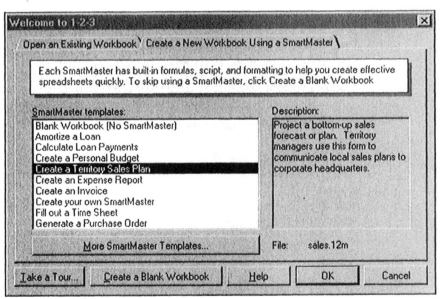

Figure 13-1: I chose this SmartMaster for the example.

3. Suppose, for the example, you want to put in sales data for Territory 1 that you will then mail. I clicked the tab for the worksheet labeled Territory 1 and typed in some sample data.

4. I saved the sheet as sales_forecast. Figure 13-2 shows the sample worksheet. Now you're ready to mail it.

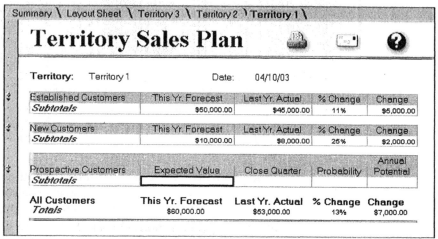

Figure 13-2: Here's a sample worksheet ready to mail.

Sending a Workbook Using TeamMail

To send mail from within 1-2-3 or any of the main SmartSuite programs, use TeamMail:

1. From the File menu, choose TeamMail. The TeamMail dialog box comes up. See Figure 13-3.

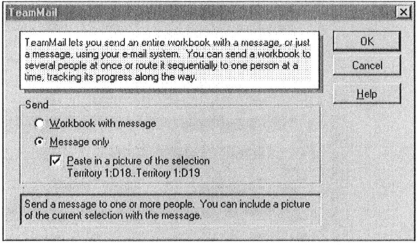

Figure 13-3: Use this dialog box to make choices about your mailing in TeamMail.

2. In the Send box, you can choose to send the entire workbook with a message or just a message. If you choose Workbook with message, you send a message and attach the workbook to your mail message. If you choose Message only, you can send a message and not attach the worksheet. (With the Message only choice, you have the option of pasting a picture of the selection into the message.)

Tip

You may want to send the actual range for another person to use in 1-2-3, instead of sending a picture. You can do that, but you have to use TeamReview, discussed in Chapter 14.

For the example, select Message only if it isn't selected already. Click the box that says "Paste in a picture . . ." to deselect it, and click OK.

3. You may be prompted for a password. If so, put in the password and click OK. A TeamMail dialog box comes up for putting in recipients for the message, as shown in Figure 13-4.

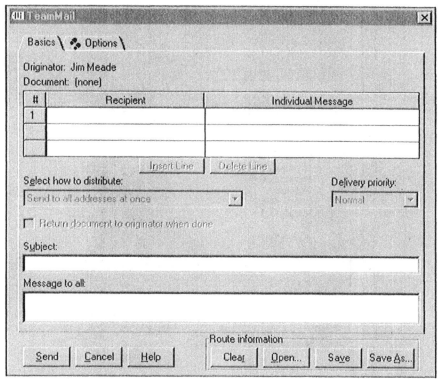

Figure 13-4: Put in mail recipients here.

4. If you aren't sure of an address and want to use the address book in your mail program, click the icon on the right side of the recipient cell. Your address book will come up (Figure 13-5). You can select names from there, and click the Name button to place them in the list. Then click OK to return to the TeamMail dialog box.

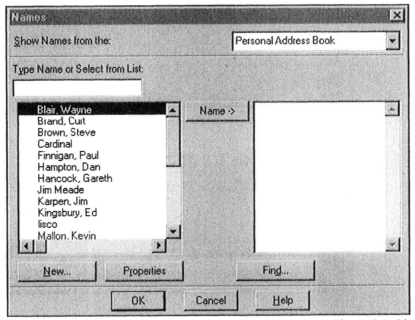

Figure 13-5: Though you're working inside 1-2-3, you can still use the address book from your mail program.

You repeat the process of putting in recipients and messages for as many recipients as you like.

5. Once you have put in the recipient information, if you want to put in a message for the individual, click in the cell in the Individual Message column for the recipient. Type in the message. For the sample, I typed "I won't need your reply 'til Friday."

6. To send the message, click the Send button. SmartSuite places the message in the Outbox of your mail system. To deliver it, use your mail system's delivery commands.

Routing Mail

If you select Workbook with Message in the TeamMail dialog box, you can route your mail to people sequentially. Perhaps you want to send a workbook first to a co-worker for a quick review, then to a worksheet design specialist, then to a manager.

To route mail:

1. Enter recipients in the Recipient list in the order you want them to receive messages. In the Select how to distribute list box, click Route from one address to the next.

    Figure 13-6 shows a sample TeamMail box set up for routing.

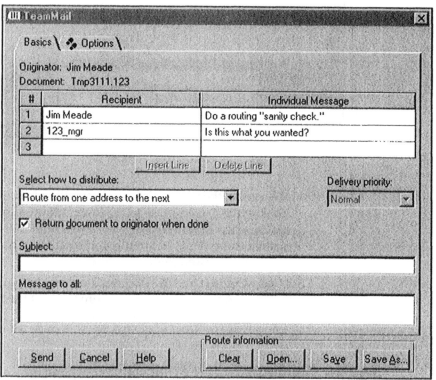

Figure 13-6: Here's how to set up a worksheet for routing.

2. If you know you will be routing mail repeatedly, you can save the routing information. In the Route information box at the bottom, click the Save button. In the Save dialog box that comes up, shown in Figure 13-7, type in a name for the file containing the routing information. Accept the file type as Routing information(*.sfr). Click Save.

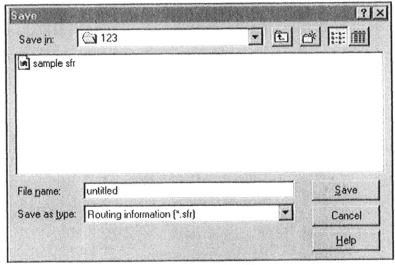

Figure 13-7: Type in a name for the routing file.

3. You can use the routing information with other messages by clicking the Open button in the Route Information box, then selecting the file and clicking the Open button. If you decide against using the saved routing information, click the Clear button in the TeamMail dialog box.

4. If you want to have the document returned to you after it has been routed to all the others, be sure to select the box for Return document to originator when done.

Sending Mail From Other SmartSuite Programs

TeamMail is the same whatever SmartSuite program you're in. What you can decide to send, though, varies from program to program. Here is a look at the possibilities for sending e-mail from the other SmartSuite programs.

Sending Mail From Approach

Sending e-mail from any of the other SmartSuite programs is essentially the same as sending it from 1-2-3. You can compose and send mail messages right in Approach, without even switching to your mail application.

In the case of Approach, you can send selected Approach data or an Approach database. And, as in 1-2-3, you can route mail from one recipient to another in order if you wish. The following sections develop a sample using Approach.

Starting Approach & Opening a Sample Database

As with 1-2-3, you first open Approach and display the database you want to work with. For this example, I used a sample database created in Chapter 6. Here's what to do:

1. Start Approach in your favorite way. I clicked the Approach icon in SuiteStart.

2. In the Welcome to Lotus Approach dialog box, choose the file you want to work with. For the example, I clicked surfnet.apr, developed in Chapter 6 in this book.

3. Click OK. The database I want to mail displays.

Sending Approach Data Using TeamMail

You can send either a snapshot of the current view, or you can send the Approach file with the current view, all views, or data from sources you designate. If you want to send a snapshot of the current view, display the view before starting TeamMail. If you want to send just certain records, select them before starting TeamMail. For the example, I sent the Approach file with the current view. To send Approach data by TeamMail:

1. From the Approach menu, click File.

2. Click TeamMail.

3. Click Send New Message. The TeamMail dialog box comes up (Figure 13-8). Though similar to the TeamMail dialog box for 1-2-3 (Figure 13-4), the box reflects Approach and is not identical to the 1-2-3 box.

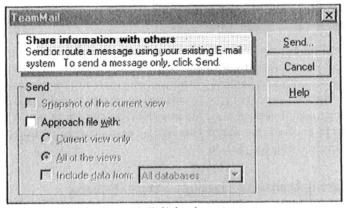

Figure 13-8: The TeamMail dialog box comes up.

4. In the Send box, click what you want to send. For the example, I clicked "Approach file with" box, then clicked the button for "All of the views."

5. Click the Send button.

6. You add the recipients, type in the message, and send the message exactly as you did for 1-2-3 earlier. Once you are done, click Send in the TeamMail dialog box. The message is placed in the Outbox for your mail system, which you will have to use to actually send the message.

Sending Mail From Word Pro

Word Pro, like Approach, is identical to 1-2-3 once you have made your choices in the TeamMail dialog box. But you can make choices in the TeamMail dialog box that apply specifically to a word processor. You can choose simply to send a message, as in any SmartSuite program. Or you can select text before starting mail, and then send the selected text with a message. Or you can send the document as an attachment, which the recipient can then save and use in Word Pro.

Starting Word Pro & Creating a Document

To use TeamMail, you first start Word Pro and either open or create a document. For this example, I created a new document—a planning calendar that one might distribute to members of one's team. Here's how:

1. Start Word Pro in one of the usual ways. For the example, I clicked the SmartSuite drawer in SmartCenter, then double-clicked the Lotus Word Pro icon.

2. In the Welcome box, you can choose any SmartMaster or none. For the example, I clicked the tab for Create a New Document from a SmartMaster, clicked Browse for More Files, then clicked Calendar in the type box. Next, I clicked monthcal.mwp in the look box, then clicked OK.

   A blank calendar comes up.

3. I clicked in the calendar and typed in some information, then clicked the Save SmartIcon and saved the document as "planner."

Choosing What to Send

For any of the SmartSuite programs, you can send just selected text or send the complete file as an attachment. In earlier sections in this chapter, I have talked about sending just a message (1-2-3) or sending a complete file (Approach). For Word Pro, I again talk about sending selected text. Here's how to do it:

1. With your document displayed, from the File menu, click TeamMail. The TeamMail dialog box for Word Pro comes up. See Figure 13-9.

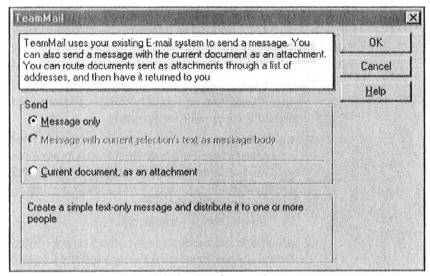

Figure 13-9: The TeamMail dialog box for Word Pro comes up.

In the Send box, you have three options. You can send a message only. You can send a message with the current selected text as the message body. Or you can send the current document as an attachment (which is often useful when sending a document out for review).

2. For the example, click the Message Only button, if it isn't selected already.

3. Click OK.

The TeamMail dialog box displays. It is identical for all the SmartSuite applications. Figure 13-3 shows it for 1-2-3.

Tip

You can route a document. See the discussion in "Routing Mail" earlier in this chapter.

To send the Word Pro file when you've completed the TeamMail dialog box, click the Send button. You place the mail in the outbox of your mail system.

Sending Mail From Freelance

The beauty of working in a suite is that certain activities become quite automatic as you do them from one program to another. If you've used TeamMail in 1-2-3, Approach, or Word Pro, you'll find it quite familiar when you turn to it in Freelance.

You cannot send a picture of the presentation, as you can with a 1-2-3 worksheet. Instead of being able to send selected material, as in the other programs, you can specify the pages that you want to send. If you send the complete presentation as an attachment, you can also include the Mobile Screen Show Player so that people who don't have Freelance Graphics can still play the screen show. Though the process of sending mail is generally the same, then, there are differences in TeamMail from SmartSuite program to SmartSuite program. Here's how to use TeamMail in Freelance.

Starting Freelance & Creating a Presentation

You can, of course, use TeamMail with any Freelance presentation. And you can start Freelance however you like. For the example, I created a sample Industry Analysis using a SmartMaster:

1. Start Freelance however you like to start it, such as by clicking its icon in SuiteStart.

2. In the Welcome screen, choose a SmartMaster, a content topic, and a look. I chose Industry Analysis as the content topic and Look stored with content topic as the look. Click OK.

3. Click in the Click Here blocks and type or choose graphics to complete some sample pages for the presentation. I created a three-page presentation beginning with a title page and saved it with the name "plastics." Figure 13-10 shows my sample title page.

Figure 13-10: An easy sample presentation.

Starting TeamMail

As with the other SmartSuite programs, choose TeamMail from the File menu to start TeamMail:

1. Click File, then TeamMail. The TeamMail dialog box comes up, with the title "TeamMail for Lotus Freelance," as shown in Figure 13-11.

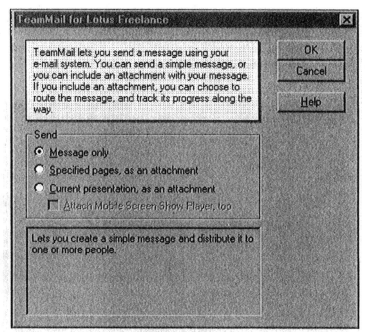

Figure 13-11: The Freelance TeamMail dialog box comes up.

You can choose three options in the Send box; as with the other SmartSuite programs, you can send a message only, specified pages, or the complete current presentation as an attachment.

For this example, I tried out the option that is unique to Freelance—sending specified pages.

Choosing Specified Pages

Often a presentation consists of multiple pages, and you may find it useful to send just certain pages—a bullet list of key points, for instance, or a chart showing industry results. For the example I chose just one page—the agenda. To specify which page(s) to send:

1. Click the radio button for Specified Pages, as an Attachment, and click OK.

    A dialog box comes up labeled "Mail Selected Pages." If you wish, you can click a button to preview a page you want to send (a useful feature. You often want to take a final look at material before mailing it.)

2. For the example, deselect the box for Select All Pages. Click the page you want to send—page 2, Agenda. The message at the bottom shows "Pages selected: 1." Figure 13-12 shows my completed dialog box.

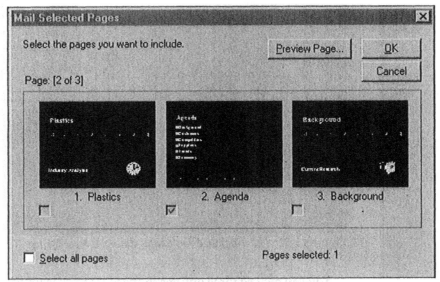

Figure 13-12: Complete this dialog box to mail selected pages.

3. Click OK.

SmartSuite now displays the TeamMail dialog box, which is already familiar to you if you've used it in 1-2-3, Approach, or Freelance.

Once you're in the TeamMail dialog box, you work the same as in 1-2-3 or any of the other programs. Enter recipients. If you wish, put in individual messages for the recipients. If you want to have the document returned to you when it has gone to all recipients, click the box for Return document to originator when done. You can type in a subject for the mailing, which people will see in the Subject box in their own mail system. If you wish, you can type in a message that all will see. And, if you wish, you can route the message, as explained in the section "Routing Mail." When you have completed the TeamMail box to your satisfaction, click Send. SmartSuite places the mail in your outgoing box in your mail system.

Moving On

E-mail is becoming as integral to modern business as the Internet. In fact, the Internet and e-mail go hand in hand any time you send e-mail over the Internet.

SmartSuite has recognized the importance of e-mail and has integrated it into all its key programs. You don't even have to leave 1-2-3 or the other programs to mail them to others in your group or to any others. Because TeamMail is standard from one program to another, once you become familiar with it in one place you'll readily be able to use it in others.

Of course, often you'll mail documents to members of your team for their review. Speaking of teams, the next chapter talks about SmartSuite's team computing capabilities.

PART FIVE

Advanced Features

14

Teaming Up With SmartSuite

People always have to put their two cents in when you write a report or create a presentation. They always think you should have done it their way, and that their way surely would have been the best. Wouldn't you know they would go and systematize something like that? Now, with SmartSuite Team tools, it's easy for everybody to make comments all over your work and try to get you to do things their way.

I'm kidding. I'm kidding. The best results come from groups working together, and Team tools are the ultimate mechanism for allowing other people to comment on your work.

There is more to sending a document out for review than just mailing it, as described in the last chapter. There are the matters of controlling who can edit what, for instance. There is the process of putting in review comments of your own. And there's working with review comments when they come in.

With TeamReview (sometimes but not always used in conjunction with TeamMail), you control who can edit documents you distribute for review, what privileges they have as they review your documents, and on what medium you're going to distribute your work.

Whether working with a team or working with multiple versions of your own document, you can get confused in the face of various versions. Versioning helps you manage those confusing versions.

Sometimes you get a review from just one person, but sometimes reviews come from eager critics of various sorts. To put their suggestions together and keep all their suggestions straight, you can use TeamConsolidate.

If you want to put on a nice show for your team, you can display screens using ScreenCam.

All in all, the team tools help you get in touch with the team, get feedback from members of the team, and incorporate suggestions wisely into your own work.

Using TeamReview: Getting Team Feedback

In Word Pro and Freelance, you use TeamReview to control who can do what to your review document, and how they can do it (that is, with e-mail or a file, or in Notes). I'll use Word Pro for my example. Here's how to use TeamReview in Word Pro.

Creating a Document for Team Review

You can start Word Pro however you like, and you can send any document out for review. Here's how I did it for the example:

1. Click its icon in SuiteStart to start Word Pro.

2. In the Welcome box, choose a SmartMaster. I clicked the Create from any SmartMaster tab, clicked Miscellaneous, then clicked busplan.mwp. Then I clicked OK.

3. A SmartMaster comes up for creating a business plan. I clicked the folders tab at the top of the vertical scroll bar to display the division tabs.

4. In the Overview division, I typed some sample text. I saved the document as bus_plan_rev. Figure 14-1 shows my sample document for review.

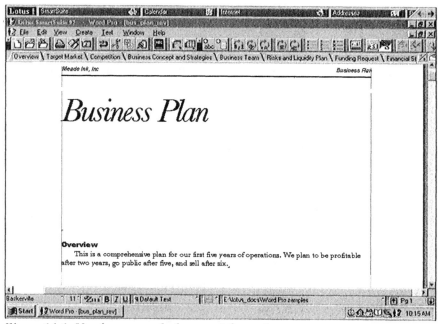

Figure 14-1: Here's my sample document for review.

Setting Review & Comment Options

You don't have to set review and comment options. Word Pro sets some as defaults, and you can simply work with them. However, you can control how review marks will appear in your document. Here's how:

1. Click File, then Document Properties, then Document.
2. In the Document Properties dialog box, click the Options tab.

   You can choose to have marked edits appear in the column in these ways:

   ■ as a bar

   ■ as a character

   ■ as no mark

You can choose to have them appear in these places:

- in the left margin
- in the right margin
- outside the margin (in the outermost right margin)

You can choose whether or not to have editor initials appear.

3. For my example, I accepted the defaults of a bar for marked edits and the left margin. I clicked the box to select "Show editor initials in comments," and I clicked OK to accept the settings.

Starting TeamReview & Assigning Reviewers

To start TeamReview, you use the File menu, just as for TeamMail. You can list the people who can access and edit the review document. Here's how:

1. From the File menu, choose TeamReview.
    The TeamReview Assistant comes up, shown in Figure 14-2. In the TeamReview assistant, you carry out all the steps for managing the review process for your document.

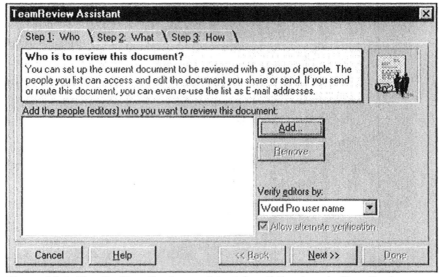

Figure 14-2: Use the TeamReview assistant for all the steps in TeamReview.

2. Click the Add button.

3. In the New Editor dialog box (Figure 14-3), type in the name of the editor. Click OK.

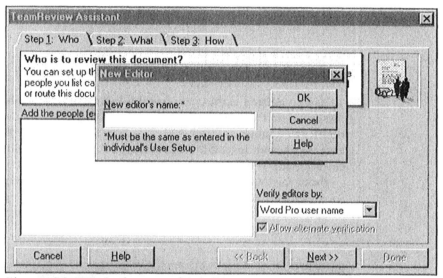

Figure 14-3: Type in the name of the editor.

4. In the New Editor dialog box, continue clicking Add and typing in names for all the reviewers you want.

Tip

If you want to remove a reviewer from the list, click the person's name to select it, then click the Remove button. Once a person has edited the document, you can't remove his or her name (which protects you from having an incorrect list of your actual reviewers).

5. You use the Who tab to control access to the document. Besides listing names, you can have Word Pro verify the editors. Click the arrow next to the Verify Editors By list box, and choose one of the options—Word Pro User Name, OS Login, or E-mail Login. For the example, I accepted the suggested choice—Word Pro User Name.

Warning

The reviewer name and type of access have to be correct. Word Pro verifies them before allowing someone access to the document.

Assigning Editing Rights

To assign editing rights, you use the What tab in the TeamReview Assistant. In this pane you can further control the review of the document. For instance, if you wish, you can make a document read-only so that people can read it but not write in it, or, to allow this status for certain people while giving additional privileges to others.

From the Who tab in the TeamReview assistant, click the Next button (or simply click the What tab).

You see a number of options for what your reviewers can do as they review the document (Figure 14-4).

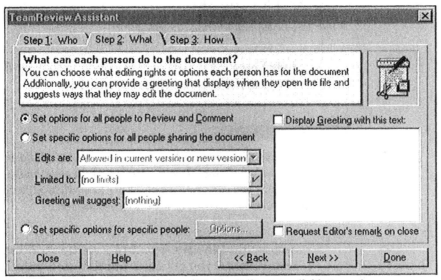

Figure 14-4: You can control the editing privileges available to reviewers.

You have three choices as you set options for the document:

■ **Set options for all people to Review and Comment.** If you click the first radio button—Set Options for All People to Review and Comment—your options apply to all reviewers. When someone opens the document, they will see the Word Pro Review & Comments Tools icon bar. Marked edits will be active, and markup options will match the author's default settings. Reviewers will be able to edit in a new version of the document only. (Later in this chapter I talk about document versioning.)

■ **Set specific options for all people sharing the document.** If you wish, you can set specific options that apply to all readers of your document. You would click the button next to Set specific options for all people sharing the document, then click the arrow or check mark next to the list box to choose an option. Figure 14-5 shows the choices if you click the arrow for the Edits are box, and Figure 14-6 shows the choices for the Limited to box.

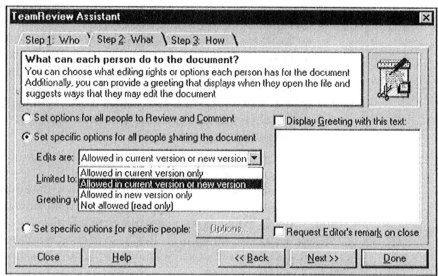

Figure 14-5: You would use this list to make a document read-only.

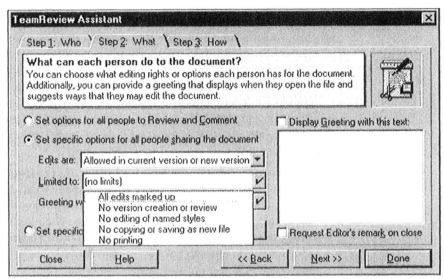

Figure 14-6: You can limit edits here, perhaps not allowing any printing.

- ■ **Set specific options for specific people.** You could even go so far as to set specific editing options for specific people who will review the document. To do so, you would click the radio button for Set specific options for specific people, then click the Options button. A TeamSecurity dialog box would appear, as shown in Figure 14-7. You could then control Access, Editing Rights, and a number of Other possibilities. You would click OK to return to the TeamReview Assistant.

For the example, I clicked the first radio button—Set options for all people to Review and Comment.

You can also choose to display a greeting. Click the box for Display Greeting with this text, then type the greeting in the box. For the example, I typed "Hi. Let's try to get this out by Friday."

If you wish, you can require all editors to enter a remark when they close the document. To do so, you would click the box next to Request Editor's remark on close.

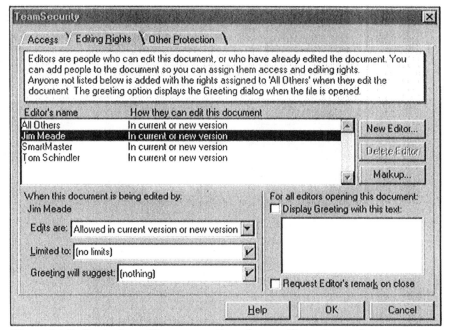

Figure 14-7: Control specific access options for specific reviewers here.

Deciding How to Distribute a Document

In Word Pro and Freelance, you can distribute a document a number of different ways—not just in e-mail. In 1-2-3, you distribute using TeamMail. Here's how to decide how to distribute a document:

1. In Step 2 of the TeamReview Assistant— "What" (for assigning editing rights)—click the Next button.

2. Click the arrow next to the Distribute document by box, and click the distribution method you want. Figure 14-8 shows the box with the list displayed. For the example, I accepted the default of Saving document to file.

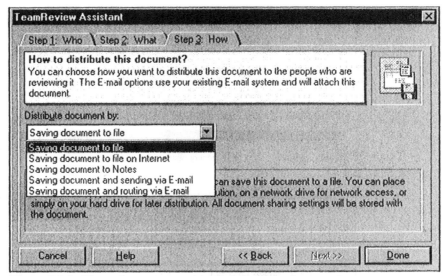

Figure 14-8: Choose how you want to distribute the document.

These are your distribution options:

- Save the document to a file, either on a floppy disk, on a network, or just on your own hard drive.
- Save the document to an FTP server on the Internet.
- Save it to Lotus Notes (as I'll discuss later in Chapter 16).
- Use TeamMail to send it by e-mail.
- Use TeamMail to route it to reviewers in a certain order.

3. Click the Done button.

   Depending on which option you chose to distribute the document, when you click Done, dialog boxes display for you to complete the options for distributing the document.

4. Continue to complete the options for the distribution method you have chosen. For the example, I have elected to save the document as a file. A Save As dialog box comes up, shown in Figure 14-9. To distribute to others, I could place the file on a server or place it on a disk and hand it to reviewers. Click the Save button to save the document.

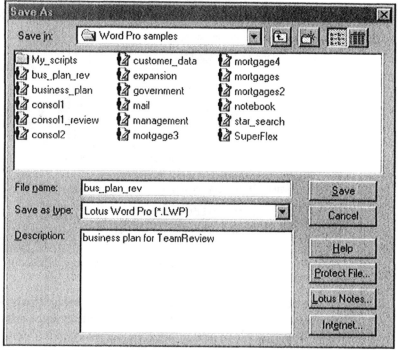

Figure 14-9: If you have chosen to distribute your document as a file, the Save As dialog box comes up.

Reviewing a Document

To review a document, the reviewer opens the document. The person may have received it via e-mail or retrieved it from Notes or even have received it on a floppy disk and copied it to his or her own hard drive.

That person then makes a number of choices about the tools to use in the review. The reviewer then makes revisions in the document before sending it back to the person who created it. To review a document:

1. As a reviewer, start your own version of Word Pro. For instance, you can click the Word Pro icon in SuiteStart.

2. Click the Open dialog box and select the document you are going to review—the document bus_plan_rev in this example. Click Open.

   The document displays, with the dialog box labeled "Document Greeting Message," shown in Figure 14-10.

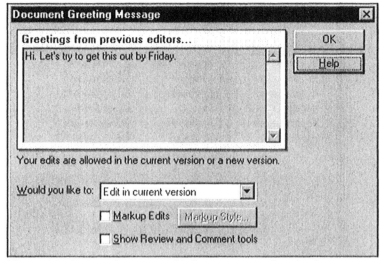

Figure 14-10: A reviewer sees this box upon opening the document.

The choices made in the TeamReview assistant display in the dialog box. You see the greeting created in the TeamReview assistant. You also see whether you can edit in only the current version or can work in a new version.

3. In the list box labeled "Would you like to," shown in Figure 14-11, choose whether to edit in the current version, edit in a new version, or open the document as read-only. For the example, I accepted the default of Edit in Current Version.

4. If you want to put in Markup Edits, click the box next to Markup Edits. You can then put in some pretty colorful markups. To see the choices, click the Markup Style button. The Markup Options dialog box displays, shown in Figure 14-12.You can choose a style for your insertions, mainly the color of text, background, and text highlighting. For the example, I accepted all the default settings and simply clicked OK.

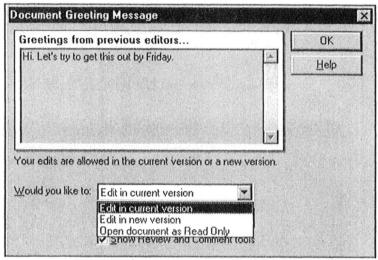

Figure 14-11: Choose whether to edit the current version or a new version.

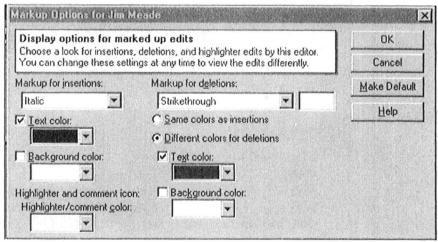

Figure 14-12: Choose a style for your insertions here.

5. If you want to see Word Pro's Review and Comment tools as you work, click the checkbox for Show Review and Comment tools to select it.

6. Click OK.

The review document displays. See Figure 14-13.

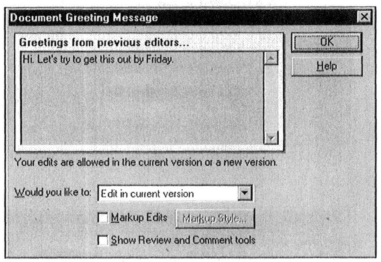

Figure 14-13: The review document comes up.

Tip

If you want to display the Review and Comment tools but did not select them in the Document Greeting Message dialog box, you can choose them from the menus. Click View, then Show/Hide, then Review and Comment tools. Of course, if the tools are displayed already and you want to hide them, use the same menu choices.

You can have a field day reviewing the document. For this example, I made some simple edits, shown in Figure 14-14.

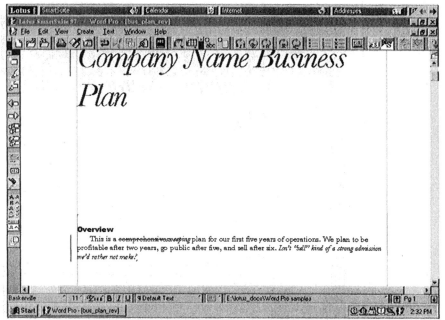

Figure 14-14: Here's a document with some sample review comments.

Working With a Reviewed Document

Once someone returns a reviewed document to you, you can use SmartSuite tools to speed your review of the returned work. To go over marked edits, use the Review toolbar. Here's how:

1. With the edited document displayed, click the Review Marked Edits SmartIcon on the Review and Comment tools bar. The Review bar displays across the top, as shown in Figure 14-15.

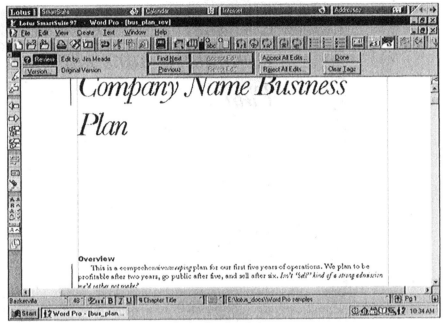

Figure 14-15: Review edits with the Review bar.

2. Place the cursor at the beginning of the document (or wherever you want to start reviewing comments) and click the Next Edit button on the toolbar. Word Pro selects the edit. For the example, it selects the term "Company Name." See Figure 14-16.

3. Click one of the buttons to deal with the edit. You can accept the insertion, reject it, go to the next edit, or go to the previous edit. If you wish, you can accept all edits. Or you can clear the tags for the edits.

   For the example, I just clicked Done to close the Review toolbar and return to the document.

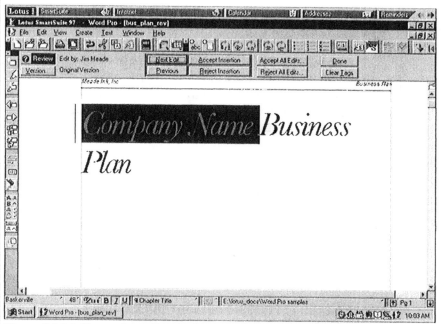

Figure 14-16: You review edits one by one. Here, the first edit is selected.

Using TeamReview in Other Programs

TeamReview in other programs is almost identical to TeamReview in Word Pro. When you use another program, of course, you use what is unique to that program. If you work with Freelance, you use drawing tools that aren't part of TeamReview in Word Pro. If you work with 1-2-3, you work with ranges instead of documents as in Word Pro. Once you know the tools in one place, though, you know them in all the other Lotus programs. Approach has TeamMail but does not offer TeamReview.

Using TeamConsolidate: Gathering Critiques Together

So far, I've talked about reviewing a document from a single reviewer. Often reviews come in from multiple reviewers. You can use TeamConsolidate to keep track of who said what and how. You can consolidate all the reviewers' comments, and then go through and accept or not accept their suggestions. Here's what to do, using Word Pro as an example.

Warning

Later in this chapter I talk about document versions. It might seem useful to compare document versions using TeamConsolidate. But you can consolidate only files, not versions.

Creating Multiple Files for the Example

To consolidate files, you have to have multiple files to put together. For the example, I created some new files in Word Pro. Here's what I did:

1. Click its icon in SuiteStart to start Word Pro.

2. In the Welcome screen, click the Create a Plain Document button.

3. Click the styles box at the bottom of the screen, and click Title for the style. Type the words **Weekly Summary**. Press Enter. The style changes to Heading 1.

4. Type these four headings, pressing Enter after each:

   - Sales
   - Promotions
   - Prospects
   - Return Business

Select them all, and click Heading 1 style in the styles box at the bottom.

5. Click Enter after the word "Sales," and type in this text: **Sales this week were brisk. We moved more product than in the average month. The attached spreadsheet shows the results.**

6. Click the Save SmartIcon, and in the File Name box, type
   weekly_report. Click Save. Figure 14-17 shows the sample
   document.

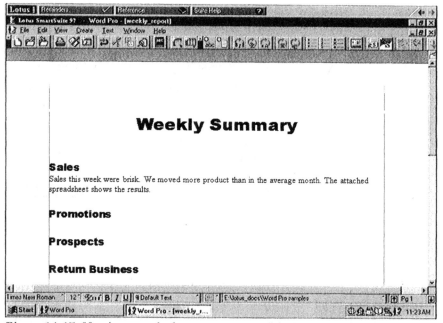

Figure 14-17: Here's a sample document to use with TeamConsolidate.

Now make changes and save the document as multiple versions.

7. Click File, then Save As, and type in the name **weekly_report** 2.
   Click Save.

8. Click File, then Save As, and type in the name **weekly_report** 3.
   Click Save.

9. Type additional text into weekly_report2 and weekly_report3 to
   make them different from the original.

For weekly_report2, I typed this text under Promotions: "Promotions
lagged a bit this week, because we were so busy selling." I saved the
changed document.

For weekly_report3, I typed this text under Prospects: "Lots of prospects are coming up on their own. I think it's the newspaper advertising."

10. Now I have three documents, and I'm ready to compare them using TeamConsolidate. I closed all the documents by clicking File, then Close in each one.

Adding Files

To compare files, you first open the original (the one you want to compare), then use TeamConsolidate. Here's what you do:

1. Click the File menu, then click weekly_report in the list of files at the bottom of the menu (a useful shortcut for opening a recent file).

2. From the File menu, choose TeamConsolidate. The TeamConsolidate dialog box comes up, as shown in Figure 14-18.

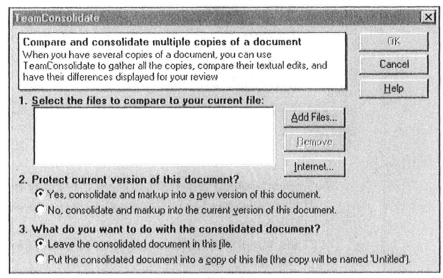

Figure 14-18: The TeamConsolidate dialog box comes up.

3. Click the Add Files button.

4. In the Browse dialog box, click the name of the file you want to work with, and click Open. Figure 14-19 shows the Browse box with weekly_report2 selected. The file then appears in the TeamConsolidate dialog box in the text box labeled Select the files to compare to your current file, as shown in Figure 14-20.

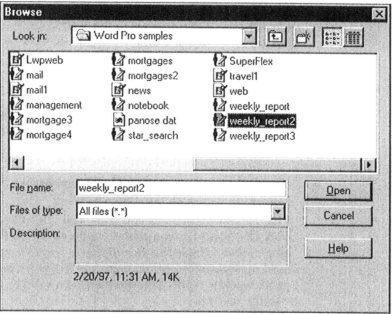

Figure 14-19: Click the file you want to work with in TeamConsolidate.

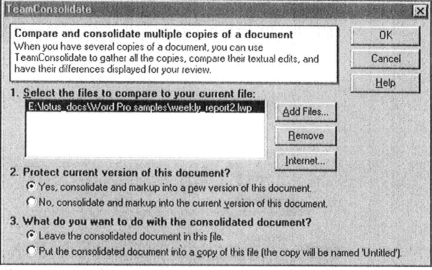

Figure 14-20: The file you want to work with appears in the TeamConsolidate box.

5. Click the Add Files button again, click weekly_report3, and click Open. The file also appears in the TeamConsolidate box, in the box labeled Select the files to compare to your current file.

Tip

You can add files from the Internet, if you wish. Click the Internet button, and choose a file from the Open from Internet box. See Chapters 7 and 8 for an explanation of opening files from the Internet.

6. If you change your mind and want to remove a file, click the file to select it, then click the Remove button.

7. When you have the files you want in the TeamConsolidate box, click OK. Word Pro consolidates all the files (three for the example) into a single file. Insertions or deletions appear in the markup style of the editor. Figure 14-21 shows the sample document, weekly_report, consolidated with weekly_report2 and weekly_report3.

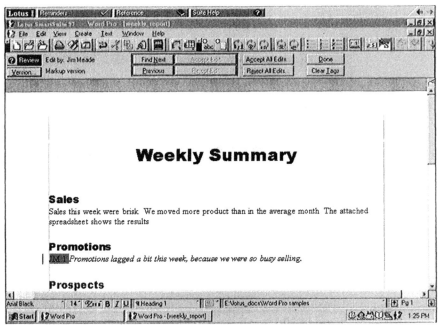

Figure 14-21: The document appears consolidated with the other documents you've selected.

To work with the edits, you would use the Review and Comments Tools icon bar at the top. See the section "Working with a Reviewed Document" earlier in this chapter for instructions on using the Review toolbar. When you're finished, click the Done button in the toolbar, save the document, and close Word Pro.

Working With Versions

In the previous section, you used multiple files to consolidate closely related documents. You can also work with multiple *versions* of the same file. One version is the current version, others are "read-only." When you work with versions, you save file space, because your SmartSuite program saves only the differences between versions.

Versioning, though, is useful for tracking the history of a document. As you work with a document, you often revise and enhance. Sometimes, you change your mind and go back to earlier renditions. The whole process can be confusing. You can use versioning to keep track of those various renditions of your document.

Creating a New Document

For this example, I again used Word Pro. You can create any document and then work with its versions. Here's what I did for the example:

1. Click its icon in SuiteStart to start Word Pro.

2. In the Welcome box, click Create a Plain Document.

3. Type in the sample text. For my example, I typed this:

```
Apple Picking
Modern science has caught up with apple picking, of
course. Automation has turned the fall ritual into
a model of efficiency.
If you have one or two trees in your back yard,
though, nothing quite matches the romantic fulfillment of
picking your own apples one at a time.
```

4. I saved the file as "apples," shown in Figure 14-22.

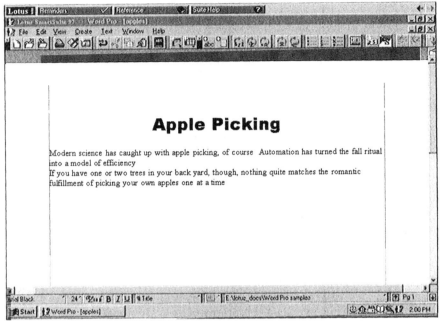

Figure 14-22: Here's the first of multiple versions of this document.

Creating Versions of the Document

Once you have the document to work with, you're ready to create multiple versions if you wish. You can then refer back to various versions as you contemplate editorial changes. Here's what to do:

1. Open the file you want to save in a different version. The example uses "apples," just created.

2. From the File menu, choose Versions. The Versions dialog box comes up, with the title Versions for file: apples, as shown in Figure 14-23. You can do all your work with versions in this one box— create them, rename them, delete them, or save them as a file.

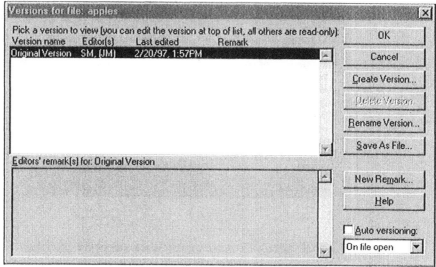

Figure 14-23: Create and work with versions here.

Tip

> *There is a second way to create versions. From the Word Pro Create menu, choose Version. In the Create Document Version dialog box, Figure 14-24, name the version, and click OK.*

3. To create a new version, click the Create Version button. The Create Document Version dialog box comes up (Figure 14-24).

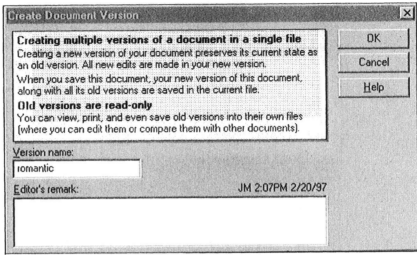

Figure 14-24: You can create new versions here instead of using the File menu.

4. In the Version name box, type in a name for the version. I typed "romantic." Click OK. If the dialog box comes up with your filename on it ("apples" in this example), click OK. The Versions dialog box then displays two versions of the document—the original, named Original Version, and the new one, named "romantic" in this example. See Figure 14-25.

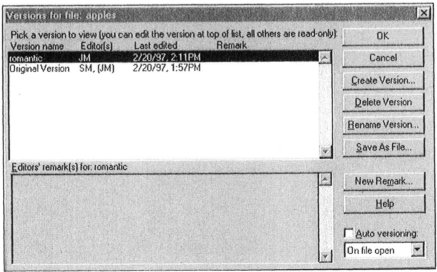

Figure 14-25: The Versions dialog box shows the new version and the original one.

5. You can think of the Versions dialog box as a control center for working with various versions. To edit any version, click it to select it, and click OK. To return to the Versions dialog box, click File, then versions.

Here's a summary of what you can do in the Versions dialog box:

- **Delete versions.** Press the Delete Version button in the Versions dialog box. As you review and modify various versions, you may decide to simplify matters by eliminating some altogether.

- **Rename versions.** Since versions are a useful way to track the progress of a document, you make versioning more useful by assigning meaningful names. For instance, describing a version as the "romantic" version tells you more than simply naming it "version 2." To rename a version, click it to select it in the Versions dialog box. Click the Rename Version button. In the Rename Version dialog box, Figure 14-26, type in a new name for the version.

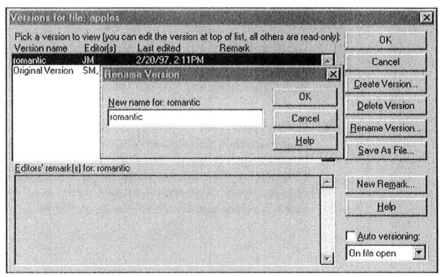

Figure 14-26: To rename the version, type in a new name here.

- **Save versions as separate files.** If you want to use TeamConsolidate on your versions, or if you just want them to be separate files, you can use the Versions dialog box to save them as files. Click the Save as File button, type in a name for the file, and click Save.

■ **Add remarks.** You can put in editor's remarks, which are then visible when you or someone else reads a version. Click the New Remark button. In the Editor's Remark dialog box, as shown in Figure 14-27, type in your remark, and click OK.

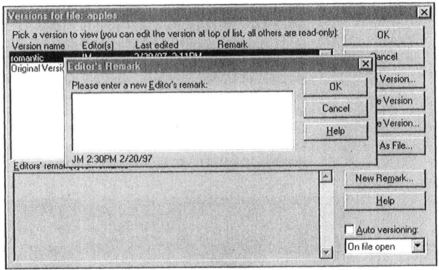

Figure 14-27: Type in your remarks here. They'll appear as an editor's comments.

■ **Create versions automatically.** If you know you want to be able to work with multiple versions of a document, you can have Word Pro create the versions automatically. Select Auto versioning. Click on the list box and choose when you want versions created—On file open, every day, every week, or On file save. Figure 14-28 shows the choices in the Auto versioning list box.

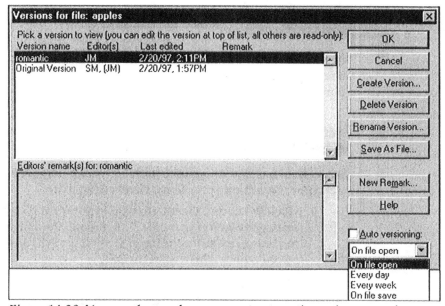

Figure 14-28: You can choose when you want automatic versions created.

Saving a Final Version

Having responded to edits and made all your changes, you probably want to create a final version. You use versioning to do that. Here's what to do:

1. With the document displayed in Word Pro, choose Create, then Version.

2. In the Create Document Version dialog box, type in a new name for the document in the Version name box. I type "apples_final." Put in a remark if you like, in the Editor's remark box, and click OK. Click OK again if another message box comes up.

   You have saved the final version of your document, which you can readily find again. (Of course, life being what it is, it may not be final for long. You can work with it just as you would any other version.)

Using ScreenCam: Putting on a Show

Sometimes you want to demonstrate software to other members of your team. With Lotus ScreenCam 97, you can record a "movie" of all mouse pointer movements and other screen events.

Recording a Movie

ScreenCam has an icon in SuiteStart, so you can start it the same way you start other SmartSuite programs. Here's what to do:

1. Click the Lotus ScreenCam icon in SuiteStart. The program starts, shown in Figure 14-29. To record a movie, you just click the button to start recording. ScreenCam then records all your screen activity. Here's what to do:

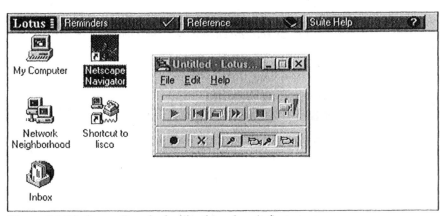

Figure 14-29: ScreenCam looks like this when it first starts.

2. Click File, then New.
3. Click the record button (a red dot).

Tip

To see what any ScreenCam control does, place the pointer on it and read the bubble help. If a control is not available, ScreenCam dims that control.

4. A dialog box comes up with the title Lotus ScreenCam 97 - Stop Panel Visible. See Figure 14-30. Click OK.

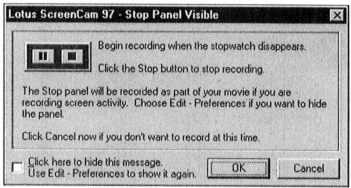

Figure 14-30: You see this panel when you start recording. Click OK.

5. A Stop panel appears on the screen. Wait until you see the Stop panel before recording.

6. Perform the screen activities you want to record. You can record whatever you want. For my example, I showed how to create a calendar from a Word Pro SmartMaster. I clicked the Word Pro icon in SuiteStart, clicked Create a New Document from a SmartMaster, clicked Browse for More Files, clicked Calendar for the type of SmartMaster and monthcal.mwp for the look, then clicked OK.

7. Click the Stop button on the Stop panel to stop recording.

   You've recorded your movie.

Playing a Movie

Using ScreenCam is pretty much the same as using your VCR. To play a movie once you've recorded it, just click the Play button. Here's how:

1. Now that you've recorded a movie, click the Play button (a green triangle) to show the movie. ScreenCam plays back the movie.

2. If you want to play a movie other than the one you've just re-corded, open it first. Click the File menu, then Open. In the Open dialog box, click the filename you want, and click Open. Then play the movie in the usual way—by clicking the Play button.

Tip

Often you may want to pause a movie you're replaying, so that you can explain things to your audience. The Play button turns into a Pause button while the movie is playing. Just click Pause to pause the movie. Click Play again to resume.

You can see a thumbnail of your movie in the Open dialog box. Just click the filename, and the thumbnail appears, as shown in Figure 14-31. You can also view the movie right from the Open dialog box. Right click the filename, then choose Quick View from the menu.

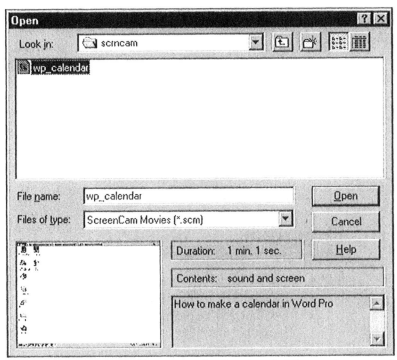

Figure 14-31: Click the filename, and a thumbnail of the movie appears in the box in the lower left of the Open dialog box.

Saving a Movie

Saving a ScreenCam movie is like saving any other Win 95 file. Here's what to do:

1. In the ScreenCam menu, click File.

2. Click Save.

3. In the Save As dialog box, type in a name for the movie. I used the name wp_calendar.

4. Click Save.

    ScreenCam saves the movie and you have it available for future use.

Embedding a Movie

You may want to embed a ScreenCam movie in another application you're using. Then, when someone is reading a document, that person can click on the embedded movie to see the movie. For the example, I embedded the movie wp_calendar in a Word Pro document. Here's what to do:

1. Click its icon in SmartStart to start Word Pro, and, in the Welcome screen, click Create a Plain Document.

2. Type in some sample text if you like. I typed, "Here's that screen demo I promised."

3. From the Word Pro Create menu, click Object.

4. In the Create Object dialog box, for Object type, click Lotus ScreenCam 97 Movie. Then click Display as icon. Figure 14-32 shows the Create Object dialog box.

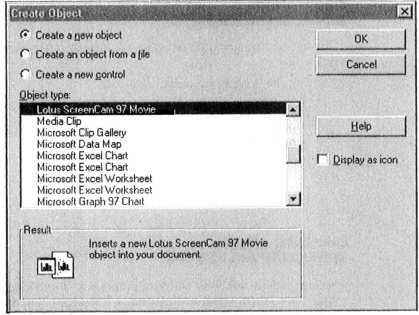

Figure 14-32: Choose Lotus ScreenCam 97 movie as your object type.

5. Click the button for Create an object from a file.

6. Click the Browse button, and locate the file you want to embed—wp_calendar for the example. Click OK.

7. Click OK in the Create Object dialog box. The ScreenCam movie appears as an icon in the application, as shown in Figure 14-33. To play the movie, you double-click the icon.

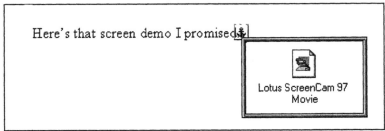

Figure 14-33: You can embed a ScreenCam movie in your document, like this.

You don't have to use ScreenCam as a team tool. You can create movies for yourself. Often, though, you want to show others how to perform a series of activities on the screen. ScreenCam is an ideal team tool for sharing information with colleagues.

Moving On

Breakthrough technologies can be deceptively simple. Before people knew about telephones, for example, they probably didn't think they had that much need to call people up anyway.

Team tools are a breakthrough technology. People have long been sharing documents, consolidating them, and working with various versions of documents. Perhaps most didn't see the need for tools to assist them in working with the team. Once you've tried the SmartSuite Team tools, though, they soon become indispensable. You can review documents, consolidate them, track versions, and put on a show for colleagues. You can work more efficiently with the group than ever before, and avoid costly errors by copying and referring to materials accurately.

SmartSuite offers other tools that are every bit as indispensable as the Team tools—standard tools you can find in every SmartSuite program. Once you learn them for one program, you know them for all the others. The next chapter talks about SmartIcons, SmartMasters, and the Lotus InfoBox.

15

Making the Most of Standard Tools

The standard tools in SmartSuite have evolved over the years from individual tools in individual products to standard tools in all the products. The tools that have come to the forefront are not just collected tools from the various products but the best of the tools from the products.

The members of SmartSuite started out as individual products. Freelance Graphics was not always Lotus Freelance Graphics, and it certainly wasn't always "Lotus Freelance Graphics 97 edition" as it is now. Lotus 1-2-3 was always *Lotus* 1-2-3, but all the other members of the suite originated somewhere else. Back in the distant past, each of those products had its own approach to menus, screen icons, dialog boxes, or whatever else might go into a user interface. Even Lotus SmartSuite 96, though it was evolving toward a standard interface and standard tools, had somewhat the feel of separate products living together as best they good.

No more. Lotus has now taken the best of its standard tools from each of its products and made those tools standard across all the products. Lotus SmartSuite 97 has made great strides toward becoming not a collection of products so much as a single product.

There are still differences among the products, of course. The other products don't match Freelance for its content SmartMasters. Word Pro offers cycle keys as a special form of SmartIcon not yet implemented in the other products. If you look, you can find differences. The point, though, is that now you do have to look.

Mostly the tools are standard from product to product, and the tools available in all the products are the best from each. The tools are supposed to be intuitive, too. You shouldn't have to spend much time learning them. Taking a little time to become familiar with them—say, for instance, by spending a little time in this chapter—can save you big bunches of time later on, and make you more effective in your daily business activities using SmartSuite.

In this chapter I look first at SmartIcons—those deceptive little buttons on the page that help you do things fast. Then I look at SmartMasters, Lotus's way of putting all kinds of expert assistance at your disposal. Then I take a tour through the Lotus InfoBox, that cute little box in the corner of the screen that can save you much irritation and lots of time as you format documents.

Getting the Most From SmartIcons

SmartIcons are quite simple as a basic concept. You click on a SmartIcon in any SmartSuite program to implement a single command. Any command—every command—available from the menus has a SmartIcon as well. Here are some of the things you do with SmartIcons:

- You display SmartIcons for the commands you use most frequently. Then, you can implement those commands with a single click.

- You can arrange SmartIcons onto bars, and you can display bars of SmartIcons for particular activities you are doing. (For instance, there's a SmartIcon bar for working with the Internet, another for Comment tools.)

- You can make bars of your own.

- You can move the SmartIcon bars around on the page to suit your convenience.

- You can make SmartIcons of your own and assign scripts to them.

Displaying SmartIcon Sets

Unless you hide them, some SmartIcons display all the time as you use the SmartSuite products. Here's how to display the SmartIcons in Word Pro:

1. From the View menu, place the mouse pointer on Show/Hide.

2. Be sure that SmartIcons is selected.

Tip

There are slight variations among the products as you display SmartIcons. In 1-2-3, you first click the View menu, on the View menu and not a submenu as in Word Pro, click Hide SmartIcons to hide the SmartIcons or Show SmartIcons to display them when hidden.

Seeing What a SmartIcon Does: Bubble Help

Icons used to pose a "hieroglyphics" problem for users. People just couldn't tell what many icons would do. Clicking an icon to find out what it does can be disastrous. For instance, you could accidentally close the file you're working in.

Lotus SmartIcons come with bubble help to tell you what each SmartIcon does. To use it, simply place the mouse pointer over an icon. Help appears in a bubble. Figure 15-1 shows bubble help for the Save SmartIcon.

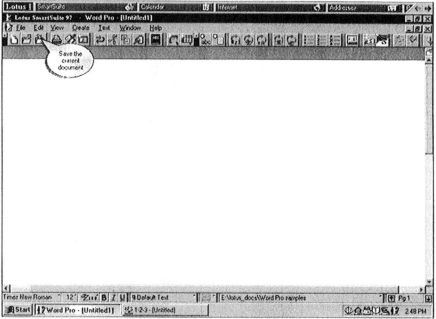

Figure 15-1: Put the pointer over an icon to see Help for it.

Working With Cycle Keys

Word Pro offers a special set of SmartIcons called *cycle keys*. For instance, if you place the pointer over the key with the letters B I U on it, the bubble help says "Cycle through attribute options." Instead of clicking and implementing one command, as with other SmartIcons, you click and cycle through a series of commands. With the attribute options cycle key, you cycle through bold, italic, bold italic, and underlining for selected text. Cycle keys allow you to display fewer SmartIcons yet have many commands at your fingertips.

You can even set up cycle keys to do what you want. Here's how to do it:

1. From the File menu, click User Setup, then CycleKey setup.

2. In the CycleKey Setup dialog box, Figure 15-2, customize your keys.

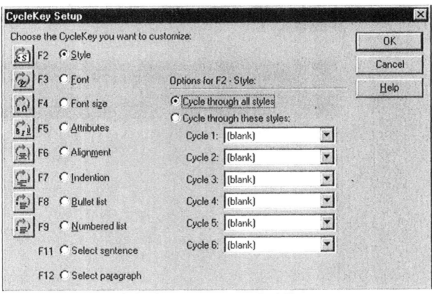

Figure 15-2: Use this dialog box to set up your CycleKeys.

Suppose you wanted to assign styles to F2. If you don't customize the key, F2 allows you to cycle through all styles in the SmartMaster you're using.

3. Click the radio button for "Cycle through these styles."

4. Click the arrow next to the Cycle 1 list box, and choose a style.

5. Repeat step 4 for the Cycle 2 list box and as many of the others as you like.

6. Click OK when you're done.

When you press the function key—F2 in this example—you then cycle through the choices it offers. F2 offers choices for styles.

Moving the SmartIcon Bar Around

You may be in the habit of thinking of SmartIcons as stationary. However, you can actually move them around the screen to suit your needs as you work.

Here's how:

1. Place the mouse pointer over the area next to the button for the SmartIcon bar, so that the pointer takes the shape of a hand.

2. Drag the icon bar wherever you want it in the workspace.

   Figure 15-3 shows the Word Pro Universal SmartIcon bar dragged to the middle of the screen. You might put them there, for instance, if you were working with a frame in the middle of the screen and wanted to have them as close as possible. Figure 15-4 shows the Universal SmartIcon bar dragged to the left of the screen, where it anchors. Some people get into the habit of anchoring the icons at one or another side of the screen and may want to place them there permanently.

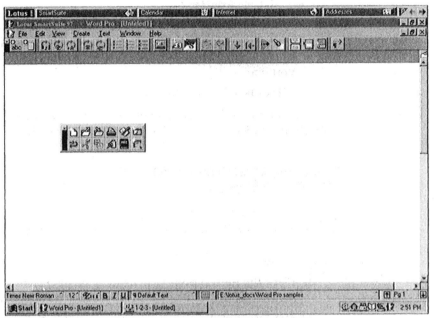

Figure 15-3: You can drag SmartIcons to the middle of the screen.

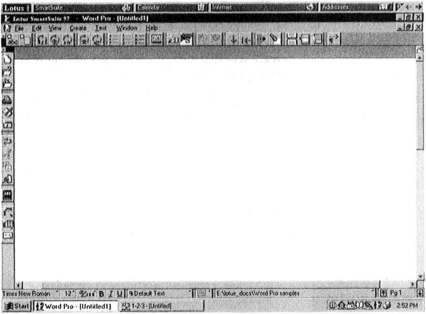

Figure 15-4: You can drag SmartIcons to the left of the screen and anchor them there.

Choosing Large or Small SmartIcons

Small SmartIcons have the advantage of taking up less space on the desktop. You can display more of them without having them get in the way of whatever you're working on.

Large SmartIcons, though, are easier to see than small ones. If you use a small number of icons but use them frequently, you may choose to go for the large ones. Here's how to change the size of SmartIcons:

1. Click File, then User Setup.

2. Click SmartIcons Setup.

3. In the SmartIcons Setup dialog box, click the arrow for the Icon size list box, and choose Regular or Large SmartIcons.

4. Click OK.

Figure 15-5 shows the SmartIcons Setup dialog box with the Icon Size list box displayed.

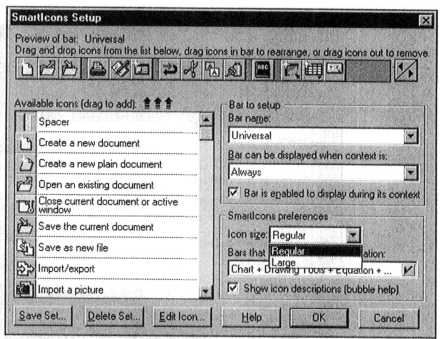

Figure 15-5: Choose Regular or Large SmartIcons here.

Moving SmartIcons Within the Bar

You also use the SmartIcons setup dialog box to rearrange SmartIcons on the bar. I find that I like to put the SmartIcons I use most often on the left, those I use least often on the right. Also, I like to drag certain icons I use often onto the Universal SmartIcon bar, such as the Show Script Editor SmartIcon. Here's how to move SmartIcons around on the bar:

1. Click File, then User Setup.
2. Click SmartIcons Setup.
3. In the SmartIcons Setup dialog box, drag icons from the list below onto the bar at the top of the dialog box (not the actual SmartIcon bar at the top of your screen).
4. To rearrange icons on the bar, drag them to the positions you want.

Figure 15-6 shows a SmartIcon being dragged on the Universal SmartIcon bar.

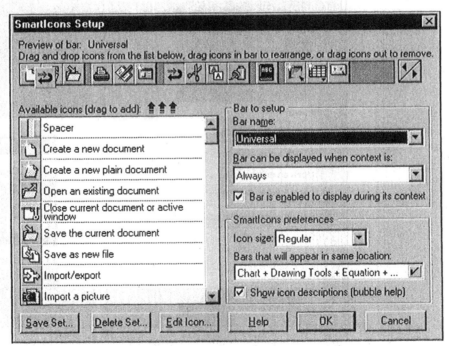

Figure 15-6: Drag SmartIcons to put them where you want them.

Creating a Custom SmartIcon Set

You may want to keep the Universal SmartIcon set intact, yet create other SmartIcon sets for your own purposes. Here's how:

1. Click File, then User Setup.

2. Click SmartIcons Setup.

3. In the SmartIcons Setup dialog box, drag the icons you want onto the bar at the top of the dialog box, and place them in the order you want them.

Unless you save the set under a new name, then you add your SmartIcons to the Universal SmartIcon bar.

4. To save the set as a new set, click the Save Set button.

5. Click Save As New.

6. In the Save As New SmartIcons File dialog box (Figure 15-7), type in the name for the set, and click OK.

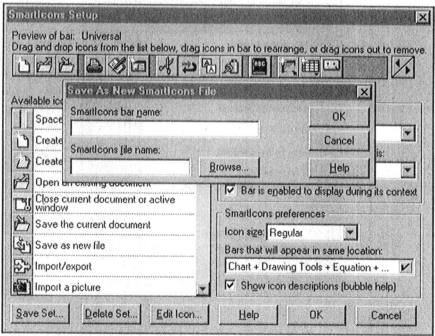

Figure 15-7: Name a new SmartIcon set here, and click OK.

Creating a Custom SmartIcon

You can create custom icons of your own and assign scripts to them. Here's how to do it in Word Pro:

1. Click File, then place the mouse pointer on User Setup.

2. Click SmartIcons Setup.

3. In the SmartIcons Setup dialog box, click the Edit Icon button.

4. In the Edit SmartIcons dialog box (Figure 15-8), you find all the tools to create your custom SmartIcon.

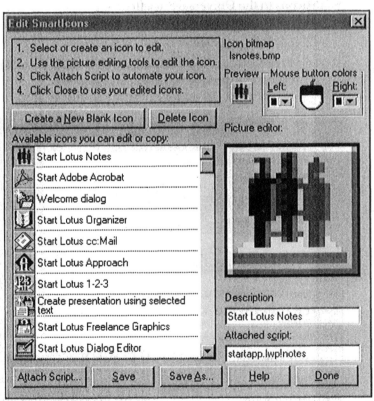

Figure 15-8: Find all the tools you need here to create custom SmartIcons.

5. In the Available icons list, click on an icon you want to customize.

6. Use picture editing tools on the right side of the dialog box to change the picture.

7. If you want to attach a script, click the Attach Script button and, in the Lotus Word Pro - Choose Script dialog box (Figure 15-9) choose the script to attach to the icon, and choose Open. The scripts available would be those you may have created yourself.

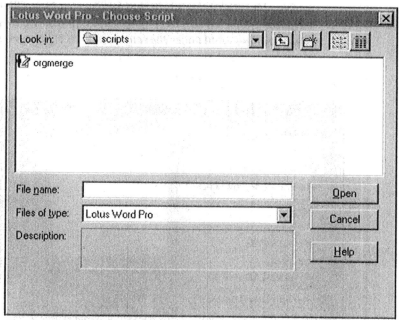

Figure 15-9: Choose a script here to attach to your custom SmartIcon.

8. Click the Save As button, and type a name for your new SmartIcon.

9. Click Done to return to the SmartIcons Setup dialog box.

10. Click OK to close the SmartIcons Setup dialog box.

Tip

The steps for creating a custom SmartIcon are not identical from one SmartSuite program to another, though they are quite similar. Figure 15-10, for instance, shows the Edit Icon dialog box in Freelance. Though it is similar to the one in Word Pro, shown in Figure 15-8, it has differences. To begin in the Freelance Edit Icon box, for instance, you don't just click an icon. You click either the button for New Icon from Blank or the one for New Icon from Current. Despite the slight differences, though, the processes are similar and offer the same results in both programs.

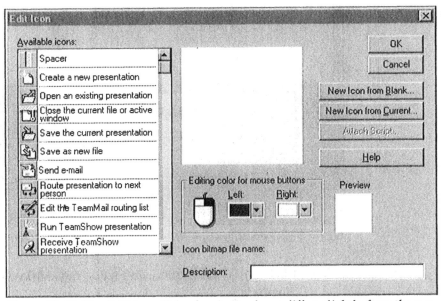

Figure 15-10: The Edit Icon dialog box in Freelance differs slightly from the one in Word Pro.

SmartIcons, then, are deceptively simple little critters. They're easy to use—just click on one. It doesn't take much to choose the ones you want and display them. If you use the same commands over and over, though, there's no better way to save time than to put SmartIcons for those often-used commands right where you can click them readily.

Mastering SmartMasters

Like SmartIcons, SmartMasters seem so simple that you can use them almost brainlessly. Just choose one and use it. However, it's worthwhile to get acquainted with SmartMasters, simple as they are. Many people are in the habit of using no special SmartMasters, or perhaps using just one.

SmartMasters are templates, which means that they provide an initial layout for a document. They contain the right fonts to use with each other and with the layout. (Choosing fonts and placing them properly in titles, subtitles, and text is a considerable job, one best left to artists like those who create SmartMasters.)

They have "click here" blocks that guide you in choosing content and placing text on the page.

SmartMasters produce different types of documents. In Word Pro, for instance, there are SmartMasters for memos, letters, and newsletters, among other things. 1-2-3 has SmartMasters for amortizing a loan, creating a personal budget, filling out a time sheet, and much more. Freelance has SmartMasters for creating a business plan, industry analysis, a meeting, and much else. Approach has SmartMasters for a blank database, a video and actor database, a survey builder, and more.

In using a SmartMaster, you get the benefit of a designer's expertise. The designer may be an artist, a business expert, or a combination. You just have to fill in the blanks.

Finding & Choosing SmartMasters

The SmartSuite programs make SmartMasters pretty easy to find. Any time you start a program or create a new document, you get the option of using a SmartMaster. Try it, for instance, with 1-2-3. Here's how to choose a SmartMaster when you start the program:

1. Click its icon in SuiteStart to start 1-2-3.

2. In the Welcome to 1-2-3 dialog box, click the tab for Create a New Workbook Using a SmartMaster.

    The SmartMaster templates list box lists the SmartMasters available. Figure 15-11 shows the list of 1-2-3 SmartMaster templates.

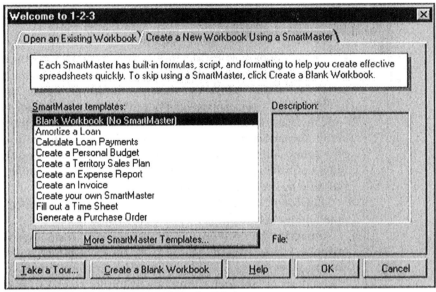

Figure 15-11: Find 1-2-3 templates in this box.

3. To see a description of a SmartMaster, click the SmartMaster in the SmartMaster templates list box. The description appears on the right in the Description box.

4. To choose a SmartMaster, click the SmartMaster to select it, then click OK. Figure 15-12 shows 1-2-3 with a workbook using the Calculate Loan Payments SmartMaster.

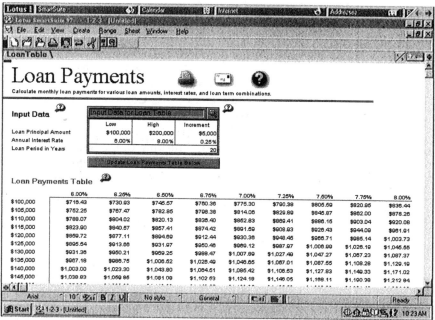

Figure 15-12: This SmartMaster makes you look like an expert at calculating loan payments.

Tip

> To choose a SmartMaster once 1-2-3 is running, click File, then New Workbook. In the New Workbook dialog box, choose a SmartMaster just as in the Welcome dialog box.

5. If you want to find a SmartMaster other than those in the New Workbook dialog box, click the button for More SmartMaster Templates.

Using Content SmartMasters

In the early days of the evolution of SmartMasters, SmartMasters had strictly to do with styles—fonts for your type, font sizes, perhaps page layouts. In SmartSuite (and in competitors like Microsoft Office) you can now find what Lotus refers to as "Content SmartMasters."

After all, experts can do more to help prepare a document than just set you up with the right typefaces to work with. They can provide expert help. Freelance is probably the king of the SmartSuite programs when it comes to offering content SmartMasters. It offers 30 content SmartMasters. Here's how to use a Content SmartMaster in Freelance:

1. Click its icon in SuiteStart to start Freelance.

2. Click the tab labeled Create a New Presentation Using a SmartMaster.

3. In the Select a Content Topic list box, click the name of a topic. For the example, I clicked Sales - Ken Wax. A description of the content topic appears on the right, as shown in Figure 15-13.

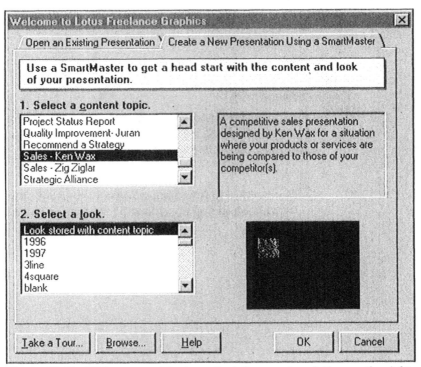

Figure 15-13: Click a content topic on the left; see a description on the right.

4. Choose a look if you like, in the Select a look box. If you don't choose another look, though, you accept the one labeled Look stored with content topic—one whose look and feel match that of the subject at hand.

5. Click OK. A presentation comes up where the expert has already provided content for a series of pages in the presentation. First, click OK in the Welcome screen.

6. In the New Page dialog box, click the Content Pages tab. Figure 15-14 shows the choice of content topics.

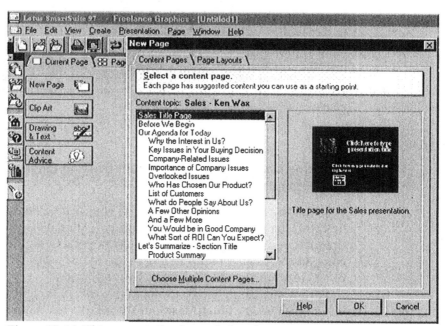

Figure 15-14: This presentation has a choice of pages containing actual content.

7. For the example, I clicked Sales Title Page in the Content topic list box, and I clicked OK. Figure 15-15 shows the presentation page, where you click and "fill in the blanks" to the leading questions provided by the content expert.

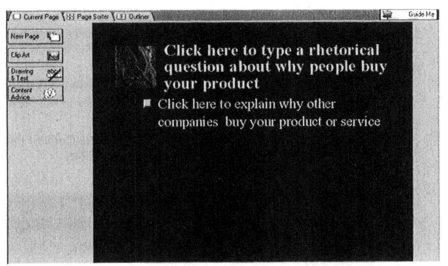

Figure 15-15: The content expert provides leading questions. You fill in the blanks.

Creating New SmartMasters From Existing Ones

Whether to assist yourself or others on your team, you can create SmartMasters from existing SmartMasters. After all, a content topic or a design template may be useful but may not exactly fit the needs of your company. You can set it up so it does meet your needs, and then allow others to work from the customized SmartMaster.

For instance, suppose you wanted to create new stationery from the existing Stationery SmartMaster in Word Pro. Here's how:

1. Create a new document, and in the New Document dialog box choose the SmartMaster you want. For the example, I chose Letter as the type and letter2.mwp as the look. Figure 15-16 shows the New Document dialog box where I chose the SmartMaster. Click OK. Figure 15-17 shows the SmartMaster on the page.

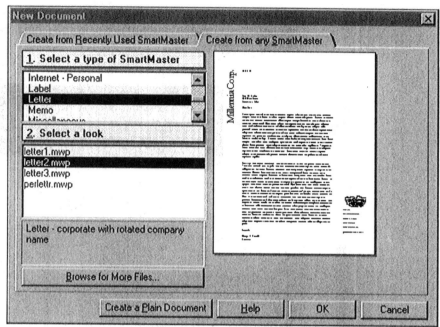

Figure 15-16: Choose the type and look you want.

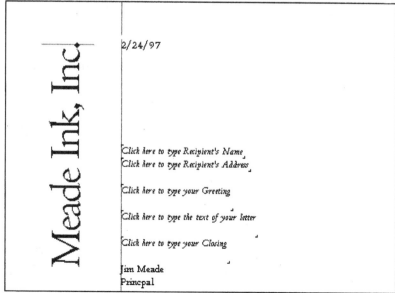

Figure 15-17: Here's the SmartMaster before I created a new one from it.

2. Make your changes in the open document. For the example, I changed the company name on the left to Aegis Products, as shown in Figure 15-18.

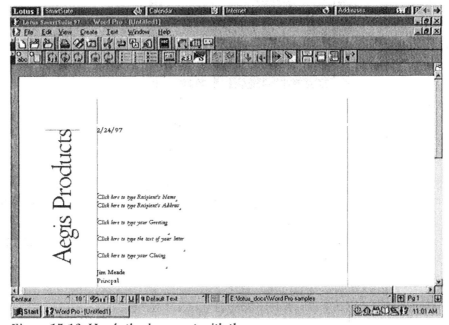

Figure 15-18: Here's the document with the new company name.

Once you've customized the document, you save it as a SmartMaster. Here's how:

1. From the File menu, choose Save As.

2. You can save the SmartMaster in any folder, but it's easiest to find if you save it in your default directory of SmartMasters. For the example, I found the folder smasters, then double-clicked the folder wordpro.

3. In the Save as dialog box, type in a name in the File Name box. For the example, I typed aegis_letter.

4. In the Description box, type in a description. I typed Company stationery. (You don't have to type in a description, but descriptions are helpful later when you look up the SmartMaster.)

5. Click the arrow at the right of the Save as type list box, and choose Lotus Word Pro SmartMaster (*.MWP). Figure 15-19 shows my completed Save As dialog box.

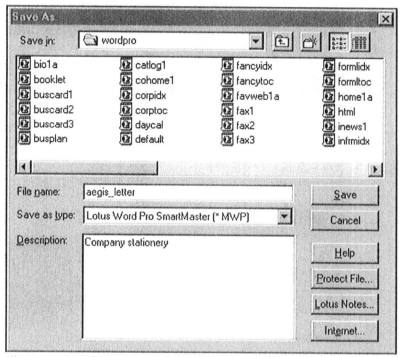

Figure 15-19: Choose SmartMaster as the type when creating a new SmartMaster.

6. Click the Save button. A dialog box comes up offering further options. For the example, I clicked OK to accept the defaults. Word Pro saves the document as a SmartMaster.

Here's how to find the new SmartMaster:

1. Click the Create a New Document SmartIcon.

2. In the New Document dialog box, you could click the SmartMaster aegis_letter.mwp at the top of the list of recently used SmartMasters. For the example, though, click the tab for Create From Any SmartMaster.

3. For type, click Letter. The new SmartMaster appears in the Select a Look list box, Figure 15-20.

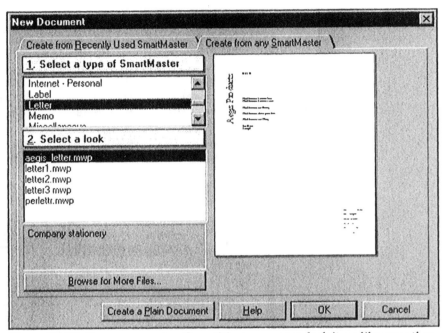

Figure 15-20: Once you create a SmartMaster, you can look it up like any other SmartMaster.

Creating Click Here Blocks in SmartMasters

You can even put your own click here blocks into SmartMasters you create. Here's how to put one into the SmartMaster just created:

1. With Word Pro running and the SmartMaster you want to work with on the page, click on the page where you want to place the Click Here Block. I clicked at the end of the letter, after name and title.

2. Click Create, then Click Here Block.

3. In the Create Click Here Block dialog box, choose Behavior if you wish. (I accepted the default.) Type in Prompt text. I typed

"Click here to type postscript." Figure 15-21 shows my completed Create Click Here Block dialog box.

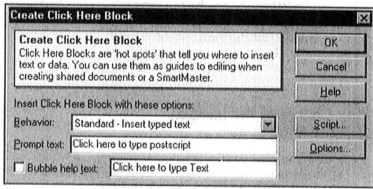

Figure 15-21: You can put in any prompt text you like.

4. Click OK. The new Click Here block appears in the document, as shown in Figure 15-22.

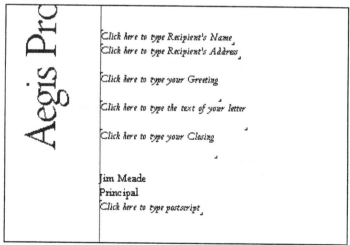

Figure 15-22: You can create Click Here Blocks of your own.

Tip

If you add a new Click Here Block and want it to appear in future SmartMasters, you have to remember to save the document with the new click here block as a SmartMaster. Otherwise, the new Click Here Block appears only in the current document.

Taking Charge of the InfoBox

Often, complex problems have very simple solutions. Such is the case with the Lotus InfoBox, shown in Figure 15-23. It is what you may think of as a sophisticated properties dialog box.

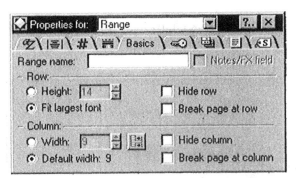

Figure 15-23: In the InfoBox, you choose among many available properties for many available objects.

The problem the InfoBox solves is that modern office software products like those in SmartSuite offer a lengthy list of possibilities for dealing with a lengthy list of document properties. In Word Pro, for instance, you can change properties of text, pages, frames, tables, table cells, headers, footers, columns, OLE objects, and drawings. How can you help users readily find the item they want to format, then readily see and choose the possibility they want? How can you put all the possibilities into one readily accessible box?

The InfoBox does the trick. It looks the same in all members of the suite, and it works the same way in all. It's no more complicated than choosing from a printed catalog, but it saves endless searching (as if, in a catalog, you had no index but had to thumb through all the pages until you found what you wanted).

Perhaps best of all about the InfoBox is that any change you make in the InfoBox appears simultaneously in the document. You don't have to exit the box and go back to the document to see the change. And you don't have to settle for seeing a simple preview of the change in a preview box in the InfoBox. Instead, you see the actual change.

Because the changes appear simultaneously in the document, an InfoBox offers true WYSIWYG (what you see is what you get) as you experiment with fonts and other looks.

Creating a Sample Document

Though the InfoBox is the same in all SmartSuite programs, I used Word Pro to show the box and how it works. Here's what I did:

1. Click its icon in SuiteStart to start Word Pro.

2. In the Welcome box, click Create a New Document from a SmartMaster, click the Browse for More Files button, and click Newsletter as the type of SmartMaster. Click news2.mwp as the look, and click OK.

3. Click and type in the click here blocks to type in sample material. Figure 15-24 shows my sample document.

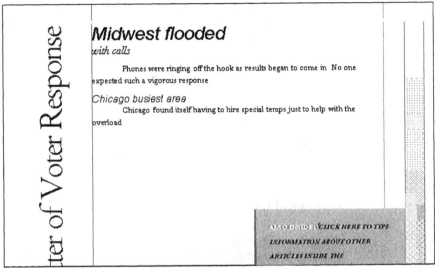

Figure 15-24: I created this sample newsletter with which to use the InfoBox.

Once you have any document open in any of the SmartSuite programs, you can use the InfoBox with it.

Opening the InfoBox

You can open the InfoBox by choosing from the menus. If you do that, though, you have to know the name of whatever you want to modify (such as frame or page or text). If you use the right mouse button, though, you can just point and click. Right-clicking is the easiest way to get to the InfoBox.

To open the InfoBox, click the right mouse button in the appropriate area or object and choose the related Properties option from the menu. Suppose, for instance, you wanted to change the look of the headline in the sample shown in Figure 15-25. Here's what you do:

1. Place the cursor on what you want to work with. For this example, I selected the headline, "Midwest flooded."

2. Right-click. Click Text Properties. The InfoBox comes up, shown in Figure 15-25.

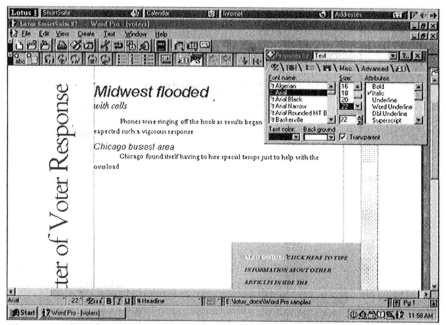

Figure 15-25: After you choose Text Properties, you see the Infobox.

Making Changes

Once you have placed the cursor where you want and opened the InfoBox, you can enjoy the power of this simple tool. Click on a tab, and click on a characteristic you want. You see the change as soon as you click on a choice. Experiment as much as you want, and see all the possibilities in the document as you work.

Tabs in the InfoBox come with bubble help of their own. Click anywhere on the box to make sure it is active. (It's good to click in the title bar, so you don't accidentally make any changes.) Figure 15-26 shows bubble help for the InfoBox.

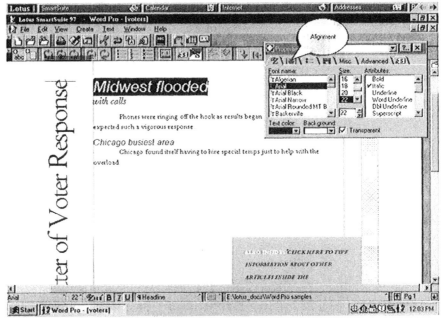

Figure 15-26: Tabs in the InfoBox have bubble help.

Suppose, for the example, you want to try a new font and size. Here's what to do:

1. With the text selected and the InfoBox displayed, click on the typeface you want to try. I clicked Arial Black.

2. Click the size you want to try. I clicked 24. The changes show up simultaneously in the document, as Figure 15-27 shows.

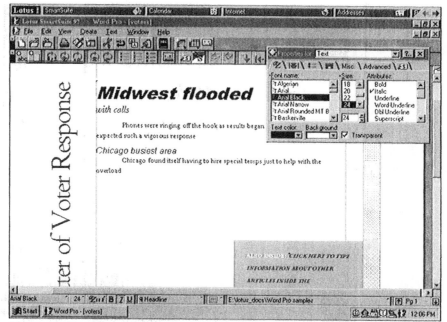

Figure 15-27: Changes you make in the InfoBox show up simultaneously in the document.

You can change all kinds of other text characteristics by clicking tabs in the InfoBox and making choices. Suppose you wanted to center the headline. Here's what to do:

1. With the sample text still selected, click the tab whose Bubble help says "Alignment."

2. Click the tab to center text. Figure 15-28 shows the InfoBox with the text centered.

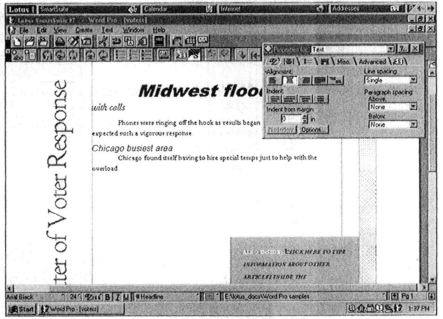

Figure 15-28: Click the centering tab in the Alignment box to center text.

Choosing a Different Property To Work With

The easiest way to get to the property you want in the InfoBox is to place the cursor where you want (such as in Text), right-click, then choose what you want—such as Text Properties. You can also choose properties to work with from within the InfoBox, though. Here's how:

1. Click the arrow in the list box at the top of the InfoBox. Figure 15-29 shows the choices in the Properties list box.

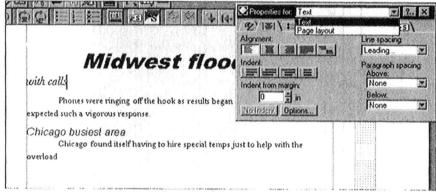

Figure 15-29: Choose the properties you want to work with.

2. Click the property you want to work with. For the example, I clicked Page Layout. A set of tabs and choices for Page Layout replaces those for Text in the InfoBox. See Figure 15-30.

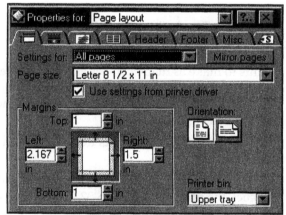

Figure 15-30: If you choose a different property, you get a new set of tabs and choices.

If you want to work with a property not listed in the Settings list box in the InfoBox, click in the document to select the property, then right-click, and choose the property you want. Suppose you want to work with a frame in a sample document. Click the frame, then right-click. Figure 15-31 shows the menu that comes up. To use the InfoBox for Frame Properties, you would then click Frame Properties.

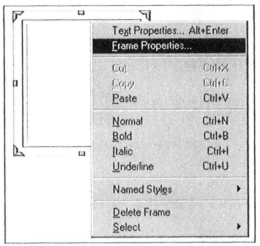

Figure 15-31: Select the frame, then right-click to see a shortcut menu containing a choice for Frame Properties.

Moving, Collapsing & Expanding the InfoBox

The InfoBox wants to make as many choices as possible available to you, yet it doesn't want to get in the way by taking up valuable screen space. You can move it around all kinds of ways. Here's how to move, collapse, and expand the InfoBox:

1. To move the InfoBox, drag it by its title bar, as with any Windows dialog box.

2. To collapse the InfoBox so that only the title bar and tabs show, double-click the title bar. Figure 15-32 shows a collapsed InfoBox. To return the InfoBox to full size, double-click the title bar again. Or you can just click one of the tabs.

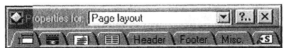

Figure 15-32: It's handy sometimes to show just the title bar and tabs. Just double-click on the title bar of the expanded InfoBox.

Tip

The InfoBox has a menu in the top left you can use to restore, move, collapse, or close the InfoBox, or to get Help. Just click the icon in the top left of the InfoBox to display the menu.

The InfoBox is a rich compendium of useful commands for changing the properties of whatever you might be working with in any of the SmartSuite programs. Deceptively simple—like its companions SmartIcons and SmartMasters—it can save time and improve productivity for those who become familiar with it. Once you become familiar with it in one SmartSuite program, you know the InfoBox in all SmartSuite programs.

Moving On

Users of office products used to tend to specialize. They would be "spreadsheet users" primarily, or word processing specialists, or (less commonly) graphics specialists.

In the modern SmartSuite, though, specialization is becoming less and less the rule. When you master one program, you become adept at others as well, and there is little reason any longer to stay within the confines of a single program or two programs.

Nothing is more powerful at making all of SmartSuite accessible to users than standard tools. Once you become familiar with SmartIcons, you can implement commands with a single click in any program. You can choose the SmartIcons you want and display them the way you like best—in any program.

Having once found out how SmartMasters can make you an instant design expert and even a content expert, you're likely to begin to make use of the possibilities SmartMasters provide. If you feel a bit tentative with one of the programs, a SmartMaster can get you off to a running start. You don't have to be a designer to look great in Freelance, for instance. Just choose a SmartMaster, and type text into click here blocks.

Once you have used the InfoBox in one place, you can use it in any SmartSuite program. The choices available in the box vary from object to object and from program to program, but the InfoBox works the same way in all of them.

Another tool appreciated by many Lotus users is Lotus Notes. Not everyone who uses SmartSuite uses Lotus Notes. Those who do, though, find that SmartSuite and Notes interact smoothly with each other. The next chapter talks about using SmartSuite with Notes.

16

Using Lotus Notes With SmartSuite

Just as the Internet is a central location where SmartSuite users can save and retrieve information, Lotus Notes is a central place—an intranet—where Notes users in a company can exchange information.

 Tip

Not every SmartSuite user is a Notes user, and you well may not use Notes. If you don't have Notes on your computer—or your network—then you probably don't have much use for this chapter . . . unless you're just curious or think you may use Notes one day.

Of course, you don't have to use Notes to use SmartSuite. Those who do use Notes, though, will find that SmartSuite products come with special tools that allow them to enjoy the power of Notes while working with SmartSuite.

For instance, you can save SmartSuite documents to Notes databases, where other team members can find and use them. Likewise, of course, you can open documents from Notes.

Besides exchanging complete documents with Notes, you can set up SmartSuite applications to share certain Notes fields. Fields created in SmartSuite documents can be available for Notes applications.

For many companies that use Lotus products, Notes is the central software on the company intranet for gathering, working with, and distributing data. SmartSuite, a sister product to Notes, offers strong integration with the popular intranet product.

Saving a Spreadsheet to Notes

You can save your SmartSuite documents as attachments to Lotus Notes documents in a database. Notes databases are collections of information useful to people in the company. A database might contain information on such things as "Company Procedures" or "This Client's Recent Activities." A spreadsheet might shed information on those results. An expense report prepared for the client, for instance, would document activity with him. Suppose, for instance, you wanted to save a 1-2-3 expense report as an attachment to a Notes database. Here's what to do:

1. Click its icon in SuiteStart to start 1-2-3.

2. Create a sample document. For the example, I clicked Create a New Workbook Using a SmartMaster, then clicked Create an Expense Report, and clicked OK. I typed in sample data and saved the file as expense. Figure 16-1 shows the sample spreadsheet.

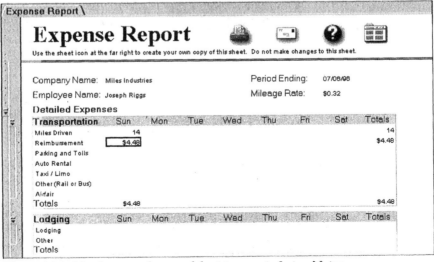

Figure 16-1: Here's a sample spreadsheet to save to Lotus Notes.

Now you're ready to save the spreadsheet as a Notes attachment.

3. Click File, then Save As.

4. In the Save As dialog box, Figure 16-2, click the Lotus Notes button.

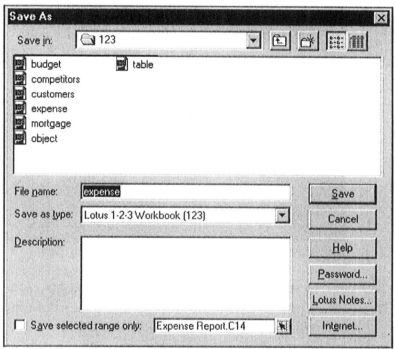

Figure 16-2: Click the Lotus Notes button to save to Notes.

5. In the Save to Lotus Notes dialog box, Figure 16-3, choose a server in the Server box. My server is "local."

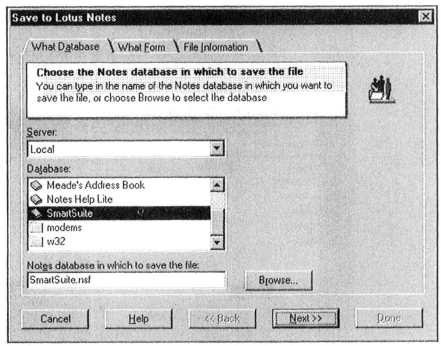

Figure 16-3: Choose your Notes server and database here.

6. In the Database list box, click the Database you want to save to. I clicked a database named SmartSuite, which I created earlier.

Creating a Notes Database

Notes doesn't come with default databases you can use. It starts up with databases for mail, help, and your address book. To create your own databases, click the File menu in Notes, then Database, then New. In the New Database dialog box, type in a title. Notes provides a filename automatically. Once you have the database, you still have work to do to design it and put in folders and views. Views are different ways of looking at the information—such as all clients that owe you money (or even "all clients" period). Folders are collections of documents. Where Views categorize documents by a particular criterion, Folders can contain any document.

7. Click the Next button. The tab for "What Form" displays, shown in Figure 16-4. In the Form box, click a form. The form is a Notes "blank form" used to guide you in putting in the information that the database contains. In the Field box, click a field, then click Next. The field in Notes, as in any database, is one particular instance on the form.

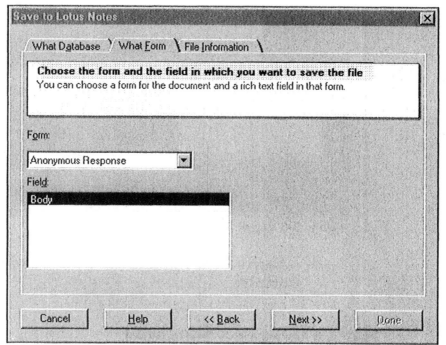

Figure 16-4: Choose a form and a field here.

8. Click Next. The File Information tab displays, as in Figure 16-5. In the File name text box, type in a name for the file. I typed "expenses." In the text box labeled "Enter text to display in field" type in some text.

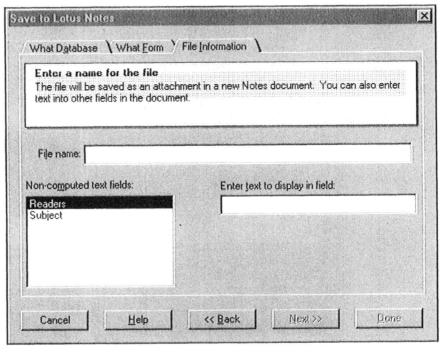

Figure 16-5: Type in a file name and display text.

9. Click Done. Notes saves the file as an attachment to the Notes document.

Opening a Spreadsheet From Notes

If you can save spreadsheets to Notes from within 1-2-3, then you of course ought to be able to open them from Notes into 1-2-3 as well. That way, you can work with the Notes attachments without ever leaving 1-2-3. I have a sample document named expenses.123 in Notes. Here's how to open a sample document from Notes:

1. Start 1-2-3.

2. From the File menu, click Open.

3. In the Open dialog box, shown in Figure 16-6, click the Lotus Notes button. The Open from Lotus Notes assistant starts up. See Figure 16-7.

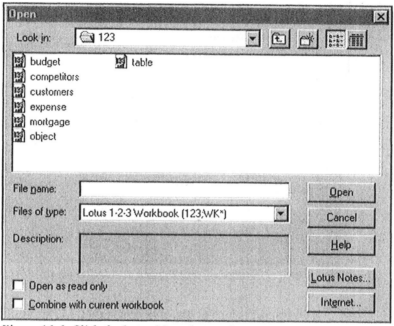

Figure 16-6: Click the Lotus Notes button here.

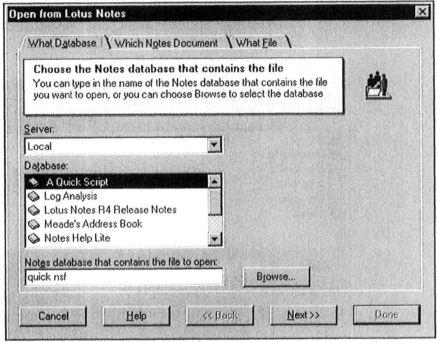

Figure 16-7: Use the assistant to open a Notes attachment from 1-2-3.

4. From the Server list, choose a server. My server is "local." From the Database list, choose a database. Click Next.

5. In the Which Notes Document tab, shown in Figure 16-8, choose a view and a document. Click Next.

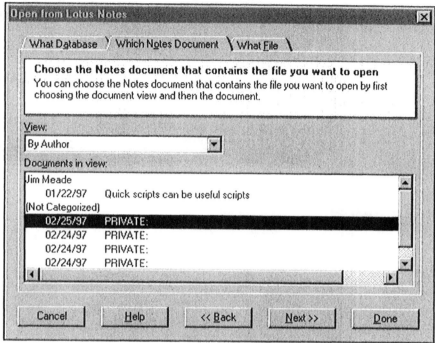

Figure 16-8: In this tab, choose the view and the document for the Notes attachment.

6. In the What File tab, Figure 16-9, click the file to open—the spreadsheet expenses.123 for the example. Click Done. 1-2-3 opens the Notes attachment as an untitled spreadsheet in its own window.

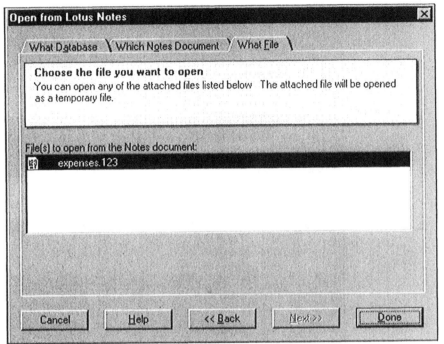

Figure 16-9: Click the spreadsheet you want to open, then click Done.

Embedding a SmartSuite Document in Notes

You can embed SmartSuite documents as objects in Notes databases. Then Notes users can work with the SmartSuite document simply by double-clicking the embedded SmartSuite object.

Here's how to do it, using Word Pro as the embedded object:

1. Start Lotus Notes. In my setup, I clicked the Win 95 Start button, clicked Programs, clicked Lotus Applications, then clicked Lotus Notes.

2. In Notes, click its icon to choose a database to work with. I chose SmartSuite on Local.

3. Click Create, then Design, then Form. A new blank form appears, as shown in Figure 16-10.

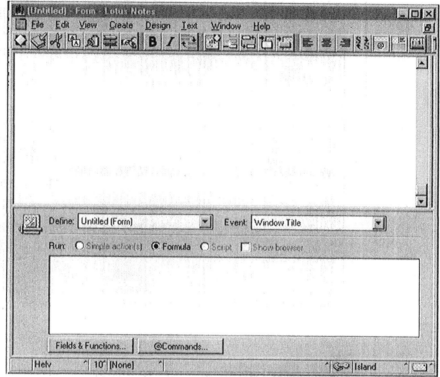

Figure 16-10: In Notes, a new, blank form comes up.

4. Place the cursor where you want to put the object for the Word Pro document.

5. Click Create, then Object.

6. In the Create Object dialog box, click the object you want to embed. For the example, I clicked Lotus Word Pro 97 Document, as shown in Figure 16-11. Then click OK. Notes embeds the Word Pro document.

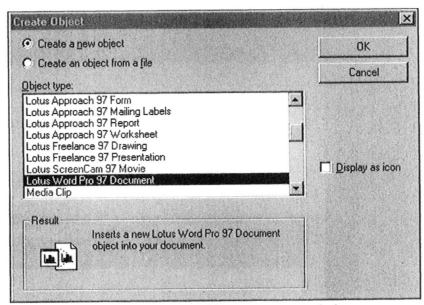

Figure 16-11: Click the SmartSuite object you want to embed.

Tip

> *If you want to embed a particular document as an object in the Notes form, in the Create Object dialog box, click the button for Create an Object From a File, and specify the existing document.*

Exchanging Fields With Notes—Notes F/X

Not only can you exchange documents between SmartSuite documents and Notes, you can exchange specific fields using Notes/FX. Fields, as I mentioned, are particular instances that appear on Notes forms. An expense form, for instance, might have a field for "last_name" and one for "meals," for example.

To exchange data between Notes and Word Pro, for instance, you add a field to a Notes form that corresponds to a Word Pro field defined for Notes/FX.

Suppose, for instance, you wanted to set up a Word Pro bookmark as a Notes/FX field. Here's how to create a Notes/FX field in Word Pro:

1. Click its icon in SuiteStart to start Word Pro.

2. Type in the sample text. For the example, I typed "The number of candidates is 50,000." I saved the document as "candidates," as shown in Figure 16-12.

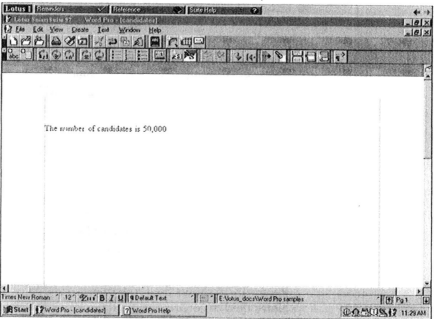

Figure 16-12: Create and save a sample Word Pro document.

3. Select the text you're going to exchange with Notes. For the example, I selected 50,000.

4. From the Create menu, choose Bookmark.

5. In the Bookmarks dialog box, type the name for the bookmark.

6. At the bottom, click the box for Notes/FX field. Figure 16-13 shows my completed dialog box.

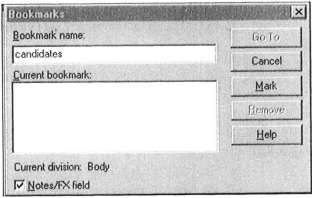

Figure 16-13: Name the bookmark and mark it as a Notes/FX field.

7. Click the Mark button.

Word Pro marks the field as a Notes/FX field. To exchange the field with Notes, you would set up a corresponding field in a Notes form and embed the Word Pro object in Notes.

Here's how you set up the field in Notes:

1. In your Notes database, click Create, then Design, then Form.

2. Click Create, then Field.

3. Type in the name of the Word Pro object defined as a Notes/FX field—"candidates," in my example.

4. Enter the Notes field name of a Word Pro document field or the name of an object that is defined for Notes/FX in the "Name" box.

5. In the "Type" box, specify the type of field. I accepted "Text." Figure 16-14 shows the Properties box in Notes for setting up the Notes field to correspond with the Word Pro field.

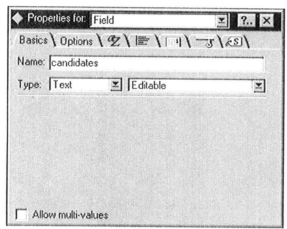

Figure 16-14: Set up the Notes field to correspond with the Notes/FX field in Word Pro.

Once you set up the fields in the two documents, they are linked. Information stored in one will be available in the other.

Moving On

Many people may use SmartSuite without using Notes. For those who do use Notes, though, SmartSuite comes with built-in tools for exchanging information with Notes. You can save documents to Notes and retrieve them from Notes, and you can set up specific fields to exchange information with Notes.

Notes has powerful capabilities to use along with SmartSuite. No matter how many capabilities like Notes the SmartSuite designers may build into the program, though, they can't think of everything. People will still want to automate SmartSuite to solve specific needs of their own. The way to do this is by using LotusScript, described in the next chapter.

17

Writing New SmartSuite Code: LotusScript

SmartSuite's developers try to think of everything you might possibly want to do. Goodness knows that, with a family of products that even includes specialty items like Organizer and ScreenCam, SmartSuite does allow you to do an unimaginable number of things as it is.

But people (and companies) nevertheless have their special needs. Sure, you can use Approach to create forms. But you may want to be able to check the responses when people fill in the forms, and give them instructions for changing their answers. Well, that is too specialized for the program itself. SmartSuite's developers can't know what you might want to ask or what additional instructions you might want to give. If you want to create a special application of your own, such as one to check responses and provide suggestions, you can do it. You create that program with LotusScript.

LotusScript is a structured programming language, like Microsoft's Visual Basic. The language—and tools that go with it, like the Script Editor—are identical for all the programs that have it, and for Lotus Notes. (LotusScript is in most of the SmartSuite products, but you won't find it in SmartCenter or Organizer.)

LotusScript allows you to develop applications across all the SmartSuite programs and Notes, though doing so is an advanced activity. For instance, you can't simply record your keystrokes in an application that combines, say, Word Pro and Freelance, then play it back as a script. You have to write original code to create a script that works across programs, which means you have to be a programmer. But the capability of programming across products is nevertheless there in this structured programming language.

LotusScript, in its overall design, is something truly ambitious. But you can nevertheless use it in modest ways as you first become familiar with it. In this chapter, you find out just the basics about this BASIC language—how to record a script, how to edit one, and how to get the benefit of the Integrated Development Environment (the program you use to work with scripts).

Working With Scripts

Programmers work with scripts by typing lines of code into the right place—in LotusScript, a place called the *IDE* (Integrated Development Environment). The Script Editor, part of the IDE, is the main place that you work.

You start the Script Editor from within any SmartSuite program and type in your scripts. When you store a document (spreadsheet, presentation, or whatever), you store the script along with the document. However, you can play back the script from any document, not just the one where you created it.

Tip

Remember that each document has its own scripts and its own IDE. It's possible to have the IDE open for one document yet be typing text into another.

The easiest way to create a script is to record keystrokes as you work. There are limitations to recording keystrokes as a way to create scripts, though. To get code that is exactly what you want, you do well to type in original code. In this section, I talk about both recording scripts and writing them from scratch.

Rarely does a script come out right the first time. Generally, you run it, then edit it to get it right. This section talks about both running and editing scripts.

You can also go through a process of formally debugging scripts. You can put in breakpoints where the script will stop executing and you can then check your code between breakpoints. During debugging, SmartIcons display at the top and the Script Editor doubles as a Debugger.

For the examples in this chapter, I use the IDE in Word Pro, though I could as easily use the IDE in any of the programs that has LotusScript.

Recording a Script

The easiest way to create a script is to have the SmartSuite program record your keystrokes as you perform an activity. The program saves the keystrokes and mouse movements as codes, which you can then edit if you want.

Recording scripts is much like recording macros in other programs. For instance, Ami Pro (the predecessor of Word Pro) allowed you to record macros. In both cases, you would type in keystrokes, and the program would record your activity as code. The macro language is a different programming language from LotusScript, though.

You can record scripts in Word Pro, Approach, and 1-2-3, but not in Freelance. (You can write original LotusScript code in Freelance, but the graphics program doesn't offer the capability to record keystrokes and convert them to code.)

Suppose, for instance, you performed some standard formatting activities often and wanted to have a script that would do them for you. You could record the script in Word Pro. Here's how:

1. Click its icon in SuiteStart to start Word Pro. In the Welcome screen, click Create a Plain Document. I typed the sample text— "Memorandum: I want to advise all of you about upcoming pay raises." I saved the document as "memo."

Suppose you now wanted to record a script that would make a word bold and colored blue. Here's how:

2. Put the cursor in the word you want to work with—Memorandum in my example.

3. Click Edit, then Script & Macros, then Record Script. The Record Script dialog box comes up, shown in Figure 17-1.

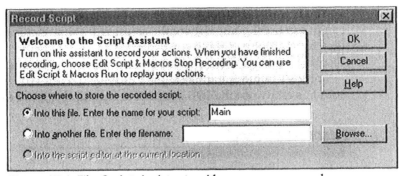

Figure 17-1: The Script Assistant guides you as you record.

4. Type in a name for the script. I typed "Main." Click OK. The cursor turns into a circle with a line across it, and the Status Line at the bottom says "recording." Perform the activities in the script.

5. For the example, I right-clicked and clicked Text Properties to open the Lotus InfoBox. In the InfoBox, for Text color I chose blue.

6. From the Edit menu, choose Script & Macros, then Stop Recording. The Script Editor comes up with the recorded script in it. See Figure 17-2.

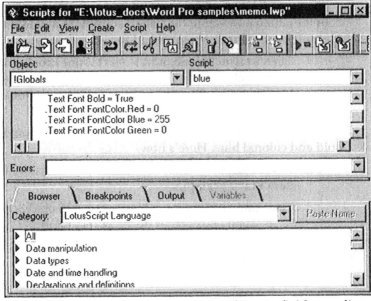

Figure 17-2: The Script Editor comes up when you finish recording.

The script editor contains code for what you have just recorded.

Tip

Often a recorded script contains unnecessary keystrokes. It's just a fact of life that in recording a script you may take one or two or more detours along the way. Recorded scripts are not always the most efficient, but they are easy to create because you don't have to know programming.

7. Click the X in the top right of the Script Editor to close it.

Running a Script

Once you've created a script, you can run it. The script "blue" should change a word to bold, blue text. Try it out:

1. In the current Word Pro document, place the cursor in any word you want. I put it in "upcoming."

2. From the Edit menu, choose Script & Macros, then Run.

3. In the Run Script dialog box, click Run Script Saved in the Current File. In the list box, click Blue, as shown in Figure 17-3. Click OK. The script runs and turns the current word to blue and bold.

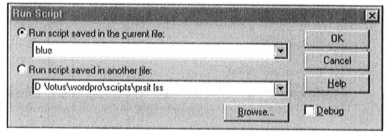

Figure 17-3: Choose the script you want to run.

Editing a Script

One step toward writing scripts yourself is to edit scripts you've recorded. Here's how to edit the script recorded in this chapter:

1. With the document still open that contains the script, click Edit, then Script & Macros, then Show Script Editor.

2. Be sure that the script you want to edit is the one displayed. For the example, the script blue is listed in the Script box on the right side of the IDE. See Figure 17-4.

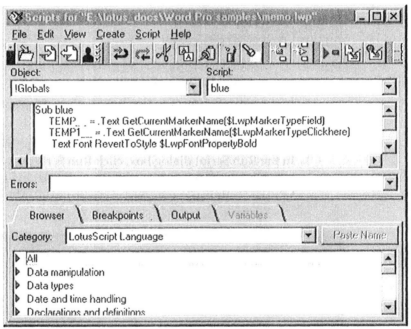

Figure 17-4: Be sure the script you want to edit is the one displayed in the IDE.

3. Suppose, for the example, you wanted to simplify the script so that it just changed items to blue. Select and delete all the lines of code except the one that looks like this:

    `.Text.Font.FontColor.Blue = 255.`

    Figure 17-5 shows the edited script.

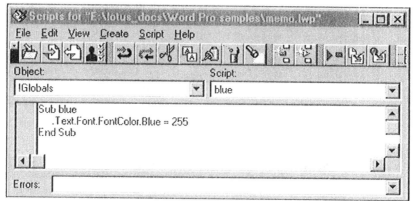

Figure 17-5: The sample script looked like this after I edited it.

4. To save the edited script, in the Script Editor, click File, then Save Scripts. Click OK in the message box, if it comes up.

5. To try out the edited script, click in any word in the document that isn't blue already, and run the script as described in the section "Running a Script."

6. Click in the X in the top right of the script editor to close it.

Writing a Script From Scratch

Sometimes it is useful to record scripts, as I've just described. As you begin to become familiar with LotusScript, though, you'll begin to write scripts of your own. To do so, you write code in the Script Editor. Here's how:

1. With Word Pro still running, click the SmartIcon to create a new document. In the New Document dialog box, click Create a Plain Document.

One of the simplest scripts to write is one using a message box. You can try it out.

2. From the Edit menu, choose Script & Macros, then Show Script Editor.

The script editor comes up, showing a blank script with the name Main in the Script box, as shown in Figure 17-6. The commands "Sub Main" and "End Sub" are already in place, showing LotusScript where the current "subroutine" (program) begins and ends.

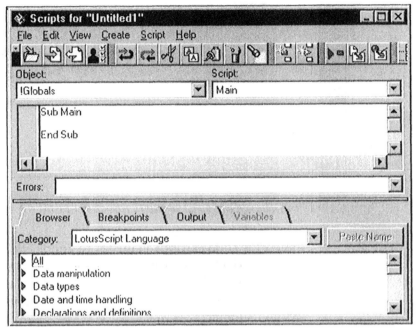

Figure 17-6: A blank script editor comes up.

3. Type this line of script: **Messagebox "Hello, World."** Be sure not to put a space in the middle of the word "Messagebox," and do put the quotation marks around "Hello, World."

4. Click at the end of the next line—End Sub. LotusScript debugs the line you've just written. If it finds errors, it turns the line to red. If there are no errors, it turns to a combination of blue and black. Figure 17-7 shows my line of script.

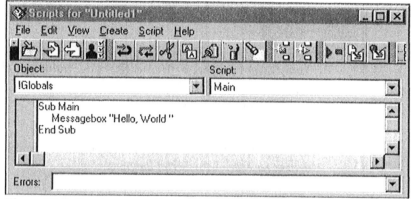

Figure 17-7: Here's my one-line script.

To try out the script, you can use a shortcut:

1. Click the SmartIcon in the IDE whose Bubble help says "Run subroutine."

The subroutine runs, and the message box displays, as shown in Figure 17-8.

Figure 17-8: With one line of script you can create a message box like this.

2. Click OK in the message box to close it.

To write original scripts, then, you type in lines of code. The process, of course, can get pretty sticky pretty fast. The Script Editor, though, is in fact more than just a place to write and run your scripts. It's a complete "Integrated Development Environment," or IDE, with all kinds of tools to help people as they develop programs in LotusScript.

Tip

To get complete information about the LotusScript language, use the LotusScript Language Reference. Here's one way to get to it:

1. In the IDE, click Help.

2. Click LotusScript.

3. Double-click "LotusScript Language Reference."

The reference is directed mainly at programmers and provides complete syntax for every LotusScript language element.

Getting To Know the IDE

Like the Standard Tools described in Chapter 15, the IDE is a collection of handy, powerful ways to get your work done as a scripter.

You use the IDE to write, edit, record, and debug your scripts. The IDE is identical in all the products that support LotusScript—Word Pro, 1-2-3, Approach, and Freelance. As you become familiar with the IDE in any one of the products, you become adept at it for all the products.

To start the IDE in any of the programs, click Edit, then click Scripts & Macros, then Show Script Editor.

The IDE comes up automatically when you finish recording a script.

As you write and debug scripts, the IDE does its best to make things easy for you, to keep you from making mistakes, to help you find mistakes if you make them, and to help you fix them.

Here's a look at the various parts of the IDE. Figure 17-9 shows the IDE in Word Pro and labels its main parts.

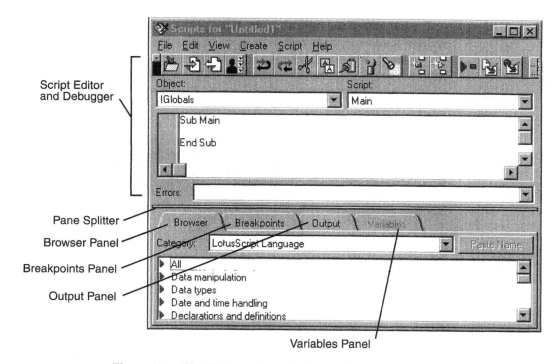

Script Editor
and Debugger

Pane Splitter

Browser Panel

Breakpoints Panel

Output Panel

Variables Panel

Figure 17-9: The IDE tries to make it easy for you to create scripts.

The Script Editor

The Script Editor is the top half of the IDE. You use it to write scripts like the "Hello, World" script in the previous section.

In the Script Editor, you write code and edit it. You check your syntax as you go along, and you get error messages for syntax that doesn't work properly.

The Script Editor is also a Debugger. You can set Breakpoints, which tell the script to stop executing at certain points. To set Breakpoints, you click in the gutter of the Script Editor (to the left of the code), as I show in the section "The Debugger." Then you can check syntax up to the Breakpoint.

For Help with the Script Editor, click Help on the menu of the IDE, then click Script Editor.

The bar across the middle of the IDE is quite useful. Called the Pane Splitter, it allows you to resize, hide, or display the panes in the window. For instance, to display only the Script Editor and not the panes at the bottom, drag the Splitter to the bottom of the screen, as shown in Figure 17-10. (The Splitter almost looks like part of the border at the bottom, but it's still there.)

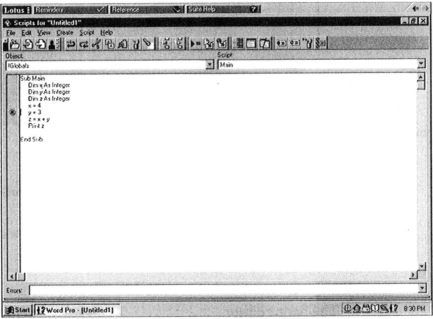

Figure 17-10: Drag the splitter to resize the screen.

You can also drag the splitter part way. To restore it to its previous position, double-click it.

The Debugger

The Script Editor is also a script debugger. Each time you complete a line of code, the debugger checks it for errors. If it finds any, it turns the line red.

Suppose, for instance you had a simple script like this:

```
Sub Main
   Dim x As Integer
```

```
        Dim y As Integer
        Dim z As Integer
        x = 4
        y = 3
        z = x + y
        Print z
End Sub
```

The script begins by defining a series of variables—a standard activity in scripting. It then assigns values to the variables and uses the Print command to output the result.

You can use the debugger to put break points into the code. The script stops executing whenever it encounters a breakpoint and allows you to check the syntax up to that point.

Here's how to put in and use a breakpoint:

1. Click in the gutter of the Script Editor where you want to place the breakpoint.

Figure 17-11 shows a sample script with a breakpoint in the gutter.

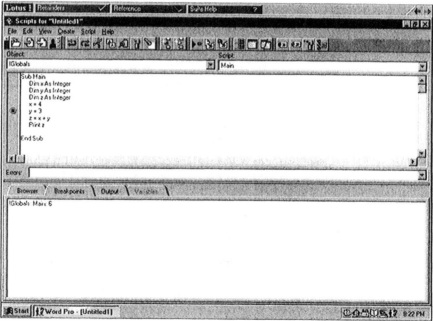

Figure 17-11: Click in the gutter where you want to put in a breakpoint.

2. Press F5 to run the current sub. (The sub is the "subroutine," the current portion of the script that you're working with.) Execution stops at the breakpoint, as shown in Figure 17-12.

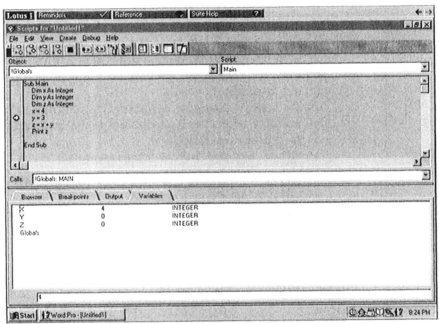

Figure 17-12: When you run the script, execution stops at the breakpoint.

3. To continue the script, click one of the icons at the top, such as the one for Continue Executing Current Script.

The debugger (which is the same as the Script Editor) gives you useful tools for systematically checking over your script.

The Utility Panels

The four tabbed panels at the bottom of the IDE are Utility Panels— Browser, Breakpoints, Output, and Variables. Each can save you time and improve accuracy as you work with scripts.

Finding Commands With the Browser

The Browser panel is really a help file. You can find any LotusScript language element, and you can use the Browser to copy and paste the element into your script. Here's what to do:

1. With Word Pro or one of the other programs running and the IDE open, be sure the Browser panel is active. Click its tab to make it active if it is not. (Opening the IDE is the same as opening the Script Editor, as you did in earlier examples. The Script Editor is part of the IDE.)

2. Click the arrow next to the category you want to work with. For the example, I clicked All. The browser displays a list of language elements, as shown in Figure 17-13.

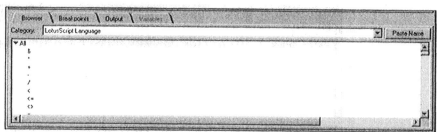

Figure 17-13: Click the arrow for the category you want in the browser.

3. Click anywhere in the list, then type the first letter of the element you want to work with. I type "m." (If several statements begin with the letter, you may have to press the letter repeatedly.) The Browser highlights MessageBox, as shown in Figure 17-14.

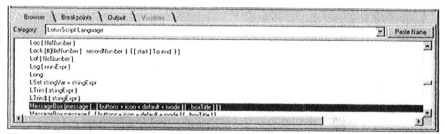

Figure 17-14: Type the first letter of a command to find it quickly in the Browser.

4. To paste the command into the Script Editor, you would click the Paste name button.

Reviewing Your Breakpoints in the Breakpoints Panel

You use the Breakpoints panel to work with breakpoints you have set in your scripts. In the Breakpoints panel, you can set Breakpoints, navigate to them, clear them, disable them, or enable them. Here's how it works:

1. Using the sample script from the section " The Debugger" in this chapter, I clicked in the margin to set several breakpoints.

2. Click the Breakpoints tab. It lists all breakpoints in the script, as shown in Figure 17-15.

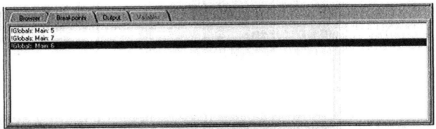

Figure 17-15: The Breakpoints panel lists all breakpoints in the current script.

3. To navigate to any breakpoint, click the breakpoint in the Breakpoints panel.

4. To clear a Breakpoint, click the item in the Breakpoints panel, then right-click the Breakpoints tab. Figure 17-16 shows the menu for the Breakpoints tab. Click Clear Breakpoint. The IDE clears the breakpoint.

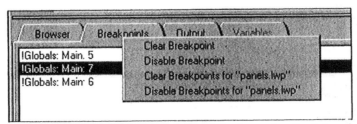

Figure 17-16: Use the menu for the tab to clear a breakpoint and perform other actions.

In a short script such as the one in this example, working with breakpoints is pretty simple. When you develop long scripts, though, the Breakpoints panel becomes quite useful.

Seeing Results in the Output Panel

When you run a script, you want to see if it produces the results you're looking for. If you use the Print command in the script, you can see the result in the Output panel. Here's how it works for the sample script from the section "The Debugger" in this chapter:

1. With the cursor in the script, press F5 to run the script.

2. Click the Output panel. The panel shows the result of the Print statement, as shown in Figure 17-17.

Figure 17-17: The Output panel shows the result of the Print statement in the script.

Reviewing Variables in the Variables Panel

As experienced scripters know, defining variables is the basis of building scripts. Variables, in scripting, are the "unknowns" that take on values in the script. (That value can "vary" depending on the actions in the script. Hence the name "variables," which derives from mathematics.)

When you debug a script, you use the Variables panel to see information about variables for the current script. Here's how the Variables panel works for the sample script from the section "The Debugger" in this chapter:

1. Place a breakpoint anywhere in the script.

2. Press F5 to run the script. Execution stops at the breakpoint, and the Variables panel becomes active, as shown in Figure 17-18.

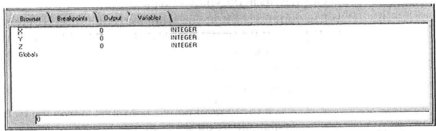

Figure 17-18: During debugging, the Variables panel shows the variables in your script.

3. To work with a variable, select it, then right-click the tab in the variables panel. Figure 17-19 shows the choices on the tab for the variables panel.

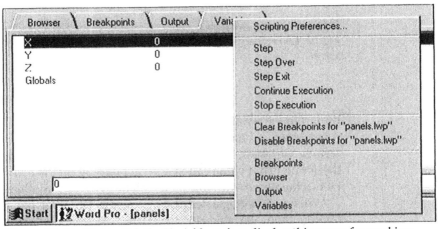

Figure 17-19: Right-click the Variables tab to display this menu for working with the selected variable.

Like most good tools, the IDE looks deceptively simple. It might appear, at first, to be just a place to type in your scripts. Actually, though, it is a collection of useful tools, including a complete Help file in the Browser panel and a useful guide to your variables in the Variables panel.

Conclusion

SmartSuite, then, is a dazzling display of automation. You can use it to automate everything from your personal information (in Organizer), to your Team Computing tools, to your activity on the Internet. There would seem, at times, to be almost no limit to what you can do with it.

When you begin to bump up against the limits of what is already in SmartSuite, though, you are not done. If you want to automate further, SmartSuite gives you the tool for creating any additional program you can dream of. That tool is LotusScript.

You have now, in this book, seen the full range of possibilities in SmartSuite. You can use it for simple things—like keeping your calendar or giving yourself reminders. You can use it to create an Internet Web page. You can use programs together, like using Approach crosstabs without leaving 1-2-3. You can use it to create new applications, with LotusScript. You can use it to do all kinds of things, and I wish you all the best as you do just that.

Index